Stories From the History of the Faculty of Law in Nijmegen (1923-2023)

Stories From the History of the Faculty of Law in Nijmegen (1923-2023)

Corjo Jansen

eleven

Published, sold and distributed by Eleven
P.O. Box 85576
2508 CG The Hague
The Netherlands
Tel.: +31 70 33 070 33
Fax: +31 70 33 070 30
e-mail: sales@elevenpub.nl
www.elevenpub.com

Sold and distributed in USA and Canada
Independent Publishers Group
814 N. Franklin Street
Chicago, IL 60610, USA
Order Placement: +1 800 888 4741
Fax: +1 312 337 5985
orders@ipgbook.com
www.ipgbook.com

Eleven is an imprint of Boom uitgevers Den Haag.

ISBN 978-94-6236-605-3
ISBN 978-94-0011-253-7 (e-book)
NUR 820

© 2023 Corjo Jansen | Eleven International Publishing

Preface

Radboud University in Nijmegen will celebrate its centenary in 2023. Founded in 1923 as the Roman Catholic University, the new academic institution had three faculties: theology, literature and philosophy, and law. The word faculty derives from the Latin word *facultas*, meaning choice or competence. In common usage, it has several additional meanings. Lokin writes at length about the meaning of 'faculty' in his book on the history of the Faculty of Law at Groningen University (1596-1970), which is rather older than the Nijmegen faculty. 'Faculty' can refer, for example, to a discipline ('I am studying law'), a building (I work 'at the faculty' – a luxury in Covid times) or an organisational entity ('the faculty is meeting').[1] Lokin establishes the meaning of the word faculty on the basis of a legal criterion: those who are authorised to decide how the study programme and examinations should be organised. Until 1970, these were the 'full' (ordinary) professors. The 'extraordinary' professors, lectors, private tutors and assistants, or other staff (who were appointed to the faculty from the mid-1950s) had only an advisory vote in faculty decisions. In this anniversary volume, I generally adopt Lokin's position.[2] Generally, because – given the small scale of the Nijmegen faculty in its early years – I also devote a few words to the persona and work of the first extraordinary professors and lectors, a category of staff that disappeared after 1980, when all lectors were made professors by law.

Chapters Two (1923-1940), Three (1940-1945), Four (1945-1970) and Five (1970-1998) offer more than just a description of the life and work of individual (extraordinary) professors and lectors. I have tried to create a 'group portrait', answering such questions as: What motivations did they share? What role did the Catholic faith play in their work? How did they respond to the rise of fascism and

---

1. J.H.A. Lokin, *De Groninger Faculteit der Rechtsgeleerdheid (1596-1970)*, The Hague: Boom juridische uitgevers 2019, pp. 31-32. The book on the law faculty at VU Amsterdam (VU) has a different format to Lokin's book or this volume. It has more than one author and contains a collection of essays about individuals (mainly professors) and several 'relevant matters' (such as the faculty association, obtaining a PhD at VU Amsterdam, the Second World War and the democratisation wave). See J. de Bruijn, S. Faber and A. Soeteman (eds), *Ridders van het Recht. De juridische faculteit van de Vrije Universiteit, 1880-2010*, Amsterdam: Prometheus*Bert Bakker 2010.
2. Lokin, *De Groninger Faculteit der Rechtsgeleerdheid (1596-1970)*, pp. 32-33.

National Socialism in the 1930s? What position did they adopt during the Second World War? How did they feel about the secularisation that began in the 1960s? I also attempt to determine their place in their discipline and in terms of the methods they used to practise their profession. This – more legal – approach distinguishes this volume from Jan Brabers' doctoral thesis, *De Faculteit der Rechtsgeleerdheid van de Katholieke Universiteit Nijmegen 1923-1982* [The Faculty of Law at the Catholic University of Nijmegen 1923-1982].[3] His work contains a wealth of statistical data on matters such as student numbers, student achievement, student life, study associations and the number of PhD defences. Because these topics have been discussed in detail in Brabers' book, I don't address them here.

The final chapter of the book, which covers the period 1998-2023, has a different format from the others. I do not discuss the lives and work of professors who are still in office as I feel it would be inappropriate to pass judgement on colleagues who I work with and am acquainted with to varying degrees. I look briefly at several significant events and developments for the faculty, some of which I have been involved in as a professor or director.[4] A conclusion ends the chapter.

From the early 1970s, the faculty began to acquire growing numbers of professors and academic and non-academic staff. This was prompted by the massive influx of students, more intensified teaching, more professional support for teaching and research, and the bureaucratisation of higher education. The faculty ranks were reinforced by more and more staff as the professors were no longer able to manage alone. It would make uninteresting reading if this book were to discuss all the academic staff appointed to the faculty. From Chapter Five onwards, therefore, I have not aimed for 'completeness' in my discussion of faculty members. The people who I do discuss can be found in bold in the list of professors in the Appendix.

The faculty, as part of the university, is shaped by university events. In this book, I focus on issues affecting the law faculty. I only discuss broader events – such as the university's founding, the occupation of the Netherlands by Nazi Germany from 1940 to 1945, the secularisation and democratisation of the late 1960s and early 1970s, and the name change from Catholic University Nijmegen to Radboud University – inasmuch as they are significant for the faculty. It wasn't always easy to make this distinction with respect to the university's past.

It has been my pleasure to make use of several earlier publications about the Faculty of Law. I would like to mention once again Brabers' *De Faculteit der Rechtsgeleerdheid van de Katholieke Universiteit Nijmegen 1923-1982.* I also refer the reader to three books on the law faculty that were published to mark university anniversaries in 2003, 2008 and 2013: *Te Recht in Nijmegen,Meesterlijk Nijmegen* and

---

3.   Nijmegen: GNI 1994.
4.   I was vice dean of research from 2000 to 2003, and dean from 2003 to 2005 and again from 2008 to 2010. I was also chair of the CPO from 2007 to 2019 and of the OO&R from 2007 (to the present).

Recht in Nijmegen, respectively.[5] These volumes contain interviews with former students and faculty professors, the biographies of several leading figures and contributions about remarkable events in the faculty's history. I also drew on another book by Brabers, *Een zoet juk* [A sweet yoke] (2014), on the rectoral addresses of the rectors magnifici. In 1923, the rector was simply the president of the senate, which was the 'gathering' of all full professors. However, the nature of this position has changed radically over the years (see Brabers' book). In the 'old days', the rectoral address provided a recap of significant issues and events during the past academic year. Many law professors have held this office, especially in the years 1923-1970, when professors would take their turn as rector, in order of seniority of appointment.[6]

Most of the sources on the history of the university's founding have been preserved. I draw mainly on the archives of Jos Schrijnen (1869-1938), the champion of the Roman Catholic University, who was also largely responsible for shaping the law faculty. He was the first rector magnificus of the university in Nijmegen. His archives are held in the Catholic Documentation Centre (KDC) in Nijmegen. I also consulted the archives of Gerard Brom (1882-1959) and Johannes Hoogveld (1878-1942), two other professors who were closely involved in establishing the university and the faculty of law. And I drew on the archives of Egidius van der Heijden (1885-1941), Bernardus Hermesdorf (1894-1978) and Josephus van der Ven (1907-1988), all of which are held in the Catholic Documentation Centre. I would like to thank the KDC director, Dr Hans Krabbendam, and the KDC staff for their assistance.

Another welcome source were the Catholic newspapers that appeared from 1923 to 1970, in which many professors of law published on a regular basis (both solicited and unsolicited contributions). These publications served as a barometer of what was on their minds and of the social problems that preoccupied them. The main newspapers I consulted are *De Tijd*, *De Maasbode*, the *Venlosche Courant*, the

---

5. Edited by W.J.M. Gitmans, A.A.H.M. Gommers, L.J.T.M. Hermans-Brand, C.J.H. Jansen, S.C.J.J. Kortmann and Y.A.J.M. van Kuijck (Deventer: Kluwer 2003), C.D.J. Bulten, L.J.T.M. Hermans-Brand and C.J.H. Jansen (The Hague: Boom juridische uitgevers 2008) and L.J.T.M. Hermans-Brand and C.J.H. Jansen (The Hague: Boom juridische uitgevers 2013), respectively.
6. Ch. Raaijmakers, J.H.E.J. Hoogveld, J.H.P. Bellefroid, E.J.J. van der Heijden, F.A.M. van Welie, W.J.A.J. Duynstee, P.W. Kamphuisen, B.H.D. Hermesdorf, J.W.G.P. Jurgens, F.J.F.M. Duynstee (twice), Ch.J.J.M. Petit, D. van Eck, G.W. Groeneveld, L.G.A. Schlichting, S.F.L. van Wijnbergen, W.C.L. van der Grinten and S.C.J.J. Kortmann. The rectoral addresses were published independently. Cf. J. Brabers, *Een zoet juk. Rectores magnifici van de Radboud Universiteit over hun rectoraat 1923-2014*, Nijmegen: Valkhofpers 2014. J. van der Grinten died in the year that he was to become rector. Titus Brandsma (1881-1942) commemorated him in: 'Prof. Mr. Dr. J. van der Grinten', *De Tijd* 7 November 1932, front page. He said in his rectoral address: "This year we are in deep mourning at the loss of one of our most celebrated and beloved Professors. At the start of this academic year we stood around the grave of Prof. van der Grinten. We stood there in such large numbers that the funeral alone was testament to the great loss suffered by the Roman Catholic University" (p. 9). On Brandsma: K. Waaijman, *Titus Brandsma*, Nijmegen: Stichting Vrienden van Titus Brandsma 2017.

Limburger Koerier, the *Overijselsch Dagblad,* the *Nieuwe Tilburgsche Courant* and *DeGelderlander.*[7]

This 100th-anniversary volume was commissioned by the Nijmegen Faculty Board chaired by the dean, Prof. Piet Hein van Kempen, professor of criminal and criminal procedural law, and by Louk Hermans-Brand on behalf of the Law Alumni Foundation.[8] I would also like to thank professors Claartje Bulten, Ybo Buruma, Bas Kortmann and Jan Lokin for their careful reading of the draft text. I am particularly indebted to Pia Lokin-Sassen, who went through the manuscript with a fine-toothed comb and made numerous suggestions for improvement. I have benefited greatly from her wisdom. I also wish to thank Dennis Arns for his help in finding illustrations.[9]

---

7. I have also made use of *De Limburger, Het Centrum, Het Binnenhof, Dagblad van Noordbrabant, De Telegraaf* and others.
8. In May 1972, the Faculty of Law established the Circle of Alumni (*Reünisten*) of the Faculty of Law of the Catholic University of Nijmegen. Its task was to promote the links between the alumni and the university. The Frans Perrick Foundation, named after the first president of the Circle, was established in 2000, with fundraising as part of its remit. The role of the Circle and the Foundation have now been taken over by the Law Alumni Foundation (SRA).
9. The manuscript was completed on 1 May 2021.

TABLE OF CONTENTS

1 | A CATHOLIC UNIVERSITY (1923)

1   INTRODUCTION

When the Roman Catholic University opened its doors on 17 October 1923, the Catholic newspapers couldn't find words enough to applaud the establishment of 'this cathedral in the service of the created intellect'. At last, Dutch Catholics – 'the people of Willibrord' (658-739), bishop of Utrecht and archbishop of the 'Frisians' – had their own *academic* stronghold. "We need clever people for our Catholic way of life, which is going from strength to strength, in both an economic and religious sense," said the newspaper *De Maasbode* in its special 'University issue' of 28 June 1923. The university's founding had the whole-hearted support of lawyer and pope, Benedict XV (1854-1922; 1914-1922),[1] who wrote to the Dutch bishops: "For our part, we cannot praise highly enough your pastoral efforts [to establish an academy] and we strongly recommend your university in the generous mildness of all those who are well-disposed to you."[2] The Prime Minister of the Netherlands, Jonkheer Charles Ruijs de Beerenbrouck (1873-1936), also a lawyer, added from his side: "With great joy we welcome the opening of the Roman Catholic University in Nijmegen. It is an event of immense historical significance for the whole of the Netherlands."[3]

The newspapers of that time were aware that the Roman Catholic University was not the first university in Nijmegen. In a special edition on 16 October 1923 to mark the university's opening, the Catholic newspaper *De Tijd* ran the headline 'Nijmegen already a university city in the 17th century'.[4] "For many, it will be a revelation to find this surprising anouncement in this special issue, and yet it is historic." This was followed by details about that old academy (known as the

---

1. During his pontificate, the *Corpus Iuris Canonici* (Code of Canon Law) was proclaimed (1918) and the Università Cattolica del Sacro Cuore was founded in Milan (1921).
2. 'De H. Stoel en de R.K. Universiteit', *De Tijd* 16 October 1923, Supplement 'Opening van de R.K. Universiteit'.
3. Ch. Ruijs de Beerenbrouck in *De Tijd* 16 October 1923, Supplement 'Opening van de R.K. Universiteit'. On Ruijs: F. Verhagen, *Toen de katholieken Nederland veroverden. Charles Ruijs de Beerenbrouck 1873-1936*, diss. Radboud University, Amsterdam: Boom 2015.
4. 'Nijmegen reeds in de Zeventiende Eeuw Universiteitsstad', *De Tijd* 16 October 1923, Supplement 'Opening van de R. K. Universiteit'.

'Quarterly Academy'), taken entirely from the booklet *Quartierlyke Academie en Apostolische of Latynsche School te Nymegen* (1795) by the well-known Nijmegen lawyer and antiquarian Johan in de Betouw (1732-1820).[5] With a nod to that old regional academy, the special supplement also contained a summary in Latin of the lectures at the new university: *Series Lectionum annuente summo numine (...) rectore magnifico Josepho Carolo Francisco Huberto Schrijnen*. It is worthwhile here to briefly reflect on the 17th-century predecessor to the new university of 1923.

2   THE OLD UNIVERSITY AND LAW FACULTY

In 1655, the Nijmegen city council created an 'illustrious' school with money that had in fact been earmarked to fund the University of Harderwijk, 'the country's university', "which was making no progress". The Nijmegen institution was formally opened on 3 May 1655. Just one year later, in 1656, it was upgraded to a university, an act that was built on constitutional quicksand as the Nijmegen city council had no authority whatsoever to establish a university. Only the States of Gelre and Zutphen had that right, which was linked to sovereignty, and they had already given their blessing to the University of Harderwijk. Thus there were questions about the validity of the foundation of the Nijmegen institution. The Court of Gelre refused to recognise the Nijmegen diplomas, which meant that lawyers who qualified in Nijmegen couldn't practise in areas where the Court of Gelre had jurisdiction. In his chronicle, In de Betouw made no mention of possible doubts about the right of Nijmegen professors to put forward doctoral candidates. On the contrary, he wrote that the professors were authorised to grant 'titles'. The young people of Gelderland appear to have been unconcerned about the possible lack of validity of their doctoral degrees. There was enormous interest in coming to Nijmegen to study, with some sixty students a year embarking on their studies there between 1658 and 1665. The teaching took place in the building of the Order of Knights of the Hospital of Saint John, the Sint Janshuis, which is now known as the 'Commanderie' of Saint John.[6]

The old University of Nijmegen had three faculties: theology, law and medicine. Of the three, the law faculty attracted the greatest number of students. This was partly

5.   *Quartierlyke Academie en Apostolische of Latynsche School te Nymegen* [1795], pp. 3-14.
6.   H. Bots & T. Kerkhoff, *De Nijmeegse Pallas. De geschiedenis van de kwartierlijke academie en medische faculteit, 1655-1679*, UMC St Radboud 2001, pp. 9-31, pp. 29-30; see previously J.J. Brinkhof, 'Enkele opmerkingen over de geldigheid van de aan de Kwartierlijke Academie behaalde doctorsgraad in de rechten', *Numaga* 1972, pp. 14-17, p. 17; A.N. Ruuls, 'Vier vragen omtrent de disputaties binnen het juridisch onderwijs aan de Nijmeegse Kwartierlijke Academie verdedigd onder P. de Greve (periode 1663-1676), benevens een poging tot beantwoording', *Batavia Academica* 1988, pp. 31-51, p. 33 and E. van Meerkerk, 'Nijmegen en de Harderwijkse academie, 1648-1679', in: J.A.H. Bots et al. (eds), *Het Gelders Athene. Bijdragen tot de geschiedenis van de Gelderse universiteit in Harderwijk (1648-1811)*, Hilversum: Verloren 2000, pp.124ff. Van Meerkerk noted (based on examples) that Nijmegen's right to propose a person for a doctorate was recognised beyond Gelre.

thanks to the reputation of the professor of law, Petrus de (1621-1677). In 1648 he had been appointed professor of Roman law in Harderwijk but the Nijmegen city council paid a large sum to wrest him away from there. In Nijmegen, he was able to earn 1200 guilders, a tidy salary at that time. De Greve taught the *Institutiones*, a textbook on Roman law for first-year law students, codified into law by emperor Justinian I (527-565), and the *Digesta*, a collection of legal writings from ancient Rome that Justinian had also codified into law. De Greve didn't just train his students in theory; he also sought to introduce them to judicial practice and therefore taught them about the Roman law that was still in force in Gelre. In his teaching he made use of Simon Groenewegen van der Made's (1613-1652) *Tractatus de legibus abrogatis et inusitatis in Hollandia vicinisque regionibus*(*A Treatise on the laws abrogated and no longer in use in Holland and neighbouring regions*). The first edition of that book dates from 1649. A Nijmegen edition of the *Tractatus* appeared in 1664, presumably as a result of De Greve's teaching.[7] Unusually for his time, De Greve made frequent reference to indigenous legal sources, such as the Reformed Land Law of the Veluwe, the Frisian Land Law, rulings of the Reichskammergericht (Imperial Chamber Court) and the Political Ordinance of Holland. His students were thus introduced to an amalgamation of local and provincial Gelderland practices, customary rights from other regions, court rulings, urban ordinances and Roman law, often referred to in Latin as the *ius hodiernum* ('contemporary law').[8] In imitation of contemporary Dutch law, termed Roman-Dutch law, this law in Gelre was referred to as Roman-Guelder law. De Greve was rector magnificus when, on 26 July 1656, in his role of doctoral supervisor, he handed the first doctoral degree to Petrus Jordan, a scion of a Nijmegen family of regents and a distant relative of In de Betouw. On 27 December 1671, De Greve was joined by a professor of law, the young Gerard Noodt (1647-1715) from Nijmegen, who would go on to achieve European fame as a professor at Leiden.[9]

French armies occupied the city in 1672, heralding the end of the University of Nijmegen. It had already been floundering before that, mainly due to an outbreak of the plague in 1665. From 1676 to 1678, a major peace conference was held in Nijmegen, with dozens of negotiators staying in the city, including representatives from the other Dutch provinces. Noodt took the opportunity at the death of his colleague De Greve to give a fine eulogy in St Stevenskerk. The church was packed with townspeople and with the diplomats who had taken up residence in the city. Noodt impressed the Frisian statesman Willem van Haren (1626-1708), who was

7.   G.C.J.J. van den Bergh, 'Simon Groenewegen van der Made (1613-1652), Petrus de Greve (1621-1677) and law teaching in Nijmegen', *Zeitschrift für Neuere Rechtsgeschichte* 2002/3-4, p. 288.

8.   M. Ahsmann, 'Teaching the ius hodiernum: Legal education of advocates in the Northern Netherlands (1575-1800)', *Tijdschrift voor Rechtsgeschiedenis* 65 (1997), pp. 436-437.

9.   On Noodt: G.C.J.J. van den Bergh, *The Life and Work of Gerard Noodt (1647-1725). Dutch Legal Scholarship between Humanism and Enlightenment*, Oxford: Oxford University Press 1988 (pp. 17ff. on Noodt's Nijmegen period).

instrumental in his appointment to the University of Franeker in 1679. As In de Betouw wrote: the University of Nijmegen "came to nothing around the year 1679, with Gerhardt Noodt, the last remaining professor, having been called away and having departed for Franeker."[10]

3   BACK TO THE TWENTIETH CENTURY: THE FOUNDING OF THE ROMAN
         CATHOLIC UNIVERSITY

There was a big difference between the old university and the new. The old "was decidedly Protestant", according to a statement in the above-mentioned special edition of *De Tijd* on 16 October 1923. As was the case with other 'Dutch' universities,[11] its costs had been covered in part by the proceeds from Catholic property that was confiscated. The entire population of Nijmegen also paid taxes for the Quarterly Academy. But that was of no use to the Catholics. This all changed with the advent of the new university in 1923.

It was not only *De Tijd* that made mention of the existence of the 17th-century academy. So too did the advisory committee set up by the Nijmegen city council in 1918, with the later professor Jozef van der Grinten (1885-1932), town clerk, as the secretary (*abactis*). In its recommendation of 17 March 1919, the committee referred to 'the renowned Apostolic School' and the 'Universitas Noviomagensis'. It described Nijmegen as an 'ancient' centre of learning. As the residence of Charlemagne (d. 814), the city had been part of the Carolingian Renaissance and there is likely to have been a school at Charlemagne's palace. The name Keizer Karel Universiteit (Emperor Charlemagne University) therefore presented itself. "The Committee felt that the name expressed both the distinctly Catholic character of the university and something of the local glory of Nijmegen. (...) After all, Charlemagne is a universal figure and therefore embodies the international mission of a Catholic University, as well as the city's tradition." An added advantage – and this mattered in university circles – was that the name could be easily 'Latinised' to 'Universitas Carolina'. Over and above these historical reasons, the city's central geographical location in the Netherlands, with its 'diverse' rail connections, argued for the establishment of a university in Nijmegen. The city could be accessed by the whole of the (Catholic) Netherlands. It was at one and

---

10. *Quartierlyke Academie en Apostolische of Latynsche Scool te Nymegen* p. 14. See C.J.H. Jansen, 'De Kwartierlijk Academie van Nijmegen (1655/1656-1679)', in: C.J.H. Jansen and L.J.T.M. Hermans-Brand (eds), *Recht in Nijmegen. Lustrumbundel ter gelegenheid van het 90-jarig bestaan van de Faculteit der Rechtsgeleerdheid van de Radboud Universiteit Nijmegen*, The Hague: Boom Juridische uitgevers 2013, pp. 3ff.
11. To spare the cost of purchasing expensive buildings, Leiden University was given the former Barbaraklooster on the Rapenburg and the Groningen academy was housed in the buildings of the Vrouwe Sywenconvent and the Broerklooster.

the same time part of a 'northern' province and a southern bishopric.[12] In 1946, shortly after the Netherlands was liberated, the question arose as to whether the university should be relocated. Former rector magnificus Bernardus Hermesdorf (1894-1978) emphasised the importance of Nijmegen's central location:

> From a geographical point of view, Nijmegen is still the preferred option. Relocation to a city in the Catholic South itself, a more central location, might mean more Catholic students from the South. Of course, any estimate remains more or less arbitrary. On the other hand, the influx of Catholic students from the North, Centre and West would in all likelihood decline. We are already hearing complaints that too few Catholic students from north of the major rivers are coming to Nijmegen. (...) Anyone who calmly reflects on relations in our country in the academic, cultural and religious spheres must admit that the Carolina is located precisely where it should be: at the bridge that connects North and South, at the bridge where two worlds can meet and find one another in *one* fatherland.[13]

The St Radboud Foundation, set up by the Dutch bishops in 1905, was the driver behind the founding of the university in Nijmegen in 1923.[14] Radboud was bishop of Utrecht from 899 to 917, the year of his death.[15] He became the patron saint of academic learning in the Netherlands. According to Art. 2 of the Articles of Association, the foundation that bore his name aimed to promote and expand 'Catholic special higher education in the Netherlands' and to establish 'a special Dutch Catholic University'.[16] It took some time for the Foundation to achieve its goal, largely due to the lack of financial muscle, a situation that in turn was exacerbated by the crisis surrounding the First World War. Nevertheless, on 1 September 1922, more than two million guilders were available to proceed with

---

12.   'Waarom Nijmegen', *De Tijd* 16 October 1923, Supplement 'Opening van de R.K. Universiteit'. The committee also mentioned that Nijmegen was the hometown of Petrus Canisius (1521-1597), who was canonised by Pope Pius XI on 21 May 1925, an event linked to the foundation of the Catholic University in 1923.
13.   KDC, B.H.D. Hermesdorf Archive (160), inv. no. 109: B.H.D. Hermesdorf, 'Moet de R.K. Universiteit in Nijmegen blijven?', *De Gelderlander* 6 April 1946, front page.
14.   According to J. Brabers, *De Faculteit der Rechtsgeleerdheid van de Katholieke Universiteit Nijmegen 1923-1982*, Nijmegen: GNI 1994, p. 8 note 27 (based on G. Brom (1882-1959)), the Geldrop wool and cotton manufacturer V.A.M. van den Heuvel (1854-1920), a member of the Dutch House of Representatives from 1898 to 1910, was the person who initiated the establishment of the St Radboud Foundation. For more about him, his family and the A. van den Heuvel & Zoon factory (1854-1980): J.C.M. van Stratum, *Bevolking in beweging 1750-1920. Historische demografie van Geldrop in economisch perspectief*, Tilburg: Stichting Zuidelijk Historisch Contact 2004, pp. 483-484, p. 488, pp. 489-490, pp. 497ff.
15.   For more about him: *Vita Radbodi. Het leven van Radboud*, explained, edited and translated by P. Nissen and V. Hunink, Nijmegen: Vantilt 2004.
16.   KDC, J.C.F.H. Schrijnen Archive (619), Schr-41: Stichtingsakte en Statuten van de Sint Radboudstichting.

establishing a university. Johannes Hoogveld (1878-1942), a priest in the archdiocese of Utrecht, was largely responsible for the successful fundraising.[17]

As well as Nijmegen, cities such as 's-Hertogenbosch, Tilburg and Maastricht competed for the honour of being home to the first Catholic university in the Netherlands. Cardinal Willem Marinus van Rossum (1854-1932), residing in Rome, stated that there was no objection in principle to collaborating with a particular city, provided that the 'freedom' of the church was guaranteed.[18] Discussions were held in 1919 and 1920 with the Nijmegen city council following recommendations from the advisory committee that had been set up in 1918. The consultations gathered pace on 5 October 1922, after a concrete proposal from Nijmegen.[19] The board of the St Radboud Foundation accepted the proposal in January 1923. The final decision to establish a Catholic university in Nijmegen was taken at a meeting of the board in Utrecht on 27 January 1923.

The St Radboud Foundation had set up an Information Commission on 29/30 September 1919 and a Preparatory Commission for the Establishment of a Catholic University on 26 October 1922. The two most important members of these committees were Hoogveld and Jos Schrijnen (1869-1938). The latter, also a priest, had been professor of comparative classical linguistics and the cultural history of Christian antiquity at Utrecht University, at the behest of the St Radboud Foundation, since 1912. Schrijnen was one of the strongest advocates for establishing the university in Nijmegen. He was attracted by the idea of the city on the Waal as an ancient Christian centre of learning. When the Roman Catholic University was founded in 1923, he was appointed professor of Greek and Latin, general linguistics and ethnology. He was also the first rector magnificus. Schrijnen and the Nijmegen commission were keen to name the university after Charlemagne in order to emphasise the secular nature of the institution and its connection with the city.[20] They didn't succeed and the St Radboud Foundation ultimately chose the name Roman Catholic University.[21] Under the Higher Education Act, the new academy had to have at least three faculties. These were to become the Faculty of Theology, the Faculty of Arts and Philosophy, and the Faculty of Law.

One important point remained: the allocation of an annual grant of 100,000 guilders from the municipality of Nijmegen to the new university. The Nijmegen city council agreed to the annual sum by the narrowest possible margin of 16 votes

---

17. 'De Stichting der R.K. Universiteit', *Het Centrum* 29 January 1923, front page.
18. KDC, J.C.F.H. Schrijnen Archive (619), Schr-8: letter from W.M. cardinal van Rossum, 20 November 1919.
19. 'De Stichting der R.K. Universiteit', *Dagblad van Noordbrabant (Breda)* 27 January 1923, front page; 'De Stichting der R.K. Universiteit', *Het Centrum* 29 January 1923, front page.
20. J. Brabers, *Een kleine geschiedenis van de Radboud Universiteit*, (in prep.).
21. According to Schrijnen, only the bishop of Den Bosch, A.F. Diepen (1860-1943), opposed the name Keizer Karel Universiteit. KDC, J.C.F.H. Schrijnen Archive (619), Schr-1: letter from Schrijnen to H.E.J.M. van der Velden, member of the Information Commission.

to 15. It was only Catholic councillors who supported the proposal. The bitterness was palpable in the editorial in *De Tijd*:

> We would have appreciated objections of an objective nature from our opponents; to our surprise and sorrow, however, we largely met with a sectarian view, as foolish as it was narrow-minded, sometimes behind a thin guise of tolerance. Thus the united attitude of the non-Catholic councillors confirms once again that many of our compatriots are still consumed by the uncharitableness towards Catholicism that at the time gave birth to the unfortunate slogan: 'sooner Turkish than Popish'. We will remember this and respond accordingly.[22]

The archival documents reveal unmistakably that the establishment of the Catholic University in Nijmegen was largely the work of Schrijnen.[23] As already mentioned, he relied on Hoogveld. The cooperation between the two priests was difficult at times. They both had big egos. Schrijnen, however, had the distinct advantage that he could count on the almost unconditional support of his brother Laurentius Schrijnen (1861-1932), the bishop of Roermond. Schrijnen said of his brother to Henricus van der Velden (1883-1923), the proposed professor-librarian of the Catholic University: "He is a tireless – and powerful – ally."[24] In Nijmegen, Jozef van der Grinten was the driving force behind establishing the university in the city. Another of Schrijnen's key supports was Gerard Brom (1882-1959), one of the first Catholic emancipators and professor of aesthetics and art history at the Catholic University from 1923.

4   Efforts by Schrijnen, Brom and Hoogveld to establish the Faculty of Law

None of the three founders of the Faculty of Law were lawyers: Schrijnen was a linguist, Brom a literature specialist and art and cultural historian, and Hoogveld was a priest who was trained in philosophy and theology. Schrijnen, Hoogveld and Brom knew each other well. They collaborated as editors of the Catholic

---

22.   'De Beslissing gevallen', *De Tijd* 8 February 1923, front page. The city council discussion appeared elsewhere in this issue. See also 'De R. K. Universiteit', *Provinciale Noordbrabantsche Courant. 's-Hertogenbossche Courant* 8 February 1923, front page. See KDC, J.C.F.H. Schrijnen Archive (619), Schr-21: letter from Schrijnen to H.E.J.M. van der Velden (1883-1923), member of the Information Commission, 28 February 1923. There, Schrijnen wrote rather cryptically: "Finally, [I] believe that it is important that you place an article in De Tijd, preferably signed, arguing that it was straightforward anti-papism in Nijmegen and not a lack of policy."
23.   See also J. Brabers, 'Schrijnen verdient een standbeeld voor het oprichten van de universiteit', Radboud University website, Geschiedenis, Radboud 100, 30 September 2019.
24.   KDC, J.C.F.H. Schrijnen Archive (619), Schr-1: letter from Schrijnen to Van der Velden, 29 December 1918. The exchange of letters between Schrijnen and Van der Velden builds a gradual picture of how the Nijmegen University came to be founded. The mayor of Nijmegen, F.M.A. van Schaeck Mathon (1853-1931), also worked to establish the university in Nijmegen. He became a member of the Board of Governors in 1923.

cultural journal *De Beiaard* (1916-1925), which made a major contribution to Catholic emancipation in the cultural sphere. Later professors from Nijmegen's Faculty of Law also published in the journal.[25]

Within the Information Commission, Jozef Beysens (1864-1945), professor of philosophy at Utrecht, like Schrijnen at the behest of the St Radboud Foundation, had expressed his preference for establishing a medical faculty and a faculty of science and mathematics rather than a law faculty and a faculty of literature and philosophy. Hoogveld replied that while he didn't dispute the need "for faculties of Roman Catholic science and mathematics, and medicine", there were compelling arguments in the short term for establishing faculties of arts and law. "Mathematics and science are not in themselves directly infused with a philosophy of life: they do of course need to be supplemented by a worldview, whereas a view of life is an intrinsic component of the study of law." If the university wished to start with a faculty of science, he feared that this would significantly postpone the university's opening date. The cost of a faculty of science was considerably higher than for arts and law. Hoogveld was supported in the Information Commission by Joop van Schaik (1882-1962), at that time a lawyer in The Hague and a member of the Dutch House of Representatives. He emphasised that "a lawyer exerts far-reaching influence in the practice of life, more so – it would seem – than a physician. After all, lawyers run the bar, hold all manner of public office, and have the greatest influence over legislation." Schrijnen also supported Hoogveld. In the end, six of the eight Commission members voted in favour of a faculty of arts and a faculty of law.[26]

After the meeting, Schrijnen set to work. As well as Van Schaik, he sounded out various leading Catholic lawyers about the organisation of the law faculty, including Antonius Struycken (1873-1923), former professor of constitutional law at the University of Amsterdam and a member of the Council of State, and R.B. Ledeboer (1863-1926), advocate general at the Supreme Court from 1908. Based in part on their recommedations, he came up with the following list of professorships and lectorships:

1. Philosophy of law; theoretical foundations of criminal law and sentencing law ['straftoepassingsrecht'] (to be taught by a professor of philosophy)
2. Criminal law, criminal procedural law and sentencing law (full professor)
3. Criminal psychology and psychiatry (extraordinary professor or lector)
4. Theoretical foundations of constitutional law, of the relationship between the Church and the State and of State governance (to be taught by a professor from outside the faculty)

---

25. In 1918 J. van der Grinten wrote an article about the overhaul of local government law and in 1921 E.J.J. van der Heijden discussed Oswald Spengler's book, *Der Untergang des Abendlandes*. Also in 1921, W.P.J. Pompe contributed to the 'University issue' of *De Beiaard* and in 1923 he wrote an article for the magazine on public interest.
26. KDC, J.C.F.H. Schrijnen Archive (619), Schr-40: Report of the meeting of 7 November 1922.

5. Social science and economics (full professor)
6. (6) Constitutional, administrative and social law; international public law and an introduction to jurisprudence (two full professors)
7. Civil, commercial and procedural law, the judiciary and private international law (one full professor and one extraordinary professor)
8. Roman law and the history of law (extraordinary professor)
9. Old Dutch law and its history (extraordinary professor or lector to be appointed in the near future)
10. Tax law (extraordinary professor or lector to be appointed in the near future)
11. Notarial law (extraordinary professor or lector to be appointed in the near future).[27]

For the law faculty, the St Radboud Foundation had tasked the Preparatory Commission to pay particular attention to philosophy of law and to canon law.[28] Despite this express wish, canon law was not part of Schrijnen's plan. His intention was to entrust the teaching of that subject to a professor in the faculty of arts and philosophy. When drafting his plan, he had been inspired by the situation at other law faculties in the Netherlands, especially in Groningen. Unique to the Nijmegen arrangement was the major emphasis on the theoretical and philosophical foundations of law and the idea of a chair in criminal psychology.

Schrijnen's plan was largely retained. In 1922, the Information Commission issued a report to the archbishop and bishops that contained slight changes in the breakdown of the professorships and lectorships. Gone was any explicit mention of the theoretical foundations of criminal and constitutional law. What remained was the desire to have the philosophy of law and canon law (now explicitly mentioned) taught by a professor from the faculty of arts and philosophy. The breakdown now read as follows:[29]

1. Criminal law, criminal procedural law and sentencing law (extraordinary professor)
2. Criminal psychology and psychiatry (extraordinary professor)
3. Social science and economics (full professor)
4. Constitutional, administrative and social law (full professor)
5. Civil law and legal procedure (full professor)
6. Commercial law (full professor)

27. KDC, J.C.F.H. Schrijnen Archive (619), Schr-86: Stukken betreffende de rechtenfaculteit. See also Schr-102: Overzicht, etc.
28. 'Het oprichtingsplan voor de R.K. Universiteit', *De Tijd* 16 October 1923, Supplement 'Opening van de R. K. Universiteit'; 'De stichting der R.K. Universiteit', *Dagblad van Noordbrabant* (Breda) 27 January 1923, front page.
29. KDC, J.C.F.H. Schrijnen Archive (619), Schr-71: Verslag van de Commissie van Voorlichting inzake de stichting eener R.K. Universiteit uitgebracht aan Hunnen Doorluchtige Hoogwaardigheden den Aartsbisschop en de Bisschoppen van Nederland over de mogelijkheid van het bezetten der verschillende leerstoelen, p. 9 (Faculteit der Rechtsgeleerdheid).

7. Introduction to jurisprudence, international public and private law (extraordinary professor)
8. Roman law and history of law (lector)
9. Notarial and tax law (lector).

Given that Schrijnen, Hoogveld and Brom were not lawyers, it seemed prudent for them to enlist Van Schaik,[30] Struycken and Ledeboer to assist in their search for suitable candidates for the law faculty. The St Radboud Foundation announced the appointments on 28 June 1923. In the next chapter, I will discuss in detail the individual law professors and their work. The Catholic newspapers devoted considerable attention to their various merits.[31] In the Information Commission, Beysens had imposed a number of criteria that prospective professors had to meet:

> The persons to be appointed must have a philosophical-religious orientation; people who are too old should not be taken on; in addition, *ceteris paribus,* Dutch people are preferred above foreigners, laypeople above clergy, secular priests above regular priests.[32]

Finding suitable people for the professorships and extraordinary professorships proved no easy task. The shortage of lawyers with a PhD qualification was keenly felt. Brom came to Schrijnen's rescue by recommending Willem Pompe (1893-1968), the son of his sister Johanna. He was offered the position of extraordinary professor of criminal law in Nijmegen. Brom and Pompe had already spoken of a professorship for Pompe before he completed his PhD in 1921. Pompe wrote to his uncle on 29 July 1920:

> You have advised me to talk to Schrijnen about it in September. Haste is of course of the essence here, but you yourself say that I make myself look ridiculous (...) by regarding myself as a candidate before my PhD defence, which I would have to do before Schrijnen. (...) If the Catholic University has to be in place next year, and if there is not yet a suitable criminalist, the

---

30. KDC, J.C.F.H, Schrijnen Archive (619), Schr-1: letter from Schrijnen to Van der Velden, 22 October 1921.
31. *De Tijd* 28 June 1923, front page; *De Maasbode,* Extra edition of the Avondblad 28 June 1923; *Het Huisgezin. Roomsch-Katholiek Dagblad voor Nederland* 28 June 1923, front page; *Nieuwe Venlosche Courant* 28 June 1923, front page and *Overijselsch Dagblad* 28 June 1923, front page.
32. KDC, J.C.F.H. Schrijnen Archive (619), Schr-71: Report to the Information Commission (etc.), p. 2. Regulars are clergy who belong to a monastic order or congregation, while seculars are clergy who do not belong to such an institution (p. 4).

public law professor or perhaps someone else could take on this subject as well for the time being (as happens at the 'Vrije' [Universiteit]).[33]

Brom was also instrumental in interesting his college friend, Egidius van der Heijden (1885-1941), in a teaching position at the Nijmegen faculty. Van der Heijden was appointed professor of commercial law (and later also civil law). And Brom played a role in sounding out Van der Grinten. At Brom's request, Van der Grinten sent information about his 'person' and his 'work' to Schrijnen.[34]

The principal problem was the professorship in civil law. The candidate proposed by Schrijnen, Maastricht lawyer Charles van Oppen (1875-1953), pulled out at the last minute.[35] Schrijnen had first asked an acquaintance from his Leuven student days, Eugène Dumoulin (1869-1938), president of the District Court of Maastricht in 1922, to fill that post. Dumoulin had refused, however: "there are so many ties that bind me to Maastricht that I cannot break them." It would be difficult, he believed, to "nominate people who have already gained such a reputation in the area of law they will have to teach that they can be considered the obvious candidates." He suggested Van Oppen for civil law: "undoubtedly someone with extraordinary aptitude, an excellent legal scholar and a man of general learning", who had also studied in Paris and Berlin.[36] Ultimately, when Van Oppen withdrew, civil law was added to Van der Heijden's teaching remit, which – it must be said – he was not exactly delighted about: "The new burden of civil law, with which they wish to honour me, weighs more heavily on me, I must confess, than I was immediately aware of."[37] Ledeboer was pleased that Van der Heijden

33.   KDC, G.B. Brom and W.J. Brom-Struick (68) Archive, BROG-1016: letter from Pompe to Brom, 29 July 1920. Ledeboer also knew Pompe well. As chairman of the Central Rehabilitation Board, he had appointed Pompe as deputy secretary in 1919. Ledeboer had ignored a request to become a professor in Nijmegen. See Brabers, *De Faculteit der Rechtsgeleerdheid van de Katholieke Universiteit Nijmegen 1923-1982*, p. 33. Ledeboer 'specially' recommended Pompe. KDC, J.C.F.H. Schrijnen Archive (629), Schr-71: Report to the Information Commission (etc.), p. 31.

34.   KDC, J.C.F.H. Schrijnen Archive (619), Schr-27: letter from J. van der Grinten to Schrijnen, 2 June 1922. Van Schaik had sounded Struycken out about possible candidates. He had 'definitely' recommended Van der Grinten. KDC, J.C.F.H. Schrijnen Archive (619), Schr-1: letter from Schrijnen to Van der Velden, 29 May 1922.

35.   Brabers, *De Faculteit der Rechtsgeleerdheid van de Katholieke Universiteit Nijmegen 1923-1982*, p. 15.

36.   KDC, J.C.F.H. Schrijnen Archive (619), Schr-27: letter from Eugène Dumoulin to Schrijnen, 18 March 1922. Van Oppen was an extraordinarily stalwart lawyer, including in wartime. For more about him: J. Meihuizen, *Smalle marges. De Nederlandse advocatuur in de Tweede Wereldoorlog*, Amsterdam: Boom 2010.

37.   KDC, J.C.F.H. Schrijnen Archive (619), Schr-27: letter from E.J.J. van der Heijden to Schrijnen, 1 May 1923.

was 'going to do' civil law. Finally there was certainty and Van der Heijden was considered an excellent candidate.[38]

One final thing. Schrijnen had clearly intended to stay well away from the politicians in The Hague. Van Schaik had brought to his attention the fact that Dr Wilhelmus Nolens (1860-1931), the parliamentary leader of the Roman Catholic State Party in the Dutch House of Representatives from 1910, who had trained as a lawyer in Utrecht, was feeling unacknowledged. Did it not make sense, Van Schaik suggested, to contact him? Besides, there was every reason to do so because Nolens had a keen interest in academia. This was also evidenced by his position since 1909 as extraordinary professor of labour law at the University of Amsterdam.[39] On 14 October 1922, Van Schaik wrote to Schrijnen:

> It has become clear to me on more than one occasion that Dr N. feels overlooked in these preparations for the establishment [of the university]. He expresses that sentiment regularly to anyone who wants to listen. Without wishing to judge whether his grievance is justified, I deem it important, for various reasons, to involve Dr N. in some way in the preparations. I myself have not yet found the form this should take; it must not, of course, have the character of rectifying past wrongs. Isn't there some task or mission that is yet to be carried out?[40]

Schrijnen ignored Van Schaik's suggestion and Nolens was not given any task associated with establishing the Roman Catholic University.[41]

5   THE PLACE OF ROMAN LAW IN THE NIJMEGEN PROFESSORSHIPS

In terms of professorships, there was one notable difference compared to other law faculties in the Netherlands. Roman law was not the responsibility of a professor, but rather a lector. According to an editorial in the newspaper *De Tijd*, this decision was in keeping with the spirit of the Academic Statute of 1921, in which Roman law did not have "so extraordinarily prominent a position as in the past". It was treated as one of the stages in the historical development of the law. The

---

38. Ledeboer wrote that the future students needed to have certainty about the composition of the faculty: "the solution that you have suggested for civil law makes me feel free to advise sending your boy to Nijmegen. (...) Now think about a father who has to make a decision. He needs to have absolute *certainty* as to the parity of the new faculty with the existing one." See KDC, J.C.F.H. Schrijnen Archive (619), Schr-79: letter from Ledeboer to Schrijnen, 29 May 1923.
39. He accepted that post on 11 October 1909, with the speech *Beteekenis en omvang van de arbeidswetgeving*.
40. KDC, J.C.F.H. Schrijnen Archive (619), Schr-43: letter from J.R.H. van Schaik to Schrijnen, 14 October 1922. The relationship with Nolens continued to be poor. For example, J.J.A. van Ginneken S.J. (1877-1945) deeply offended Nolens in his rectoral address of 17 September 1928. See Brabers, *De Faculteit der Rechtsgeleerdheid van de Katholieke Universiteit Nijmegen 1923-1982*, p. 54, note 25.
41. Schrijnen and his brother, the bishop, once visited Nolens. See KDC, J.C.F.H. Schrijnen Archive (619), Schr-1: letter from Schrijnen to Van der Velden, 1 December 1921.

establishment of a separate lectorship, not of a professorship, was the best way to do justice to the formative power of Roman law within legal thinking.[42] The lesser place of Roman law in the curriculum of the Nijmegen law faculty was grist to the mill for lawyer Antoon Arts (1873-1955), who had obtained his PhD in Amsterdam under Struycken. Arts was a conservative Roman Catholic and editor-in-chief of the newspapers the *Nieuwe Tilburgsche Courant* and the *Overijselsch Dagblad*. When the Catholic University opened in Nijmegen in 1923, he wrote in the latter paper:

> Until now, our lawyers have been kept below the social freezing point in the refrigerated chambers of Roman law. Splendid as a system, but frozen in spirit. Had they become acquainted with Canon law, which, in addition to the best of Roman formal law, also includes Germanic Christian law, their social views would be much milder and more Christian.[43]

To his regret, Arts had to conclude that Dutch universities still taught Roman law as an indispensable component in two of the four years, "whereas no attention is paid to our old Christian Germanic and indigenous law." Training in Roman law may have been essential for a lawyer's education, since Dutch civil law was largely Roman law, "but it is the wrong spirit for a truly Christian society."[44] Fortunately, things were done differently in Nijmegen. Up until the German occupation, Arts continued his battle for a stronger emphasis on 'Christian-Germanic' law alongside Roman law in the training of lawyers. He pointed out that his ideas about the place of Roman law had nothing to do with the 'new era' in which the Netherlands had found itself.[45] Arts was not a National Socialist, but his ideas aligned with the National Socialist view of the position of Roman law. The National Socialists favoured replacing Roman law with Germanic law as well asintroducing a National Socialist Civil Code based on that law, the *Volksgesetzbuch*.[46]

---

42. 'De inrichting onzer Universiteit', *De Tijd* 28 June 1923, front page.
43. 'De politiek van den dag', *Overijselsch Dagblad* 19 January 1923, front page.
44. A. Arts, 'Handelsmoraal en Recht', *Nieuwe Tilburgsche Courant* (NTC) 27 June 1930, front page (*Overijselsch Dagblad* 28 June 1930, front page). See also 'En toch...', NTC 5 October 1938, front page.
45. A. Arts, 'Terug naar het Christelijk-germaansche', NTC 5 October 1940, front page; A. Arts, 'Iets over oud-christelijk germaansch recht', NTC 5 June 1941, front page; A. Arts, 'Recht en onrecht', NTC 11 June 1941. Arts was charmed by the conservative Catholic priest W. Lutkie (1887-1968), an admirer of Benito Mussolini (1883-1945). He published his articles from the NTC in *Van blad tot boek. Verzameld Werk van Dr. A.C.B. Arts met inleidingen van Professor Mr. W. Pompe en Wouter Lutkie, Pr.*, Tilburg: Nieuwe Tilburgsche Courant 1937.
46. See L.J. van Apeldoorn, 'De fundamenten van een grootsch bouwwerk. Het Duitsche Volkswetboek. Grondregels en Boek I', *Het Rechtsfront* 1943, p. 18, pp. 26-27, pp. 37-39, pp. 45-46, pp. 54-55; H. Westra, 'Het plan voor het nieuwe Duitsche Volkswetboek', *Nieuw Nederland* 1941, pp. 431-434.

6   Objections to establishing the Roman Catholic University

The advent of a second confessional university was not welcomed by everyone in Dutch academic circles. Pompe's supervisor, the Utrecht professor of criminal law David Simons (1860-1930), wanted to exclude graduates of the Roman Catholic University from appointments as single judges because their training was too one-sided. "The Roman Catholics want to remove Catholics from the general universities and bring them to their own university, where – by its very nature – they will be limited by associating with fellow students of the same mind." They would then lack a sense of what was happening outside their own circle, which would be exacerbated if the university was located in a 'Catholic centre'. Students at the calvinist Vrije Universiteit Amsterdam had the same issue to contend with, of course, but they probably took part in the social life of the city to some extent since they were in the capital.[47]

Pieter Diepenhorst (1879-1953), professor of economics in the law faculty at the Vrije Universiteit Amsterdam from 1904, was given ample space in *De Tijd* to challenge Simons' words. Like the Vrije Universiteit, the Roman Catholic University practised the requirement of true scholarly research and a sound university education. The view that science and scholarship were an unbiased 'establishing of the the truth' was unsustainable. Each discipline was based on fundamental principles that were not the fruit of its own research. "Depending on the philosophy of life that one confesses, the general principles on which research is based are different and the method and result therefore differ." What the Roman Catholic University and the Vrije Universiteit also had in common was that they had not been created by 'public decree', but had been brought forth by the 'spiritual need of broad populations'.[48]

A year after the opening of the Roman Catholic University, Richard Boer (1863-1929), rector magnificus of the University of Amsterdam, said in his rectoral address in 1924 that there was a 'natural' gulf between a confessional and a non-confessional university. In a confessional university, there was always a threat of a yoke to free thinking, with science and scholarship subject to control. An anonymous editorial in the newspaper *De Tijd* indignantly rejected Boer's view. Liberal sectarianism was responsible for the rather undignified state of affairs at Dutch universities. "Our higher education had to rid itself of the libertine shackles, in which it could never breathe freely. Because the mentality, the atmosphere, the cultural life created around our public universities was entirely liberal and was

---

47. See D. Simons, 'Bezuiniging en rechterlijke macht', *Weekblad van het Recht* 1923/10994, pp. 1-2. Simons wrote these words on 28 February 1923. See Brabers, *De Faculteit der Rechtsgeleerdheid van de Katholieke Universiteit Nijmegen 1923-1982*, p. 10.
48. P.A. Diepenhorst, 'Goede kameraadschap', *De Tijd* 16 October 1923, front page.

suffocating to academic freedom."[49] At the editors' request, Pompe opposed Boer's view in *De Maasbode*. Pompe wrote that the Amsterdam rector magnificus had touched on an important issue, namely the relationship between faith and intellectual endeavour. Boer was convinced that there was only one path to the truth: that of academic enquiry. At a confessional university, expressed opinions would always depend on someone else's opinion, would not be a 'personal invention' and could not therefore lead to truths. Pompe argued, however, that there were more avenues to the truth, not only those of intellectual enquiry, but also those of faith. God's revelations also presented truths.[50]

The liberal, non-confessional spirit among Dutch professors, especially those at Utrecht, had not escaped the attention of the Belgian lawyer and prospective Nijmegen professor Joannes Bellefroid (1869-1959). The Utrecht professor of constitutional law, Bonifacius de Savornin Lohman (1883-1946), wrote to Schrijnen that Bellefroid focused not only on technical aspects, but also on philosophical aspects in the study of law. He had noted "that this was so absent among the left-wing members of the faculty because of the liberal views of scholarship. This attests to very keen powers of observation since the non-left-wing members rarely make deliberate mention of religion."[51]

The critical attitude of the outside world also meant that the professors at Nijmegen set a high bar for students, perhaps a little too high at times. Titus Brandsma (1891-1942) briefly addressed the issue in his rectoral address on 18 September 1933:

> It would be wrong if Nijmegen went too far in this [in the requirements imposed on students] and thereby turned away students who belong there, but it is nonetheless pleasing – within reason – that Nijmegen sets the requirements high and that there is general recognition within university circles that the requirements set by Nijmegen guarantee a high level of academic education.[52]

7   CONCLUSIONS

The young university and the fledgling law school faced two major problems when they were established: a lack of money and a lack of capable people. By pulling out all the stops, Schrijnen was able to bring both issues to a satisfactory resolution, although the university, and with it the faculty, continued to be plagued by a

---

49. 'Professor Dr. R.C. Boer en de R.K. Universiteit' and 'Een Rector Magnificus tegen de R.K. Universiteit', *De Tijd* 17 September 1924, front page.
50. W. Pompe, 'De Katholieke Universiteit. Haar bestaansrecht betwist', *De Maasbode* 19 September 1924, front page.
51. KDC, Schrijnen Archive (619), Schr-27: letter from B.C. de Savornin Lohman to Schrijnen, 7 March 1922.
52. T. Brandsma, *De Katholieke Universiteit in 1932-1933*, Nijmegen-Utrecht: N.V. Dekker & Van de Vegt and J.W. van Leeuwen 1933, p. 5.

funding shortage for decades. At least the teaching staff were of a high calibre, as the next chapter will demonstrate. Most professors and lectors barely knew one another. With little or no experience in providing academic education, they faced an immense challenge. They also had to build a faculty from scratch, when most of them were not yet living in Nijmegen. They were all aware that the founding of the university was the crowning glory of Catholic emancipation and that the creation of the new Faculty of Law was not to be taken for granted. The eyes of the bishops, Catholic politicians, Dutch lawyers and the Catholic population would be on them. They still had three months to go before the university's official opening. And – as stated in the introduction – that opening would be accompanied by sounds of jubilation. On the afternoon of 17 October, as at the opening of the 'illustrious school' on 3 May 1655, the church bells of Nijmegen rang and the cannons roared, ushering in a new life for those in academic gowns.[53]

---

53. In de Betouw, *Quartierlyke Academie*, pp. 7-10. In 1655, there were cannons on the ramparts and walls of Ford Knotsenburg. 'Officieele opening van de R.K. Universiteit', *Het Vaderland* 17 October 1923, p. 2. In 1923, the cannons were fired from a boat on the Waal.

Professors and lectors in the Faculty of Law (1923-1940)

1   Introduction

On 28 June 1923, the Catholic newspapers announced the names of the newly appointed (extraordinary) professors and lectors in the law faculty. They would take up their posts on 1 October of that year. On behalf of the Information Commission, Schrijnen had presented his list of professorships and lectorates to the board of the St Radboud Foundation in late 1922 (see previous chapter). He hadn't been able to find a candidate for every post.[1] His list read as follows:

Appointments as of 1 October 1923

1. Criminal law, criminal procedural law, and sentencing law [*straftoepassingsrecht*]: W.P.J. Pompe (extraordinary professor)
2. Social science and economics: Ch.A.M. Raaijmakers (1871-1954) (full professor)
3. Constitutional and administrative law: J.H.P.M. van der Grinten (full professor)
4. Commercial law, civil law, and history of law: E.J.J. van der Heijden (full professor)
5. Introduction to jurisprudence, international private law, international law, and civil procedural law: J.H.P. Bellefroid (full professor)
6. Roman law: G.M.G.H. Russel (1891-1961) (lector)
7. Matrimonial property and inheritance law: A.P. Louwers (1886-1944) (lector)[2]

---

1. KDC, Archive J.C.F.H. Schrijnen (619), Schr-1: letter from Schrijnen to Van der Velden, 18 June 1923. The professorship in criminal psychology and psychiatry had disappeared. Hoogveld had informed Schrijnen by telephone that the member of the Information Commission and intended curator of the Roman Catholic University, W.A. Boekelman (1869-1962), medical director of the St Antonius Hospital in Utrecht, had raised objections with the archbishop about J.E. Schulte's (1889-1946?) candidacy. Why hadn't he done so sooner? Schulte had worked for a year at St. Anthonius. Schrijnen suspected Boekelman of 'jalousie de métier'. See Brabers, *De Faculteit der Rechtsgeleerdheid van de Katholieke Universiteit Nijmegen 1923-1982*, p. 13.
2. This lectorate didn't enter the picture until 30 April 1923. Schrijnen and Van der Heijden had discussed the fact that matrimonial property and inheritance law would be useful in a 'course for the notarial profession'. It was desirable that both components of civil law should be the responsibility of a separate staff member. See KDC, J.C.F.H. Schrijnen Archive (619), Schr-27: letter from Van der Heijden to Schrijnen, 1 May 1923. On 24 November 1922, Van der Heijden had agreed to the inclusion of legal history in his teaching remit.

For philosophy of law, Schrijnen had requested his 'comrade-in-arms' Johannes Hoogveld, full professor in the introduction to philosophy, logic, ethics, metaphysics, and pedagogy in the Faculty of Arts and Philosophy, and for canon law, F.A.M. (Frans) van Welie (1886-1968), professor in the Faculty of Theology.[3] In accordance with the 1922 plan, Hoogveld and Van Welie were also appointed at the Faculty of Law.

All the professors and lectors mentioned above (with the exception of Russel) met on 14 July at Schrijnen's home, where they agreed that they would not give any inaugural addresses. They also discussed the organisation of the law faculty (the division of lecture hours, the lecture material, test and examination requirements, etc.). They were unanimous in the view that they should set high standards for students in order to avoid a situation in which the faculty became a refuge for students who had failed elsewhere. "Without wishing to detract from others," wrote Hermesdorf in his personal chronicle of the faculty's past, Van der Heijden and Van der Grinten had "done an enormous amount of work": they were the driving forces within the young faculty.[4]

2   THE FIRST GENERATION OF NIJMEGEN LAW PROFESSORS AND LECTORS

2.1   *Egidius van der Heijden*[5]

The later Nijmegen professor, Gerard Brom, had approached his friend Van der Heijden as early as 1919 to fill a professorial post in the law faculty. His answer was as follows: "Your letter coloured my Sunday with the golden aspect of my youthful illusions. Your message was therefore dear to me, also because it convinced me that the recognition that I had little opportunity to nourish after completing my doctoral thesis has not died." Van der Heijden did warn, however, that he had attained a position as a lawyer, "such that I would wish for in material terms", and that this position would make the choice difficult for him. He

---

3. KDC, J.C.F.H. Schrijnen Archive (619), Schr-71: Verslag van de Commissie van Voorlichting (etc.), p. 9. For their work in the faculty of law, I refer to Brabers, *Faculteit der Rechtsgeleerdheid van de Katholieke Universiteit Nijmegen 1923-1982*, p. 41 ff.

4. KDC, B.H.D. Hermesdorf Archive (160), inv. no. 334: Enkele persoonlijke herinneringen uit het verleden der juridische faculteit (c. 1973).

5. P.W. Kamphuisen, 'Mr. E.J.J. van der Heijden (Gouda, 12 Augustus 1885-Nijmegen, 24 Mei 1941)', in: *Jaarboek van de Maatschappij der Nederlandsche Letterkunde* 1941, pp. 38-42; Brabers, *De Faculteit der Rechtsgeleerdheid van de Katholieke Universiteit Nijmegen 1923-1982*, p. 14 ff. and C.J.H. Jansen and G. van Solinge, 'Egidius Johannes Josephus van der Heijden (12 augustus 1885-24 mei 1941)', in: C.J.H. Jansen and G. van Solinge, *Verspreide Geschriften van E.J.J. van der Heijden*, Serie Monografieën vanwege het Van der Heijden Instituut, part 67, Deventer: Kluwer 2001, p. XIII ff.; C.J.H. Jansen, 'Prof. mr. E.J.J. van der Heijden (1885-1941) in het licht van zijn tijd', in: *50 jaar Van der Heijden Instituut 1966-2016*, Serie vanwege het Van der Heijden Instituut, part 148, Deventer: Wolters Kluwer 2017, p. 17 ff.

promised that he would publish again: now that "I am assured of 'primum vivere', I can 'deinde filosofari'."[6]

> Van der Heijden (1885-1941) was born in Gouda into a middle-class Catholic family. He began his law studies in Utrecht in 1903, completing them in 1908 with a *cum laude* doctorate under the supervision of Willem Molengraaff (1858-1931), a leading Utrecht academic in the field of commercial law. Van der Heijden's doctoral thesis, entitled *De ontwikkeling van de Naamlooze Vennootschap in Nederland vóór de codificatie* [The development of the public limited company in the Netherlands before codification] encompassed history, economics and law. From 1908 to 1923 he worked as a practising lawyer in Rotterdam. He was politically active during his professorship and held many additional positions, including memberships of three standing government committees. He was also chair of the standing committee to prepare for legislation of the purchase on instalment credit terms. Van der Heijden initiated the establishment of the *Rota Carolina*, the Nijmegen moot court that has been part of the Nijmegen curriculum since 1924. First and foremost, however, Van der Heijden believed that legal training had to be rigorously academic. "Practical application skills, on the other hand, can only be achieved once the theoretical training is completed. The appropriate training ground for that is life. As far as our discipline is concerned, practical training is not part of the essential task of the university."[7]

In *De Tijd*, Molengraaff praised Van der Heijden as one of his best former students.

> My familiarity with the person and the work of Van der Heijden, his appetite for study, his interest in the deeper questions of law, in addition to his familiarity with practice, lead me to have high expectations of his future work as a professor, both in the training of his students and in the academic practice of private law.[8]

Van der Heijden became a notable professor of law in the Netherlands. He was editor and co-founder of the journal *De Naamlooze Vennootschap*, which began publication in 1922, and he wrote the authoritative *Handboek voor de Naamlooze Vennootschap* [Handbook of the Public Limited Company] (first edition 1929). In Van der Heijden's view, lawyers wishing to engage in scholarly endeavour had to adopt a dogmatic approach to the law. This required the study of the foundations and principles on which legislation was based, including from a legal-historical and comparative law perspective. Van der Heijden believed that including dogmatics had three tasks:

---

6.   KDC, Brom Archive (68), no. 537: letter from Van der Heijden to Brom, 31 March 1919. Van der Heijden received a supplement to his salary.
7.   E.J.J. van der Heijden, 'Voldoet de universitaire opleiding van den jurist aan de daaraan uit wetenschappelijk oogpunt te stellen eischen? Zoo neen, welke wijzigingen behooren daarin dan te worden aangebracht?', *HNJV* 1931-I (first part), p. 11.
8.   W. Molengraaff, 'Professor Van der Heyden', *De Tijd* 28 June 1923, Tweede blad, p. 6. According to *De Maasbode* 28 June 1923 in an 'extra edition of the evening newspaper', Van der Heijden was "the right man in the right place".

1) to examine the concepts with which positive law works and the judgments it forms (formal dogmatics); 2) to identify the ideas to which positive law gives expression (material dogmatics); 3) to test positive law against the rules that apply to the legislator (philosophical dogmatics).[9]

In 1924, together with Pompe, Van der Heijden joined the editorial board of the Social Catholic weekly *De Nieuwe Eeuw*, which was founded in 1917. The journal's editor-in-chief was Max van Poll (1881-1948), who had earned his reputation as editor-in-chief of a wide range of regional publications, including *De Gelderlander.De Nieuwe Eeuw* focused on 'world events' of a political, legal and economic nature. According to the *Provinciale Geldersche en Nijmeegsche Courant* of 22 January 1924 (p. 2), the paper became the 'official organ' of the 'young Roman Catholic University in Nijmegen.' In 1927 Van der Grinten joined the editorial team, which was then given the name 'Raad van Medewerking' [Board of Cooperation]. Thus three law professors from the young faculty were working in close collaboration on the publication of a weekly journal.[10]

Van der Heijden – a practising Catholic – saw it as his mission to anchor the law in Catholic morality. Law was more than what was defined by a human legislator. In other words, law should not be practised in a manner akin to natural science, which was based on facts and experimentation. Positive law was about (moral) norms. The foundation for the validity of these norms could not be traced back to a fact, but to the will of Him who laid down the law which all must obey.[11] Behind the rules of law was a higher reality, which emanated from the nature of things. *Natural norms in positive law*, Van der Heijden's 1933 rectoral address, was the most important expression of this philosophy.

Kamphuisen described Van der Heijden as having an intuitive sense of what was just in a specific case. At the same time, he had a sharp analytical mind, as attested to time and again by his tongue and his pen. His emotions would point to the solution of a problem, and his mind to the appropriate arguments to support that solution.[12] Was justice a living, law-making factor, alongside and at times even above the law? Van der Heijden answered this question with a resounding yes. Catholic teaching had never allowed room for the view that legislation and law

---

9.   KDC, E.J.J. van der Heijden Archive (817), no. 29: E.J.J. van der Heijden, Rechtsdogmatiek, p. 3.

10.   'Redactiewijziging van het Weekblad "De Nieuwe Eeuw"', *De Tijd* 7 January 1927, p. 9. The daily editing was in the hands of Van Poll and G.C.J.D. Kropman (1887-1968), an Amsterdam lawyer and editor of *De Tijd* and *Het Centrum*. The journal ran into difficulties in 1937 due to a "lack of interest from the Catholic people". See 'De Nieuwe Eeuw. Een Katholiek weekblad in gevaar', *De Tijd* 4 January 1937, front page. Hermesdorf also published in *De Nieuwe Eeuw*.

11.   E.J.J. van der Heijden, 'Recht en vrijheid' (1934), in: *Verslagboek Cultureele Week van het Nijmeegsche Studentencorps Carolus Magnus*, p. 51 and p. 54, to be found in KDC Nijmegen, E.J.J. van der Heijden Archive (817), no. 31. See also E.J.J. van der Heijden, 'Voorwoord', in: E.J.J. van der Heijden, *Handboek voor de naamlooze vennootschap naar Nederlandsch recht*, 2nd edition, Zwolle: W.E.J. Tjeenk Willink 1931, p. V.

12.   *Jaarboek van de Maatschappij der Nederlandsche Letterkunde* 1941, p. 39.

were synonymous.[13] The criticism that such a view would lead to legal uncertainty was outmoded. "People began to refuse any longer to pay for the illusion of legal certainty with the certainty of injustice."[14]

Van der Heijden was averse to interference from outside, whether from a secular or ecclesiastical authority. As Brom said at the memorial service for Van der Heijden: "he had the apostolic temerity, if necessary, to tell even high authorities the truth to their faces because, as he declared with his sense of responsibility, 'if they are not good, it is our fault to have made them so by our silence'."[15] He was guided by his own moral compass against any proclaimed authority.

2.2   Jozef van der Grinten[16]

Van der Grinten was a generalist in the area of public law. He wrote about constitutional, municipal, provincial, administrative and international law and was interested in (parliamentary) history, general state doctrine and current politics. Based on his experience as town clerk, he attached great importance to the practical orientation of scholarship. Like all his colleagues, Van der Grinten was a practising Catholic, a fact that was also reflected in his articles. On 28 November 1923, two months after being appointed professor, he voiced his opposition, based on the Catholic doctrine of the state, to what he considered to be the 'false' fascist doctrine of the state. That doctrine was based on the individual legal consciousness, the subjective insight of the individual that replaced the objective ethical principle. The fascists were concerned with overthrowing legitimate state authority, whereas the Catholic doctrine of the state demanded obedience to lawful authority, "i.e. the authority which must be regarded as such in accordance with an objectively

---

13.   See E.J.J. van der Heijden, 'Recht en billijkheid', *De Nieuwe Eeuw* 1924, no. 381 (in response to P. Scholten, *Beschouwingen over recht*, Haarlem: De Erven Bohn 1924).

14.   See E.J.J. van der Heijden, 'De Advocaat in dezen tijd', *De Nieuwe Eeuw* 1924, no. 335; E.J.J. van der Heijden, 'Natuurlijke normen in het positieve recht' (1933), in: *Verspreide Geschriften van E.J.J. van der Heijden*, Deventer: Kluwer 2001, p. 246.

15.   Derived from a biography by G. Brom: 'Prof. mr. E. van der Heijden. Een geleerde en christen', *Limburgsch Dagblad* 31 May 1941, p. 14. For a report of a conversation between the Archbishop of Utrecht and an outspoken Van der Heijden, see: Brabers, *De Faculteit der Rechtsgeleerdheid van de Katholieke Universiteit Nijmegen 1923-1982*, p. 498 ff.

16.   P.W. Kamphuisen, C.Ch.A. van Haren and F.G.J.M. Peters (eds), *Verspreide Opstellen van Prof. Mr. Dr. J.H.P.M. van der Grinten*, Nijmegen-Utrecht: Dekker & Van de Vegt and J.W. van Leeuwen 1934; C.A.J.M. Kortmann, 'J.H.P.M. van der Grinten (1885-1932)', in: L.J.T.M. Hermans-Brand and C.J.H. Jansen (eds), *Recht in Nijmegen*, Den Haag: Boom Juridische uitgevers 2013, p. 57 ff; R. Reussing, 'De vroege geschiedenis van de (lokale) bestuurswetenschappen. Jos van der Grinten als bondgenoot van Gerrit van Poelje', *Bestuurswetenschappen* 2018 (72) 1, p. 64 ff.; J.B.A.M. Brabers, 'Jozef Hubertus Petrus Maria van der Grinten (1885-1932)', *Biografisch Woordenboek van Nederland* (available online).

reasonable assessment of the facts." Irritation with democracy should not, in his view, lead to unbalanced theories with unforeseeable consequences.[17]

> Van der Grinten (1885-1932) began his law studies at the University of Amsterdam (UvA) in 1903. He was reputed to be one of the most gifted students of Struycken, a well-known (Catholic) constitutional lawyer. Van der Grinten obtained his doctorate in law on the basis of theses (*Stellingen*) in 1907 and his doctorate in constitutional law – again on the basis of theses – in 1911. He had been appointed deputy clerk at the provincial registry of Gelderland in 1909 and (deputy) clerk at the Nijmegen town's office in 1910. On 11 September 1915 he accepted the post of secretary of the town council in Nijmegen. Following his appointment as professor in Nijmegen, he would hold numerous positions on boards. He was on the editorial board of *Themis* and *Studia Catholica*. He had a particular interest in municipal and administrative law (administrative case law, case law in crisis cases, unlawful acts of government). Unfortunately, he left behind no textbooks, but perhaps that wasn't his style. He died young, at the age of 47.

In his 'In memoriam' for Van der Grinten, Kamphuisen wrote that 'the feeling of the old academic community' was perhaps stronger in Nijmegen than at any other Dutch university. He wrote that there was "no part of the Universitas Carolina where not something, indeed a great deal, of Van der Grinten's spirit has remained." He had been the secretary of the board of the university for an almost continuous period, which had enabled him to "stamp his signature on the University's style."[18]

Van der Grinten's method can be characterised as historical-dogmatic. He was concerned about the purity of terms. For example, he made a sharp distinction between leadership ('*bestuur*') and management ('*uitvoering*'). Not all leadership was management, not all management was leadership, while leadership could be management. Management could, for example, also involve legislation, such as the drawing up of a general order in council. Equating the two terms damaged

---

17. J. van der Grinten, 'De Gezagsleer van het Fascisme', *De Tijd* 28 November 1923, front page. He took a position against the weekly *Katholieke Staatkunde* edited by Dutch fascist E.G.H. Verviers (1886-1968), who was influenced by cultural pessimist O. Spengler (1880-1936), whose ideas Van der Heijden had opposed in *De Beiaard* in 1921 (p. 414 ff.). Verviers joined the NSB in 1933. Van der Grinten relied on J.Th. Beysens, *Hoofdstukken uit de Bijzondere Ethiek*, II, *Wijsgeerige Staatsleer*, Hilversum: P. Brand 1917. Verviers accused Van der Grinten of dancing to the tune of Bishop Diepen van Den Bosch. Diepen had written in many newspapers that Verviers' views were contrary to the Catholic doctrine of the state and that his weekly journal could no longer be called 'Catholic'. See 'Katholieke Staatkunde', *Onze Courant* 1 December 1923, front page. See E. Verviers, 'Trieste vertooning', *De Maasbode* 6 December 1923, front page and E. Verviers, 'Het episcopaat en de Katholieke Staatkunde', *Nieuwe Rotterdamsche Courant* 8 December 1923, front page.
18. P.W. Kamphuisen, 'In memoriam Prof. Mr. Dr. J.H.P.M. van der Grinten', in: Kamphuisen et al. (eds), *Verspreide Opstellen van Prof. Mr. Dr. J.H.P.M. van der Grinten*, p. I.

constitutional dogmatics.[19] Van der Grinten was also a democrat in heart and soul. It was he who wrote: "In our own country at least, there is no reason for grand-style reform. Our country is completely unsuitable for Caesarism, in whatever sense of the term. Democracy is undoubtedly the system of mediocrity. It knows no cult of the great man. It is averse to ideas of dictatorship, mindful of the wise words of Montesquieu (...): *il faut que le pouvoir arrête le pouvoir*."[20] Many felt that Van der Grinten literally worked himself to death on behalf of the university and the faculty.

2.3   Joannes Bellefroid[21]

Bellefroid was a Belgian, or rather a Fleming, by birth. He experienced first-hand the misery and destruction that the First World War brought to his country. During the war he expressed his sympathy for Flemish activism, whose supporters strove for greater independence for Flanders within Belgium and fought to make Ghent University a Dutch-speaking institution. In those years Bellefroid was appointed to the Flemish Mining Board. When the war ended, he had to flee to the Netherlands. Given his experiences in and after the 'Great War', it should come as no surprise that he was an ardent supporter of the Catholic Dutch Peace Alliance ('Katholiek Nederlandsch Vredesverbond), which called for world peace. "By virtue of our Faith and our Religion, we Catholics are specially called on to love, pursue and promote peace on earth. No sooner was our king Jesus born than the Angels greeted Him as the Prince of Peace and His coming to this world as the harbinger of peace." The Peace Alliance wanted to help ensure that future conflicts between states would be peacefully resolved through mediation, arbitration or international justice.[22]

> Bellefroid (1869-1959) already had an academic past before his appointment in Nijmegen. At the end of the 19th century, he had studied law in Leuven and in 1891 he began work as a lawyer in his native city of Hasselt. From 1896 he also taught criminal and criminal procedure law and notarial practice at the University of Liège. Bellefroid was also politically active in

---

19. Van der Grinten, 'De begrippen "Bestuur" en "Uitvoering"', in: Kamphuisen et al. (eds), *Verspreide Opstellen van Prof. Mr. Dr. J.H.P.M. van der Grinten*, pp. 177-179. See also his article 'Wat is administratief recht?' in *Verspreide Opstellen*, p. 167 ff.
20. Van der Grinten, 'Het Parlementarisme' (1928), in: Kamphuisen et al. (eds), *Verspreide Opstellen van Prof. Mr. Dr. J.H.P.M. van der Grinten*, p. 138.
21. R. Victor, 'Een verjaardag. Prof. J.H.P. Bellefroid', *Rechtskundig Weekblad* 13 (1949/1950), col. 913 ff.; B.H.D. Hermesdorf, 'Een voortreffelijk ambassadeur', *Rechtskundig Weekblad* 13 (1949/1950), col. 923 ff.; F.F.X. Cerutti, 'Prof. mr. J.H.P. Bellefroid', *De Tijd* 13 February 1959, p. 4; G.C.J.J. van den Bergh, 'Bellefroid, Joannes Henricus Paulus 1869-1959', *Biografisch Woordenboek van Nederland* (available online); Brabers, *De Faculteit der Rechtsgeleerdheid van de Katholieke Universiteit Nijmegen 1923-1982*, p. 26 ff.
22. 'Om den Vrede', *De Tijd* 8 September 1925, Tweede blad. Bellefroid met his colleagues Pompe and Raaijmakers within the Peace Alliance.

Hasselt. His vocation was to introduce Dutch into the French-speaking Belgian judiciary. He published a *Dictionnaire français-néerlandais des termes de droit* in 1897 (second edition 1912, third edition 1930). He also translated laws and codes into Dutch, among them the Belgian Commercial Code in 1899, the Belgian Code of Civil Procedure in 1901 and the Belgian Criminal Code in 1924. After fleeing Belgium, Bellefroid studied law in Utrecht, where he established himself as a lawyer in 1920. The rehabilitation that followed in Belgium in the 1930s was not enough to persuade him to return to his homeland. He felt at home in Nijmegen, where he had a mammoth teaching remit to fulfil. He published two books on the introduction to jurisprudence: *De Bronnen van het Stellig Recht en Haar Onderlinge Verhoudingen* [The sources of positive law and their interrelationships] (1927) and *Inleiding tot de Rechtswetenschap in Nederland* [Introduction to jurisprudence in the Netherlands] (1937). During the war Bellefroid published *Beknopt overzicht van de staatsinrichting van Nederland tijdens de bezetting* [Brief overview of the state system of the Netherlands during the occupation] (1941, second edition 1942). He wrote in the Preface: "Discussions of disputes, judgements, let alone my own political considerations, make no appearance here."

Hermesdorf wrote that Bellefroid had no predisposition to be a dry 'armchair scholar'. "He was much too involved in the practice of legal life to become a pure theoretician who would only be a burden and of no use to students."[23] Like Van der Heijden, Bellefroid regarded the search for legal principles (as part of the dogmatic method) as the ultimate in scholarly work.
"For just as all science and scholarship strive for unity in diversity, so too strives legal science for unity in the rule of law. However, legal science does not ascend any higher than legal principles."[24] Bellefroid viewed legal principles as general elements that were present in positive law. The lawyer had to track them down from living law through induction.[25] In both *Bronnen van het Stellig Recht* and *Inleiding tot de Rechtswetenschap in Nederland*, Bellefroid addressed subjects that were part of general legal doctrine. He discussed sources of law, the relationship between judge, law and the interpretation of the law, terms such as positive law, the legal system, legal fact, legal effect, subjective law and legal relationship, the state, and international law. His approach was a positive law approach, based on the system of law. Leiden professor Ben Telders (1903-1945), who – like Bellefroid – taught the introduction to jurisprudence and international law, praised this approach:

It so happens that the choice of material that underlies Bellefroid's work that is announced here (the Introduction) is an excellent one for me personally. It is quite possible that others will think

---

23.   Hermesdorf, 'Een voortreffelijk ambassadeur', col. 925.
24.   J.H.P. Bellefroid, *Inleiding tot de rechtswetenschap in Nederland*, 5th edition, Nijmegen-Utrecht: Dekker & Van de Vegt 1948, p. 30. Bellefroid had given a lecture in 1946 for the Flemish Academy of Sciences, entitled *Beschouwingen over rechtsbeginselen*.
25.   See Victor, 'Een verjaardag. Prof. J.H.P. Bellefroid', col. 921.

differently, but this healthy positivism, this avoidance of profundities and of references to
literature, of which even many a 'graduate' lawyer has neither taken note nor ever will, seems
to me entirely in keeping with the nature of an introduction intended for students.[26]

When Bellefroid was appointed rector of the Roman Catholic University in 1929,
incidentally the first non-priest to be appointed to that position in Nijmegen, it was
evident from protests in the *Bien Public* (Ghent) and *Libre Belgique* (Brussels)
newspapers that the French-speaking press had not forgotten Bellefroid's
sympathies for Flemish activism. Both papers queried whether the university had
become a hotbed of anti-Belgian sentiment. They also wondered whether, under
Bellefroid's leadership, the university would support the battle to introduce Dutch
as a language of instruction in Belgian universities. Schrijnen hastened to deny that
the Roman Catholic University in Nijmegen had become a centre for anti-Belgian
feeling. He joined the Belgian bishops who had condemned Flemish nationalism
aimed at the secession of Wallonia. In deference to the Belgian bishops, the Roman
Catholic University, "resting on the authority of the Venerable Dutch Episcopate",
wished to be inferior to no-one.[27]

2.4   Charles Raaijmakers[28]

Many will be familiar with the 'striking portrait' of Raaijmakers, drawn by Jan
Toorop (1858-1928) in 1910. The Jesuit Charles Raaijmakers was Toorop's
confessor when he lived and painted in Nijmegen. Raaijmakers was a lecturer at
the Canisius College at that time. Like Van der Grinten, he had obtained his PhD in
constitutional law and jurisprudence in Amsterdam. He was fascinated by the
encyclical *Rerum Novarum* (1891) of Leo XIII (1810-1903), who became pope in
1878. In this encyclical, the Pope expounded the social teachings of the Roman
Catholic Church: it was the Catholic response to the 'social question' that plagued
almost all countries in Europe: long working hours, poor wages, unsanitary and
dangerous working conditions, and child labour. "Justice demands (...) that the
worker be cared for by the government, that he may receive something from what
he contributes to the general prosperity, a dwelling, clothing and security of

---

26.   B.M. Telders, '[Review of:] J.H.P. Bellefroid, Inleiding tot de rechtswetenschap', *Rechtsgeleerd
      Magazijn* 1937, p. 421.
27.   'Nederland en België. Nijmegen onder Belgische censuur?', *De Tijd* 25 September 1929, front page;
      'Nijmegen en het Vlaamsch Nationalisme. Een belangwekkend schrijven van Mgr. Prof.
      Schrijnen', *De Tijd* 3 October 1929, p. 5; J. Schrijnen, 'Ingezonden Stukken', *De Tijd*
      11 October 1929, p. 11. See 'De nieuwe Rector Magnificus', *Limburgsch Dagblad* 16 July 1929, front
      page.
28.   J.B. van Dijk, 'Katholieke Tijdgenooten. Prof. Mr. Dr. Ch. Raaijmakers S.J.', *De Tijd*
      27 August 1927, Derde blad; A.C.A.M. Bots, 'Raaijmakers, Charles Adrianus Marie (1871-1954)',
      Biografisch Woordenboek van Nederland (available online); Brabers, *De Faculteit der Rechtsgeleerdheid
      van de Katholieke Universiteit Nijmegen 1923-1982*, p. 29 ff.

livelihood, in order to be able to lead a less miserable life."[29] Marking the 40th anniversary of the encyclical, Raaijmakers wrote: "I remember as if it were yesterday how, forty years ago, immediately after the publication of 'Rerum Novarum', I read it in translation (...). That old copy (...) is still on my lectern. (...) And now, after forty years of studying economics and sociology, philosophy and theology and consulting the Encyclical again and again, I am profoundly convinced that 'Rerum Novarum' is a masterpiece, an overabundant source of light and power, a goldmine from which, whoever continues to delve deeper can always unearth new treasures."[30]

> In 1895, Raaijmakers (1871-1954) earned his doctorate with a thesis entitled *Verzekering tegen werkloosheid* [Insurance against unemployment] (1895). He then joined the Jesuits and was ordained a priest in 1902. From 1902 to 1921 he taught at Canisius College in Nijmegen and from 1921 until his professorial appointment he was rector at Ignatius College in Amsterdam. He was also the provincial of the Dutch Jesuits. Like all professors at the Roman Catholic University, Raaijmakers published frequently in the Catholic newspapers of his time and in the *Katholieke Sociaal Weekblad* (on such topics as working hours and employee participation). He also wrote about a wide range of economic issues, such as government bonds, the gold standard, inflation, devaluation and unemployment. He published little work of an academic nature. His best-known book is *Economie en Ethiek* [Economics and Ethics](1926), in which – above all – he pointed out the normative aspect of economics and argued that the empirical approach to economics was too prevalent in academia. For secondary school students he wrote the successful *Beginselen der Staathuishoudkunde* [Principles of Economics] (1914), which ran to 15 editions!

Economics – or political economy (*Staathuishoudkunde*) as it was then called – had a long history as a university subject, going back in the Netherlands to the 18th century. In 1876 it became a compulsory examination subject in the *kandidaats* (undergraduate) course and a compulsory doctoral course for a PhD in constitutional law. As in other law faculties, the subject failed to take off in Nijmegen. Economics and law were – and continue to be – related but entirely distinct disciplines.[31] Raaijmakers therefore didn't occupy a prominent place in the young Nijmegen law faculty. Pompe, the youngest of the Nijmegen professors, might have done so, however, if he had not departed prematurely for Utrecht.

---

29. *Rerum Novarum. Encycliek van Paus Leo XIII van 15 mei 1891 over de toestand der arbeiders*, no. 27.
30. Ch. Raaijmakers, 'Bron en Goudmijn', in: *Veertig Jaren "Rerum Novarum" 1891 – 15 May – 1931, De Tijd* 10 May 1931, Tweede blad, p. 7.
31. See J.P. Duyverman, 'Feiten en feitjes – betreffend de groei van de economische wetenschap in Nederland', *De Economist* 126 (1978), p. 1 ff. (p. 12). See also: P.M.M. Klep and I.H. Stamhuis (eds), *The statistical mind in a pre-statistical era: The Netherlands 1750-1850*, Amsterdam: Aksant 2002.

2.5   *Willem Pompe*[32]

Pompe had his sights set on an academic career, preferably in Nijmegen, quite early on. He began corresponding on the subject in 1919 with his uncle, the future Nijmegen professor Gerard Brom. The Catholic faith had forged a strong bond between the two men. Brom was Pompe's spiritual adviser for almost his entire life, as evidenced by a letter that Pompe wrote to his uncle at the beginning of the Second World War:

> Since my grammar school days (...) I have been indebted to you for much of my spiritual training as a Catholic intellectual. In particular, I would like to thank you for the Catholic enthusiasm, the *sentire cum ecclesia*, not only – and I have this in common with my entire student generation – through your writings and lectures, especially in *De Beiaard*, but in personal conversations and letters.[33]

In 1917 Pompe embarked on his PhD under Simons, professor of criminal law at Utrecht: "it is now in my 24th year, this week, that a new period of life begins for me, between being a student and being a man."[34] He thought it would take him two years, during which time he would earn a living as a tutor. His relationship with Simons was cool: they barely spoke.

> I receive no advice from my supervisor; my contact with him is very accidental, in part because Simons appears to have consciously adopted laissez-faire tactics.[35]

This distant relationship between supervisor and student continued right through to Pompe's PhD conferral in 1921. Simons was therefore not welcome at the celebration dinner ("a men's dinner, family and friends"): "the supervisor, unknown to our family and still reserved towards me, will not be joining us."[36] Pompe had worked from 1919 to 1921 as deputy secretary of the Central Rehabilitation Board in The Hague. The board's chair was R.B. Ledeboer, advocate

---

32.   G.Th. Kempe, 'Levensbericht Willem Petrus Joseph Pompe (10 maart 1893-26 juli 1968)', *Jaarboek van de Koninklijke Nederlandse Akademie van Wetenschappen* 1968-1969, p. 3 ff.; C. Kelk, 'Willem Petrus Josephus Pompe (1893-1968)', in: T.J. Veen and P.C. Kop (eds), *Zestig juristen. Bijdragen tot een beeld van de geschiedenis der Nederlandse rechtswetenschap*, Zwolle: W.E.J. Tjeenk Willink 1987, p. 345 ff.; Brabers, *De Faculteit der Rechtsgeleerdheid van de Katholieke Universiteit Nijmegen 1923-1982*, p. 33 ff.; C. Kelk, 'W.P.J. Pompe (1893-1968)', in: C.J.H. Jansen, J.M. Smits, L.C. Winkel (eds), *16 juristen en hun filosofische inspiratie*, Nijmegen: Ars Aequi Libri 2004, p. 89 ff.

33.   KDC, G.B. Brom and W.J. Brom-Struick Archive (Brom) (68), BROG-1018: undated letter from Pompe to Brom (c.1942). In another, undated, letter presumably from 1918, he had already written that he thanked and honoured Brom as a spiritual father.

34.   KDC, Brom Archive (68), BROG-1018: letter from Pompe to his uncle and aunt, 11 March 1917.

35.   KDC, Brom Archive (68), BROG-1018: letter from Pompe to Brom, 16 April 1919.

36.   KDC, Brom Archive (68), BROG-1018; letter from Pompe to Brom, 1921.

general at the Supreme Court and, as Schrijnen's advisor, closely involved in the establishment of the Roman Catholic University.

Pompe consciously chose to enter legal practice after completing his doctorate. To this end, he contacted Joop van Schaik in The Hague and Van der Heijden, later a Nijmegen colleague, in Rotterdam. "My plan now is to first become a lawyer. The books, the 'intellectual life' have become too much for me. Practice and transition will restore me to health."[37] He started work at the Amsterdam office of his college friend, Piet Witteman (1892-1972). A year later, in 1922, Pompe left for Deventer, in part because this would allow him to combine various practical pursuits: the practice of law ("hopefully including some criminal law"), the secretariat of the Centre for Catholic Social Work, an administrative law position, which was beneficial for his insights as a judge, and the deputy secretariat of the Roman Catholic Employers' Association in the Archdiocese of Utrecht (which he would pass on to Hermesdorf, his old classmate and later professor at Nijmegen, in 1924). Deventer also offered opportunities for intellectual discourse, with both Catholics and non-Catholics. Pompe saw his time in Deventer as a transitional period:

> After my bookworm years, however, I consider these practical exercises as a further education towards a better understanding. I always have the University in mind as the ultimate goal.[38]

Pompe was appointed extraordinary professor, presumably because of his youth (just 30 years of age) and limited work experience.

> After his doctoral thesis, *Beveiligingsmaatregelen naast Straffen* [*Security measures alongside penalties*] (1921), Pompe (1893-1968) had almost no academic publications to his name. He had, however, published in Catholic newspapers and journals, such as *De Tijd*, *De Maasbode*, *De Beiaard* and *De Nieuwe Eeuw*. In 1927 he was given a full professorship, which included criminology. In 1928 Pompe succeeded his supervisor Simons in Utrecht. The exact reason for his departure has never been clear. In any event, he wanted little to do with the episcopal influence in Nijmegen.[39] In 1943, during the German occupation, Pompe was forced to resign his Utrecht professorship and go into hiding.[40] After the war, he was appointed a member of the Special Court of Appeals. He attended the trial of the Nazi ringleaders in Nuremberg in June 1946. Pompe had become the founder of the 'Utrecht School' of criminal justice, which was characterised by the multidisciplinary study of criminal law and a focus on the delinquent. His most important work is the *Handboek van het Nederlands(ch)e Strafrecht* [Handbook on Dutch criminal law] (first edition 1935, fifth edition 1959).

---

37. KDC, Brom Archive (68), BROG-1018: letter from Pompe to Brom, 25-10-1921 and undated.
38. KDC, Brom Archive (68), BROG-1018: letter from Pompe to Brom, undated (c. 1922).
39. Brabers, *De Faculteit der Rechtsgeleerdheid van de Katholieke Universiteit Nijmegen 1923-1982*, p. 49.
40. F. Broeyer, *Het Utrechtse universitaire verzet, 1940-1945. 'Heb je Kafka gelezen?'*, 2nd edition, Matrijs: Utrecht 2015, pp. 205-206, p. 209. Pompe had taught under duress from April 1943 until he went into hiding. He was a member of the 'Dubbel Zeven', a group of professors who were regarded as the hub of academic resistance in Utrecht (p. 83).

In his doctoral thesis, and later – as a Nijmegen professor – in his *Preadvies voor de Vereeniging tot het bevorderen van de Beoefening der Wetenschap onder de Katholieken in Nederland* [Preliminary report for the Association for the advancement of science and scholarship among Catholics in the Netherlands] (1924), Pompe was concerned with the foundations of criminal law. He believed that any criminal law had to be rooted in the function of punishment as retribution for guilt. After all, individuals were endowed with free will, by which they could do, or refrain from doing, something. Criminal law was necessary in order to uphold the rule of law. It was embedded in an objective moral order, which was known to humankind. The principle of retribution did not apply in absolute terms. Punishment wasn't always necessary where there was guilt. Sentencing was there to maintain the rule of law: it could only be justified if punishment was demanded in the interests of upholding the law. In formulating his ideas on criminal law, Pompe was inspired by Thomas Aquinas (1225-1274) and Beysens, a neo-Thomist professor at Utrecht, whose lectures he had attended.[41] As part IV of *Hoofdstukken uit de Bijzondere Ethiek* [Chapters from special ethics], Beysens had published a work entitled *Wijsbegeerte van het Strafrecht* [Philosophy of Criminal Law] (1919), which influenced Pompe's views on the foundations of criminal law.[42] According to his close colleague Gerrit Kempe (1911-1979), Pompe held faithfully to these views throughout his life; they simply became deeper and broader, in part due to his experiences during the war years.[43]

Finally, I would like to point out Pompe's passionate defence in 1923 of Christian democracy. His article was characteristic of Catholic opinion at the time. Pompe believed that Christian democracy – unlike pagan democracy – was guided by the notion that everyone should give of themselves to the best of their ability, in the interests of all – in other words, for the common good. Pompe urged that the general 'ideal and higher' aspect of this Christian democracy should not be lost sight of:

---

41. 'Katholieke tijdgenooten. Professor mr. W. Pompe', *De Tijd* 24 March 1928, also included in *Het Centrum* 30 March 1928, p. 2. See 'De rechtsgrond der straf naar katholieke inzicht', *Algemeen Handelsblad* 9 June 1926, Avondblad, p. 2. In 1937, Pompe and his colleague Hermesdorf from Nijmegen, who had also studied for five years under Beysens, contributed to the tribute that Beysens – "this doyen and maestro of the new-scholastic philosophy" – received in the form of a double issue of *Studia Catholica*. 'Mgr. Dr. Beysens. Een huldeblijk', *De Tijd* 18 August 1937, front page.
42. See D. Simons, 'De wet der vergelding', *W.* 1925/11322, 2; D. Simons, 'Straf- en beveiligingsmaatregel', *W.* 1925/11358, p. 8 and 'Katholieke Leer', *Het Vrije Volk. Dagblad voor de Arbeiderspartij* 29 June 1925, p. 4.
43. Kempe, 'Levensbericht Willem Petrus Josephus Pompe', p. 5, p. 7.

May the Catholic spirit, the solidarity, the righteousness and charity, be strengthened among us, and then, in the spirit of Christian democracy, not only *for* the workers, but also *by* the workers on their part for others.[44]

2.6 Adriaan Louwers and George Russel[45]

Louwers' appointment as lector in matrimonial property and inheritance law and Russel's appointment as lector in Roman law were both opportunistic. They had not published in the field of their lectorships, a situation that wouldn't change during their time in those positions. Willem van Basten Batenburg (1862-1936), a member of the Administrative High Court (Centrale Raad van Beroep) in Utrecht (from 1903 to 1933) and of the Dutch House of Representatives, had recommended Louwers as a man with extensive knowledge of the law and a keen understanding of private law matters. What Van Basten Batenburg based this judgment on is not known. Perhaps it was Louwers' reputation as tutor in civil law and commercial law at Utrecht, from 1917 to 1919. Isaac Hijmans (1861-1937), professor of Roman law in Amsterdam, praised Russel's eloquence and acumen when defending his *cum laude* thesis, *De Onderneming in het Privaatrecht* [The enterprise in private law] (1918). In his book, Russel had revealed his feel for the practical. In Hijmans' view, Russel had never lost sight of the connection with modern discourse, not even when dealing with 'antiquity' – from which he had unearthed a wealth of facts.[46]

Louwers (1886-1944) was town clerk in Veldhoven from 1909 to 1916. In 1917, after more than a year in Utrecht, he completed his law studies with a doctorate by theses (*stellingen*). He was appointed registrar of the district court in Tilburg in 1919 and subdistrict court judge in Venlo, Limburg on 23 February 1926. Louwers became a town dignitary, taking a seat on the many committees and commissions that abounded within Catholic society. The most curious committee to which he belonged was the Committee of Honour for the Roman Catholic Netherlands and Germany, under whose auspices a football match was organised in Venlo.[47]

---

44. W. Pompe, 'Democratie', *Overijselsch Dagblad* 6 November 1923, front page, also in *Nieuwe Tilburgsche Courant* 12 November 1923, front page. Pompe had also written to Brom on 22 December 1940: "Politics is not for me." KDC, Brom Archive (68), BROG-1018.
45. Brabers, *De Faculteit der Rechtsgeleerdheid van de Katholieke Universiteit Nijmegen 1923-1982*, p. 35 (Louwers), p. 35, pp. 62-64 (Russel). P.L. Nève, 'Toetsing van het belastingrecht aan een/het rechtvaardigheidscriterium. Enkele kanttekeningen', in: Y. Buruma et al. (eds), *Recht door de eeuw. Opstellen ter gelegenheid van het 75-jarig bestaan van de Faculteit der Rechtsgeleerdheid van de Katholieke Universiteit Nijmegen*, Deventer: Kluwer 1998, p. 291 ff. (pp. 292-298).
46. For the characterisations of Louwers and Russel, see the descriptions in *De Tijd* 28 June 1923. The Utrecht professor C.W. Star Busmann (1878-1966) had informed Schrijnen: "In my opinion, Mr Russel's thesis shows without any doubt a perceptiveness and a scholarly acumen." See KDC, J.C.F.H. Schrijnen Archive (619), Schr-27: letter from Star Busmann to Schrijnen, 10 January 1919.
47. Catholic Netherlands lost its first game to Catholic Germany, 2-1. Louwers met leaders such as Nolens, Charles Ruijs de Beerenbrouck and Schrijnen in this committee.

Russel (1891-1961) was a lawyer in Amsterdam. From 1923 to 1961, he rarely came to Nijmegen, except for Saturdays when he had to give lectures. His specialism was tax law. In his work in this area, he was driven by "an ideal of justice, by a passionate desire to help weak citizens against what he saw as overly powerful tax authorities."[48] In 1928, he was relieved of his lectorship in Roman law and was given tax law and tax policy.[49] After the war, he made the headlines when defending his brother, the Eijsden notary Charles Russel, who had been a member of the fascist Black Front (later National Front) and who was even Gauleiter of Limburg until 1 November 1940. Charles Russel had executed 81 deeds for the deportation of Jews during the war. He was arrested in 1944 on suspicion of collaboration. With the help of his brother, the lawyer, (and a petition that his brother organised among the inhabitants of Eijsden), Charles Russel came through the post-war purge unscathed. Miraculously, he was not held to account for issuing the Jewish transportation orders.[50]

In 1928, Russel was the first professor of tax law in the Netherlands. One of his 'favourite' subjects was whether or not taxes should be paid as a duty of conscience and the right of the state to impose taxes. He addressed this issue in a series of articles in *De Tijd* in 1932 and returned to it once more in his farewell speech in 1961. In Russel's view, the state's right to impose taxes followed from the natural moral law, which stipulated that the state could not levy more tax than is necessary for the performance of its task. Positive law should provide the basis for taxation. The basis of this law would show whether the tax payment required by law was also mandatory in conscience. A person was not obliged in conscience to comply with the tax law or to settle a specific tax claim if its foundation was unjust and therefore immoral.[51] Russel was forthright on this point: "bad laws make bad people." He had spent his entire working life battling against the 'exorbitant power' of tax officials and investigators, who assumed powers that were not founded in law. When Russel retired in 1961, *De Telegraaf* ran the headline: "Prof. Russel: Fiscal warrior with holy respect for the law."[52] How modern these words appear today.

48.   'Prof. Russel herdacht door Nijmeegse universiteit', *De Tijd-Maasbode* 21 December 1962, p. 4.
49.   Brabers, *De Faculteit der Rechtsgeleerdheid van de Katholieke Universiteit Nijmegen 1923-1982*, pp. 62-64.
50.   R. Schütz, *Kille mist. Het Nederlandse notariaat en de erfenis van de oorlog*, Amsterdam: Boom 2016, pp. 326-328.
51.   G. Russel, 'Belasting-ontduiking', *De Tijd* 7 April 1932, front page; G. Russel, 'De natuurlijke zedenwet. Belastingheffing. Een verplichting tot betaling', *De Tijd* 7 May 1932, front page and 'Wetten voor den belastingplicht', *De Tijd* 17 May 1932, front page.
52.   J. Fahrenfort, 'Prof. Russel: Fiscale Houwdegen met heilig respect voor de Wet', *De Telegraaf* 15 June 1961, p. 7 and 'Prof. Russel neemt afscheid van Nijmegen. "Na-oorlogs belastingrecht is vol buitensporigheden"', *De Tijd-Maasbode* 3 June 1971, p. 3.

3   THE SECOND GENERATION OF LAW PROFESSORS AND LECTORS

Following Pompe's departure for Utrecht in 1928 and Van der Grinten's death in 1932, the St Radboud Foundation was obliged sooner than expected to fill vacancies. Past experience had shown that this was no easy task. Willem Duynstee (1886-1968) took over criminal law from Pompe, and Pieter Kamphuisen (1897-1961) succeeded Van der Grinten in constitutional and administrative law. Bellefroid's retirement in 1939 – at the age of 70 – was anticipated. Bellefroid had three successors. Robert Regout (1896-1942) was appointed extraordinary professor of international law, Duynstee had responsibility for introduction to jurisprudence and in 1939 Dirk van Eck (1911-1969), as lector, was given the criminal law and criminology component of Duynstee's professorship. Finally, Johannes Jurgens (1895-1963) was appointed professor of private international law and civil procedural law in 1940. He succeeded the seriously ill Van der Heijden in commercial law. I will not discuss the life and work of Van Eck and Jurgens in this section as they did not play a significant role until after the liberation of the Netherlands in 1944/1945.

Pompe's succession ended in a confrontation between the faculty, in particular Van der Heijden, and the bishops, especially Mgr Diepen, the bishop of Den Bosch, who had an axe to grind with the headstrong Van der Heijden. On behalf of the faculty, he had nominated Cor Kropman (1887-1968), a well-known Amsterdam lawyer and journalist, as Pompe's successor. Van der Heijden and Kropman knew one another from the editorial board of *De Nieuwe Eeuw*. Kropman had not published any work of an academic nature. Brabers has described the conflict between the faculty and the episcopate in detail in his doctoral thesis.[53] What it boils down to is this: the bishops wanted to assess not only the scholarly merits of nominated candidates, but also their religious beliefs, political views and lifestyle, whereas the law faculty appeared to be solely concerned with the former aspect. Kropman proved to be a critic of the Roman Catholic State Party (RKSP) and supported the founding of an anti-capitalist Catholic party. The bishops therefore pushed Kropman unceremoniously aside and appointed Willem Duynstee, a blank canvas when it came to criminal law.

---

53.   Brabers, *De Faculteit der Rechtsgeleerdheid van de Katholieke Universiteit Nijmegen 1923-1982*, p. 59 ff.

3.1   Willem Duynstee[54]

Duynstee's first major publication – *Burgerlijk recht en zielzorg* [Civil law and pastoral care] (first edition 1919) – dealt with the interface between law and pastoral work. Duynstee's primary fascination, however, was with natural law. He first expounded his views on natural law in 1929, in an address to the Netherlands Association for Philosophy of Law (VWR), with the unsurprising title of *Natuurrecht* [Natural law]. In 1939, he elaborated on these views in *Het natuurrecht*, which appeared on behalf of the Dutch Association for Thomist Philosophy. In 1940, Duynstee published an overview of the historical development of natural law, entitled *Geschiedenis van het natuurrecht en de wijsbegeerte van het recht in Nederland* [History of natural law and philosophy of law in the Netherlands]. The book begins with a survey of the few earliest Dutch practitioners of philosophy of law in the Middle Ages and ends with the work of the Dutch philosophers of law from the period 1880-1890. Its main focus is the work of Hugo de Groot (1583-1645) and the influence of Samuel von Pufendorf (1632-1694), Christian Wolf (1679-1745) and Immanuel Kant (1724-1804) in the Netherlands. Lastly, *Over recht en rechtvaardigheid* [On law and justice], containing his most comprehensive views on natural law, was published in 1956.

As already mentioned, Duynstee hadn't published a single word on criminal law at the time of his appointment as professor. This was to change fairly quickly.[55] His inaugural address was entitled *De leer der straf van den H. Thomas van Aquino* [St Thomas Aquinas' doctrine of punishment] (1928). In his work on criminal law, he established connections with criminology, constitutional law, philosophy of law, moral theology and psychology. He wrote extensively on the nature of punishment and the foundations of criminal law. He developed a theory of retribution inspired by Aquinas, thereby following in the footsteps of his predecessor Pompe. Like Pompe, Duynstee saw punishment primarily as retribution for a crime committed, whereby a violation of the God-created order was rendered undone.[56] Duynstee's great inspiration was Thomas Aquinas, whose ideas permeated Duynstee's

---

54. On Duynstee, see: Brabers, *De Faculteit der Rechtsgeleerdheid van de Katholieke Universiteit Nijmegen 1923-1982*, p. 64 ff.; C.E.M. Struyker Boudier et al., *De "oude Duyn" herdacht*, Nijmegen: Katholieke Universiteit Nijmegen 1987; J. Elgershuizen, 'Pater Prof. Mr. Willem Duynstee', in: *Een kroniek van vijfenzeventig jaar Nebo*, Nijmegen: Paters Redemptoristen 2003, pp. 50-53; A. Stadhouders, 'Willem Duynstee', in: *Jaarboek Numaga* 2004, pp. 43-44; C.J.H. Jansen, 'W.J.A.J. Duynstee', in: Hermans-Brand and Jansen (eds), *Recht in Nijmegen*, pp. 71-72; J.P. de Valk, 'Duynstee, Willem Jacobus Antonius Joseph (1886-1968)', in: *Biografisch Woordenboek van Nederland* (available online). See also: *Verspreide Opstellen* [*van*] *prof. mr. W.J.A.J. Duynstee CssR*, collected and with an introduction by P.J.A. Calon, Roermond: J.J. Romen & Zonen 1963.

55. Between 1936 and 1943 he contributed five articles to the *Tijdschrift voor Strafrecht*, with titles such as 'Objectieve pogingsleer' (on criminal attempt) (1936) and 'De oorzaak van de criminaliteit der Katholieken' [The causes of Catholic crime] (1937). Pompe had also discussed this latter subject.

56. See his inaugural lecture and his address as rector: 'Het wezen der vergelding', in: *Verspreide Opstellen* [*van*] *prof. mr. W.J.J.A.J. Duynstee CssR*, Roermond: J.J. Romen & Zonen 1963, p. 102 ff.

writings. In his study *Over recht en rechtvaardigheid*, Duynstee wrote: "We have based ourselves on St Thomas, not because Thomas was Thomas, but because we sensed in him the truth."[57] In his university farewell speech in 1956, Duynstee had but one wish for the Catholic University: "that the spirit of Thomas may always remain the foundation of what is taught at this university."[58]

> Duynstee (1886-1968) studied law at the University of Amsterdam from 1905 to 1908. He completed his studies with a doctorate by theses *(stellingen)*.[59] At the age of 21, against his father's wishes, he joined the Order of the Redemptorists (CssR). It is not known what prompted him to make this choice. It may have been a book about St Alphonsus Liguori (1696-1787), the founder of the Redemptorists and a brilliant lawyer, given to him by the Redemptorist Father Christianus Boomaars (1863-1931) as a gift during his studies. Duynstee was ordained a priest in 1913. In 1928, he took over Pompe's professorship. His teaching remit was modified in 1939, whereby he retained criminal law, but lost criminal procedural law. He also gained introduction to jurisprudence. Duynstee was rector magnificus during the first year of the German occupation (1940 to 1 May 1941). He was then ordered to resign his post by the occupying forces. In 1948, after the war, philosophy of law replaced criminal law in his teaching remit.

Duynstee regarded natural law as being of the utmost importance for the practical application of the law. It provided a firm foundation on which both judge and legislator could continue to build. Without natural law, there could be no criterion for testing the justice and validity of positive law. Letting go of natural law would lead to hopeless opportunism within legislation. With natural law as a guideline, the judge was no longer someone who applied the law blindly and mechanically, but a *iudex boni et aequi*. It was Duynstee's deep conviction that 'the good and the just' had a firm foundation in natural reason. "Then, if positive law should in any circumstances become too harsh or unfair, this can be corrected in accordance with the requirements of natural law (...)."[60]
Duynstee believed that natural law led to the dismantling of the notion that all law could be found in legislation. In his view, it supported a freer role for judges vis-à-vis the law. "People have become increasingly aware that legislative law in the full sense of the word can be unjust; judges have been given a power that the orthodox

---

57. W.J.A.J. Duynstee, *Over recht en rechtvaardigheid*, 's-Hertogenbosch: Malmberg 1956, Preface. 'Prof. W. Duynstee C.ss.R. "Wij zijn uitgegaan van St. Thomas omdat wij in hem de waarheid voelden"', *De Tijd* 21 February 1958, p. 3.
58. W.J.A.J. Duynstee, 'Wet en wetsverplichting bij St. Thomas', *Verspreide Opstellen*, pp. 135-136.
59. The name of the supervisor is not known. The name of Prof. M.W.F. Treub (1858-1931), professor of economics and statistics, is sometimes mentioned but he had resigned on 1 November 1905. Struycken, a practising Catholic, is more likely to have been the supervisor.
60. W.J.A.J. Duynstee, 'Natuurrecht', *Handelingen van de Vereeniging voor de Wijsbegeerte des Rechts* 1929, pp. 176-178 (quote on p. 178).

legal positivists would have abhorred ..."[61] Van der Heijden no doubt read these words with approval.

Duynstee was very interested in the mental health of the clergy. He was one of the first Catholic scholars to apply the results of modern psychoanalysis and psychology to pastoral care. In the mid-1950s, he came into conflict with the Vatican-based Sacred Congregation of the Holy Office, in what became known as the Duynstee-Terruwe affair. Anna Terruwe (1911-2004) was the first woman psychiatrist in the Netherlands. She had worked with Duynstee to develop a treatment for pastors and other clergy with neurotic disorders, including of a sexual nature. This treatment was deemed to contravene the morality of the Church. In 1957, Duynstee was transferred to Rome following a 'conviction' by the Holy Office. He was able to return to the Netherlands (Amsterdam) in 1960, thanks to the mediation of Cardinal Bernard Alfrink (1900-1987). Rehabilitation did not happen until 1965. He then went to live in his beloved Nebo monastery in Nijmegen.

3.2   *Pieter Kamphuisen*[62]

Kamphuisen is unjustly a relative unknown among Nijmegen law professors. He once described himself as someone "with the legs of an industrialist, the body of a lawyer and the arms of a banker."[63] As a lawyer, he was an all-rounder: he published on civil law, civil procedural law, the law of legal entities and company law, history of law, philosophy of law and on the field of his teaching remit, which was constitutional and administrative law. He shared with his colleagues a fascination with natural law, a law that – as he wrote – was given by nature and which had an altogether general validity and immutability. It provided a basis for the limitation of state power. The fundamental standard of natural law was 'to render to each their own' (*ius suum cuique tribuere*).[64] His conception of natural law was inspired above all by his close colleague Willem Duynstee, whom Kamphuisen regarded as having done ground-breaking work on the study of natural law. Admittedly, Duynstee himself argued that he owed his teachings to Aquinas, but this did not prevent him from "adding his own distinctive voice to

61.   Duynstee, 'Natuurrecht' (1929), p. 164. In other words, Duynstee rejected legism.
62.   H.J. Pabbruwe, 'Pieter Wilhelmus Kamphuisen (6 maart 1897 – 16 augustus 1961)', in: *Verzameld Werk van Prof. Mr. P.W. Kamphuisen*, Zwolle: W.E.J. Tjeenk Willink 1962, pp. VIII-XI; C.J.H. Jansen, 'P.W. Kamphuisen (1897-1961)', in: Jansen, Smits, Winkel (eds), *16 juristen en hun filosofische inspiratie*, p. 129 ff.
63.   *Verzameld Werk van Prof. Mr. P.W. Kamphuisen*, p. 571.
64.   P.W. Kamphuisen, 'Het natuurrecht' (1939), in: *Verzameld Werk van Prof. Mr. P.W. Kamphuisen*, p. 79 ff.

the chorus of natural law philosophers and from developing a doctrine that, in my opinion, removes all objections to natural law."[65]

Following Duynstee's example, Kamphuisen made a distinction between natural law (generally valid, completely immutable and inviolable by humankind or human authority) and natural-reasonable law, a law that was closely related to human nature and was based on a reasonable understanding, but which was not given by nature and which therefore had to be stated explicitly. Freedom of contract, Kamphuisen believed, was not a requirement of (strict) natural law, but a certain degree of freedom of contract was a corollary of natural-reasonable law. This meant that the state could set limits on freedom of contract. This was also demonstrated by history. Freedom of contract had been seriously undermined in the course of the 20th century. Wars and economic crises forced the government to take measures that restricted freedom of contract. Kamphuisen even made reference to 'the great flood': the emphasis was on social aspects, there was a stronger sense of belonging, and a greater concern for the common good. The individual was once again a member of a community. For lawyers too, this created a pleasant feeling in times of crisis.[66]

Kamphuisen (1897-1961), like Van der Heijden, was born in Gouda. He began his law studies in Leiden in 1919 and obtained his doctorate in 1922 with a legal-historical thesis entitled *De Codificatiegedachte in het Romeinsche Rijk* [The notion of codification in the Roman empire]. He worked for a short time as a lawyer in Middelburg. In 1928 he was appointed head of the legal department of the Algemene Kunstzijde Unie (AKU) in Arnhem, a predecessor of today's Akzo Nobel. Kamphuisen succeeded Van der Grinten, who died in 1932. Kamphuisen wanted nothing to do with the National Socialist Movement (NSB) and Nazism. He proved insubordinate and his rectorship (1941) lasted less than a year, by order of the occupying forces.[67] As a specialist in Van der Heijden's field of law, Kamphuisen wanted to take over his colleague's civil law professorship after the war (Van der Heijden had died in 1941). The Board of Governors put a stop to this, partly because he had continued as legal advisor to AKU. The message was clear and Kamphuisen resigned in 1945. An illustrious public career awaited him. He became chairman of the supervisory boards of AKU, the Bank voor Handel en Scheepvaart in Rotterdam and the Nederlandsche Handel-Maatschappij. He continued to publish. His best-known work is the volume 'Bijzondere Overeenkomsten' [On Contracts] in *Mr. C. Asser's Handleiding tot de Beoefening van het Nederlandsch Burgerlijk Recht* [C. Asser's Handbook to Dutch civil law] (1945). Other key works are *Beschouwingen over rechtswetenschap* [Reflections on Legal Science] (1938), *De collectieve en de individuele arbeidsovereenkomst* [The collective and individual

---

65. P.W. Kamphuisen, 'Contractsvrijheid' (1957), in: *Verzameld Werk van Prof. Mr. P.W. Kamphuisen*, p. 120.
66. Kamphuisen, 'Contractsvrijheid' (1957), in: *Verzameld Werk van Prof. Mr. P.W. Kamphuisen*, p. 122 ff., p. 127.
67. J. Brabers, *Een zoet juk. Rectores magnifici van de Radboud Universiteit over hun rectoraat 1923-2014*, Nijmegen: Valkhofpers 2014, pp. 52-53.

employment contract] (1956) and *Dwaling bij obligatoire overeenkomsten* [Errors in binding contracts] (1961). From 1936 to 1956 he was chairman of the Commercial Law Association. It is revealing that he continued, after 1945, to call himself a former professor at the Roman Catholic University of Nijmegen.

Kamphuisen had a keen interest in questions concerning the administration of justice, such as the relationship between the judge and the law, legal interpretation and the nature of jurisprudence. He did not care for legalism. With the triumphal advance of free interpretation of the law, "the halo that had shone so brightly around the head of the law had been tarnished: for if legislation was not the only source of law, why were its words weighed on golden scales?" Some heralds of the new theory may have gone too far: "few of today's jurists will wish to deny that the freer interpretation represents an invaluable advance for our legal system." This is because practice had shown that it wasn't possible for the legislator alone to bring redress. "That is why, especially in private law but also in public law, judges have had to reclaim their old praetorian prerogative, the power to create new law themselves, if necessary, to be allowed to work on a task, to keep the law abreast with the times."[68] Kamphuisen also addressed the role of jurisprudence. In his *Beschouwingen over rechtswetenschap* (1938), he described the importance of systematising legal scholarship as follows:

> When you say science, you are at the same time saying system. This also applies to a large extent to legal science, or jurisprudence; indeed, in my opinion, it may be said that it is only through systematisation that the practice of law as a scientific discipline becomes possible.[69]

Kamphuisen regarded comparative law and the history of law as the most important tools for constructing a system. In his *Beschouwingen over rechtswetenschap*, he also pointed to the importance of using words unambiguously in law. Lawyers often used different meanings of a term. The term 'rule of law' (*rechtsstaat*) was a good example.

> The term rule of law has become a catchphrase; it is no longer the preserve of the lawyer, but has also been seized upon by journalists, politicians (...).[70]

---

68.   P.W. Kamphuisen, 'De interpretatie in het staatsrecht' (1933), in: *Verzameld Werk van Prof. Mr. P.W. Kamphuisen*, p. 8, p. 17.
69.   P.W. Kamphuisen, *Beschouwingen over rechtswetenschap*, Nijmegen-Utrecht: Dekker & Van de Vegt 1938, p. 69.
70.   P.W. Kamphuisen, 'Eenige terminologische opmerkingen over het woord rechtsstaat' (1939), in: *Verzameld Werk van Prof. Mr. P.W. Kamphuisen*, p. 89.

The result was a Babel-like confusion. Kamphuisen's conclusion was simple: the term 'rule of law' was not suitable for 'scientific' purposes.[71]

Ultimately, he had a highly reliable moral compass, as an administrator and as a publicist. Following a discussion with the *Limburger Koerier* (LK) about the constitutional principles of the national socialist NSB, he wrote: "In the meantime, we agree with the LK that in the Netherlands too, a National Socialist state will – in practice – also mean a state of power."[72]

3.3 Bernardus Hermesdorf[73]

Hermesdorf took over Roman law from Russel in 1928. Although he hadn't written on the subject of Roman law, he had at least shown an interest in the history of law.[74] He had also published historical articles in a range of Catholic (historical) journals and newspapers (such as *De Tijd, De Maasbode* and *De Zuid-Limburger*). His appointment as lector had not gone smoothly because the faculty had quarrelled with the bishops. His name had been put forward in 1927, but the faculty refused to provide details about his religious, moral and social conduct, and that of his family, and about his suitability for teaching in a Catholic sense. The bishops eventually obtained this information themselves and appointed him lector in 1928.[75]

> Hermesdorf (1894-1978) was a practising Catholic who had attended Beysens' lectures as a student in Utrecht. He had been president of *Veritas*, the Catholic student association. In 1919 he obtained his doctorate by theses (*stellingen*) under Jean Charles Naber (1858-1950), the professor of Roman law. In 1923, Hermesdorf began work as a lawyer in Deventer. Like Pompe, he was involved in many of the social organisations of the city. Hermesdorf wrote the 'legal column' for the *Overijselsch Dagblad* from 1923 to 1926: he wrote for laypeople about new legislation ('The new Rent Tribunal Act', 'The new Criminal Procedure Code'), legal concepts that they encountered ('Commuter tax', 'Construction guarantee', 'The limited liability

---

71. Kamphuisen, 'Eenige terminologische opmerkingen over het woord rechtsstaat', p. 103. See also: 'Is het woord rechtsstaat onbruikbaar?', *Algemeen Handelsblad* 17 December 1939, Tweede blad, p. 3 and A.W.E. Brandsma, 'Rechtsstaat of machtstaat. Zowel een democratisch als een autoritair regiem kan van rechtsstaat tot machtsstaat zinken', *Limburger Koerier* 30 December 1939, front page.

72. P.W. Kamphuisen, 'Staatkundige Notities. CXXXIII', *De Venlosche Courant* 2 November 1935, front page.

73. Brabers, *De Faculteit der Rechtsgeleerdheid van de Katholieke Universiteit Nijmegen 1923-1982*, p. 68 ff.; O. Moorman van Kappen, 'Hermesdorf, Bernardus Hubertus Dominicus (1894-1978)', in: *Biografisch Woordenboek van Nederland* (available online); C.J.H. Jansen, 'Bernardus Hubertus Dominicus Hermesdorf (1894-1978)', in: Hermans-Brand and Jansen (eds), *Recht in Nijmegen*, pp. 63-64. Bibliography in: *Opstellen over recht en rechtsgeschiedenis aangeboden aan Prof. Mr. B.H.D. Hermesdorf*, Deventer: Kluwer 1965, pp. XI-XXIII.

74. See his work 'Recht en cultuur', *De Beiaard* 1925, pp. 452-458.

75. Brabers, *De Faculteit der Rechtsgeleerdheid van de Katholieke Universiteit Nijmegen 1923-1982*, pp. 58-59.

company') and recent case law ('Undue payment').[76] In 1931, Hermesdorf was appointed professor of Roman law at the Catholic University of Leuven. He resigned that professorship in 1938 when he was appointed professor of Roman law and old Dutch law in Nijmegen. Hermesdorf became a prolific writer. Generations of Nijmegen students were obliged to study his *Schets der uitwendige geschiedenis van het Romeins recht* [Sketch of the external history of Roman law] (first edition 1936, seventh edition 1972). He also adapted his predecessor Van der Heijden's *Aante(e)keningen bij de geschiedenis van het oude vaderlands(ch)e recht* [Notes on the history of old Dutch law] (1943, eighth edition 1968). His best-known publications included *Licht en schaduw in de advocatuur der Lage Landen* [Light and shadow within the legal profession in the Low Countries] (1951), *Te hoofde gaan* [Preliminary rulings] (1954), *Römisches Recht in den Niederlanden* [Roman law in the Netherlands] (part V of the prestigious series *Ius Romanum Medii Aevi*, 1968) and the posthumously published *Rechtsspiegel. Een rechtshistorische terugblik in de Lage Landen van het herfsttij* [Reflections on law. A legal-historical look back at the twilight of the Low Countries] (1980). A salient aspect was the attention he devoted to Bernard of Clairvaux (1090-1153) as a jurist. As a legal historian he was not a dogmatist, like Van der Heijden, but more of a (Catholic) cultural historian. He had a keen interest in the connection between law on the one hand and art, language and literature on the other. In 1945 Hermesdorf was appointed to the board of the National Bureau for War Documentation (now NIOD), which was tasked with collecting all the documentation on the history of the occupation period.

Hermesdorf's initial years in the Nijmegen law faculty had not been easy. The joint efforts of Van der Heijden, Van der Grinten, Bellefroid and Raaijmakers had built up the faculty from 1923 onwards, with Hermesdorf, the 'newcomer', remaining an outsider for some time. That wasn't because of his Catholicism. On the occasion of the fifteenth anniversary of the 'Carolina' in 1938, he spoke about the university tradition to which law faculties belonged: to teach the required ready knowledge about the law, and in the first instance positive law. The Nijmegen law faculty added something to this tradition: "Its aim is rather to find new forms and new possibilities for these legal values, which are of all time." Knowledge of positive law did not suffice for this: a "Catholic orientation in law and legal life" was needed in order to identify the 'deeper' grounds of the law.[77]

Just a year after his appointment as extraordinary professor, Hermesdorf asked to be appointed full professor. Whereas he had thought that he could successfully combine the practice of law and the lectorate, without detriment to either, "I have since increasingly learned that this creates a dualism, which is harmful. It is like limping in two minds. Legal practice requires considerable work and care. Moreover, study increasingly requires the whole person." More importantly, however, was that "under the current arrangement, I have far too little contact with members of the faculties, especially the law faculty. I feel this same loss to an

---

76. He had written contributions on current legislation for the *Zuid-Limburger* from 1916 to 1919.
77. 'Het derde lustrum onzer Universiteit. Prof. Mr. B.H.D. Hermesdorf, Katholieke oriënteering. Hervatting eener oude traditie', *De Maasbode* 17 October 1938, Avondblad, p. 5.

even greater extent with regard to students." Van der Heijden and Van der Grinten played for time in their letter, saying that the time was not yet ripe for an appointment other than that of lector.[78] It wasn't until 1938 that Hermesdorf was appointed as a full professor. Van der Heijden did not yet appear fully convinced of Hermesdorf's abilities, perhaps because students were dissatisfied with his lectures. However, Hermesdorf's view of Roman law aligned in many ways with that of Van der Heijden: students must be made aware that knowledge of Roman law was of practical significance for modern law. Hermesdorf also argued that history and dogmatics stood alongside one another in the practice of Roman law. "Well, the future lawyer must know what possibilities there are in the apparent rigidity of our own Dutch law, and in this respect the Roman lawyer, a practitioner and a true casuist, more than a constructive systematist, is the teacher for all times."[79] During the occupation, Hermesdorf was able to show just what he was made of (see the following chapter).

3.4 Robert Regout[80]

Robert Regout became an extraordinary professor of international law when Bellefroid retired. He had trained as a lawyer in Utrecht and Leiden.

> Regout's father Louis (1861-1915) was also a doctor in law. Robert (1895-1942) joined the Jesuits in 1915 and was ordained a priest in 1927. In 1934, Telders acted as Regout's supervisor in Leiden. Regout's doctoral thesis in international law dealt with the Catholic doctrine of the just war. In the year in which he completed his PhD, he became spiritual counsellor (moderator) to the Nijmegen students. He was also closely involved in international politics, including as an advisor to the Roman Catholic State Party and as a supporter of and speaker for the Catholic Dutch Peace Alliance. The Nijmegen professors Bellefroid, Pompe and Raaijmakers were also active within the Alliance.

---

78. KDC, B.H.D. Hermesdorf Archive (160), inv. no. 330: Hermesdorf's letter to the Faculty of Law, 22 November 1929 and letter from Van der Grinten (president of the faculty) and Van der Heijden (secretary), 6 December 1929. They called on Hermesdorf to publish a work on old Dutch law as this would significantly increase his chances of achieving the solution he desired.

79. B.H.D. Hermesdorf, *De verhouding van Romeinsch en Oud Vaderlandsch recht in geschiedenis en academische opleiding*. See also 'Romeinsch en Oud-Vaderlandsch recht bij de academische opleiding', *De Tijd* 7 February 1939, p. 2 and 'Ambtsaanvaanleg Prof. Mr. B.H.D. Hermesdorf', *De Maasbode* 6 February 1939, p. 7.

80. See M.J.F. Lindeijer and A. Welle (eds), *Robert Regout Maastricht 1896 – Dachau 1942*, Drachten: friends of Robert Regout and Omnia Faustia 2004. In this book, see: H. de Waele, 'Grond voor vertrouwen. Regout als jurist', p. 103 ff.; H. de Waele, 'Commemorating Robert Regout (1896-1942). A chapter from the history of public international law revisited', *Journal of History of International Law* 2005, pp. 81-92; Brabers, *De Faculteit der Rechtsgeleerdheid van de Katholieke Universiteit Nijmegen 1923-1982*, p. 92 ff.

In the years before the outbreak of the Second World War, Regout spoke out
openly against communism and National Socialism. In 1936 he described Soviet
communism as a wolf in sheep's clothing.

> In passing, the speaker expressed his opinion that an equally bleak opinion could be given
> about National Socialism: his impression is that the Nat. Soc. tendencies severely encroach upon
> religious and political freedoms and that this Nat. Socialism is a serious threat to our faith. (...)
> The Episcopate pointed out the great dangers of our time as follows: 1. communism, 2. National
> Socialism, 3. freethinkers; the great danger therefore threatens from different sides. For
> Catholics, there is a duty to take a direct positive action of Faith in God and Church, after which
> one will automatically turn words into deeds.[81]

Regout was appointed professor in 1939. He delivered his inaugural address on
28 February 1940, a few months after the Nazi occupation of Poland and other
European countries. His speech was entitled: *Are there grounds for confidence in the
future of international law?* Regout answered this question in the affirmative, despite
the fact that the term 'international law' had become a mockery in his time. He
believed that the study of international law was a solemn duty, "regardless of what
the near future might bring in terms of lawlessness and arbitrariness." Truth and
goodness had to be sought, even if it brought no immediate result. In his view,
strengthening the foundations of the international legal order was the most
essential and difficult task of the discipline of international law. He believed that as
international law had flourished in Christianity, it was only in Christianity that it
could find its life force. Regout supported a legal order in a League of Nations.
"The failure of the League of Nations ... is due not so much to internal flaws as to
the egotism that has misused this instrument, based on a sense of community."[82]
The German invasion must have come as a shock to Regout.[83] Following the
occupation of the Netherlands in May 1940, he published a major article, which the
Eindhovensche en Meijerijsche Courant even described as being "of decisive
importance". The article, entitled 'The legal situation in occupied territory',
discussed the occupier's rights and obligations under the Regulations concerning
the Laws and Customs of War on Land (1907).[84] He then travelled tirelessly

---

81. 'De invloed van Sovjet-Rusland in West-Europa. Mr. Rob. Regout S.J. voor de RK Limb.
     Werkgeversvereeniging. Het communisme thans een wolf in schaapsvacht', *Limburger Koerier*
     10 December 1936, front page.
82. R.H.W. Regout, *Is er grond voor het vertrouwen in de toekomst van het volkenrecht?* Nijmegen-Utrecht:
     Dekker & Van de Vegt 1940, p. 10, p. 14.
83. On 8 May 1940 (!) he defended the Dutch policy of neutrality. "We want to remain neutral. But
     we will also defend that neutrality with all our strength against any attack." See 'Onze
     neutraliteit, een Nederlandsch en een Europeesch belang', *Provinciale Noordbrabantsche en
     's-Hertogenbossche Courant* 8 May 1940, Vijfde blad, p. 1.
84. *Studiën* 133 (1940), p. 469 ff. Regout's article was also published in the 'regular' newspaper:
     'Professor Mr. Robert Regout S.J. over den rechtstoestand in bezet gebied', *Eindhovensche en
     Meijerijsche Courant* 7 June 1940, Tweede blad, p. 1.

through the Netherlands, calling on everyone to take a firm stance. He was arrested on 3 July 1940, after which his ordeal began. He died on 28 December 1942 at Dachau, one of the first German concentration camps, near Munich.

4   THE NIJMEGEN PROFESSORS AND NATURAL LAW

The distinction between natural law and positive law had been made by the Roman jurist Ulpian. In *Institutes*, he explained that private law was divided into three parts: precepts derived from nature (*exnaturalibus praeceptis*), from all peoples and from communities. He wrote that the difference between natural law on the one hand and human and civil law on the other was easy to comprehend: natural law was common to all living beings, while human and civil law was common to all people.[85] The distinction between natural law and positive law became part of the legal tradition of the Roman Catholic Church, which – after all – lived by Roman law. Almost all the professors in the Nijmegen law faculty in the first half of the 20th century engaged with the place and role of natural law in the practice of law.[86] They were inspired above all by the ideas of Thomas Aquinas and, from their own time, those of Utrecht professor Beysens, who worked in the spirit of Aquinas. Van der Heijden, Bellefroid, Duynstee, Pompe, Hermesdorf, Van der Grinten, Hoogveld and Kamphuisen were well acquainted with Beysens' work. Regout was also influenced by natural law,[87] while Duynstee wrote on that subject. The latter was also inspired by Hoogveld, his fellow professor of philosophy of law, and by Hoogveld's book *Overzicht van beginselen deralgemeene rechts filosofie naar peripateties-thomistische beginselen* [Overview of principles of general philosophy of law according to peripatetic-Thomist principles] (1935). Bellefroid also made regular references to Hoogveld in his books and – as already mentioned – Kamphuisen relied heavily on Duynstee's work.

Another thing that Duynstee and his colleagues had in common was their emphatic rejection of the old and 'new' ideas about natural law of their time (the new ideas did not go back to Thomas Aquinas). They condemned the 'old', in particular the 17th- and 18th-century views on natural law, because the natural law from that time was 'denatured'. The practitioners of natural law had detached it from its 'last' source, God, and they regarded the nature of humankind only as

---

85. See D. 1,1,1,2; D. 1,1,1,3 and D. 1,1,1,2.
86. See J.H.A. Lokin, 'Nijmeegs privaatrecht, bestaat dat?', in: *Nijmeegs privaatrecht bestaat (niet)!* Nijmegen: GNI 1999, p. 2 ff.
87. His five-part *Hoofdstukken uit de Bijzondere Ethiek* had considerable influence. Three of the five chapters dealt with legal subjects: *Eigendomsrecht* (1917), *Wijsgeerige Staatsleer* (1917) and *Wijsbegeerte van het Strafrecht* (1919). See I.J.M. van den Berg, 'In memoriam Mgr. Prof. dr. J.Th. Beysens', *Tijdschrift voor Philosophie* 8 (1946)-2/3, p. 379 ff. In 'A New League of Extraordinary Gentlemen? The Professionalization of International Law Scholarship in the Netherlands, 1919-1940', *European Journal of International Law* 2020, p. 1005 ff., H. de Waele called Regout one of the "prime exponents of natural law thinking".

individuals (and not as part of a community).[88] The Nijmegen professors rejected the 'new' view of natural law because it was based on a natural law whose content varied, known as the 'richtige Recht' (the right law). The content of this 'richtige Recht' changed according to time and place. The interpreter *par excellence* of this 'relative' natural law was the German lawyer and philosopher of law Rudolf Stammler (1856-1938). Paul Scholten (1875-1946), the Amsterdam professor of civil law and philosophy of law, was very impressed by Stammler's natural law. By his own account, Scholten avoided the use of the term natural law, "although I am aware that what I want to propose touches closely on many conceptions of what they call natural law."[89] Duynstee considered this modern natural law an 'error' as it was not based on essential immutability. In addition, this natural law did not result from the nature of humankind, but from the nature of culture. Duynstee did not place a high value on the system of natural or cultural law. However, it did have a major 'negative' significance in that "it proclaimed the complete untenability of legal positivism."[90]

According to the Catholic viewpoint, the law should be divided into the eternal and immutable natural law ('the Eternal law', 'God's world order') on the one hand and temporal laws on the other. Natural-reasonable law and positive laws belonged to temporal law. Natural-reasonable law had a share in natural law, but a 'human' government had to provide the authority. In order to be 'good' law, positive law had to satisfy the requirement of justice, which was rooted in natural law. The principle of justice was the assessment criterion for positive law. An act that was contrary to justice was bad law and lacked intrinsic legal quality.[91] The professors of Nijmegen were frequently engaged in the interpretation of natural-reasonable law. Perhaps the best-known deliberation is Van der Heijden's address as rector, *Natuurlijke normen in het positieve recht* [Natural norms in positive law] (1933), in which he discussed the meaning of such terms as morality, reasonableness, justice, good faith, due diligence, the demands of societal discourse, and decency. Van der Heijden sensed in his time a growing influence of these natural norms in positive law. "Returning to natural standards is essentially a recognition that the law is more than what humans determine, that there is a higher reality in the nature of things."[92] It was the task of the legislator and judge

---

88. See J. van der Grinten, 'De katholieke staatsleer en de vrijheidsrechten van den mensch' (1930), in: *Verspreide Opstellen van Prof. Mr. Dr. J.H.P.M. van der Grinten*, p. 83 ff. J.H.P. Bellefroid, *De Bronnen van het Stellig Recht en haar Onderlinge Verhoudingen*, Nijmegen: G.C. Richelle 1927, pp. 31-32, pointed out that the natural law of the 18th century, which "was supposedly generally and eternally valid for the whole of humanity" was in reality nothing but a combination of Roman and Germanic law.

89. See C.J.H. Jansen and E. Poortinga, 'Het onderwijs in de rechtsfilosofie van Paul Scholten', *Recht en kritiek* 19 (1993) 2, p. 191 ff. (quote on p. 201).

90. Duynstee, 'Natuurrecht' (1929), p. 163, p. 168 (quote).

91. See J.H.P. Bellefroid, *Inleiding tot de rechtswetenschap in Nederland*, 5th edition, Nijmegen-Utrecht: Dekker & Van de Vegt 1948, p. 13, pp. 28-29.

92. See E.J.J. van der Heijden, 'Recht en billijkheid', *De Nieuwe Eeuw* 1924, no. 381.

to adapt these natural standards to changing circumstances, whereby a positive law could evolve.[93]

Not only Van der Heijden, but also his colleague Kamphuisen was a defender of natural law as the foundation and touchstone of positive law. In 1939, together with Duynstee, he presented an introduction to natural law to the Association for Thomist Philosophy. Kamphuisen struggled with giving concrete form to the content of natural law standards. While all were in agreement about the basic standard – to render to each their own – the standards of natural law were necessarily so general that they rarely appeared in legislation and case law. Perhaps it was better, therefore, for scholars to designate institutions of a natural law nature, such as private property, the doctrine of *justum pretium* (just price) and the principle of *pacta sunt servanda* (agreements must be kept). His conclusion was clear: "The doctrine of natural law thus provides a philosophical foundation to law and state, it thus limits the power of the state, and thus provides guidelines; but in no way does it lock state law into a straitjacket."[94] Van der Grinten had written in similar fashion: "Natural law is therefore not worthless, but provides us with principles, which point out for each cultural period the guidelines for society and which maintain the correct balance between community and individual."[95]

To demonstrate the topicality of the natural law position, Catholic jurist C.M.O. van Nispen tot Sevenaer (1895-1995) referred to the Germany and USSR (Russia) of his day: "Not on religious grounds, but solely on the basis of natural law, the exclusion of Jews, for example, from the state in which they were born and raised, should be rejected; the execution without trial of the guilty – not to speak of the innocent – should be condemned."[96] From 1931, Duynstee gave lectures on 'eugenics', the purpose of reproduction in the light of Catholic genetics. He pointed out the popularity in a country like Germany of 'negative eugenics', which aimed

---

93.   E.J.J. van der Heijden, *Aanteekeningen bij de geschiedenis van het oude vaderlandsche recht*, 1st edition, Nijmegen/Utrecht: Dekker & Van de Vegt 1933, pp. 1-3.
94.   P.W. Kamphuisen, 'Het natuurrecht' (1939) in: *Verzameld Werk van Prof. Mr. P.W. Kamphuisen*, p. 78 ff, pp. 84-85, p. 87 (quote); P.W. Kamphuisen, 'De leer van het justum pretium herleefd' (1933), in: *Verzameld Werk van Prof. Mr. P.W. Kamphuisen*, p. 222 and p. 231.
95.   J. van der Grinten, 'De katholieke staatsleer en de vrijheidsrechten van den mensch' (1930), in: *Verspreide Opstellen van Prof. Mr. Dr. J.H.P.M. van der Grinten*, p. 94.
96.   C.M.O. van Nispen tot Sevenaer, 'De strijd om de grenzen van het natuurrecht', *NJB* 1934, p. 673 ff. and p. 685 ff. (quote pp. 692-693). Cf. C.M.O. van Nispen tot Sevenaer, 'Natuurlijke normen als ondergeschoven kinderen', *Weekblad van het Recht* 1934/12692, pp. 3-4. W. Duynstee did not regard Van der Heijden's natural standards as part of strict natural law, but as natural-reasonable law. See W. Duynstee, 'Het natuurrecht' (1939), p. 87, note 8. In his Preliminary opinion for the Association for the advancement of science and scholarship among Catholics in the Netherlands, entitled *Nulla poena sine lege* (1936), he also criticised the arbitrariness in the 'new' German criminal law. He believed that the *nulla poena* principle did not belong to strict natural law (pp. 7-8).

to make reproduction impossible through measures such as sterilisation.[97] From a natural law perspective, Duynstee rejected the sterilisation introduced in 1934 by the German (National Socialist) legislator to make it impossible for "sufferers of hereditary mental and physical illnesses" to produce offspring.

> The right to procreation is a natural right, a right that people naturally have, by the mere fact of being human. After all, the Creator has given them the power, the potential for procreation ... The right to procreate is therefore a natural right which the State cannot infringe.[98]

5   RESISTANCE TO FASCISM AND NATIONAL SOCIALISM

A 2015 report by Bas von Benda-Beckmann shows that Catholicism was an obstacle to German attempts to 'nazify' the Netherlands. In particular, the position adopted by Mgr Jan de Jong (1885-1955) was the driving force behind Catholic resistance to National Socialism in the Netherlands during the occupation.[99] This firm stance during the war didn't come from nowhere. On 11 February 1934, the Dutch bishops had published the *Vastenmandement*, a pastoral letter, in which they voiced their opposition to National Socialism, fascism and anti-Semitism. In so doing, according to Te Slaa and Klijn, the bishops inflicted a heavy blow on the power of Dutch National Socialism to attract Catholics.[100] Furthermore, in 1936, they excluded members of the NSB (National Socialist Movement) from the sacraments. Catholic newspapers, such as *De Tijd* and the *Limburger Koerier*, took a strong stand against the National Socialist threat and the anti-Jewish measures in Germany. In 1936, at the request of the Committee for Special Jewish Affairs, important Catholic clergy such as Henri Poels (1968-1948) and the Nijmegen professor Titus Brandsma, denounced the treatment of German Jews by the National Socialists in a pamphlet entitled 'Dutch voices on the treatment of the Jews in Germany.' Poels wrote:

---

97. Brabers, *De Faculteit der Rechtsgeleerdheid van de Katholieke Universiteit Nijmegen 1923-1982*, p. 128 (note 117); 'Nijmeegsch studentencorps. Lezing van Prof. Duynstee over "eugenetiek"', *De Maasbode* 23 January 1931, Avondblad, p. 3.
98. 'Sterilisatie ontoelaatbaar. Het standpunt der katholieke moraal. Recht tot voorplanting is een natuurrecht', *Limburger Koerier* 9 August 1933, front page.
99. B. von Benda-Beckmann, Rapport verkennend onderzoek 'De rooms-katholieke kerk en de grenzen van verzet in Nederland tijdens de Tweede Wereldoorlog' (available online), p. 4. Cf. C.J.H. Jansen, 'Nederlandse protesten tegen het Duitse antisemitisme in de jaren dertig van de vorige eeuw en de rol van de Rooms-Katholieke kerk daarin', *RMThemis* 2016/6, pp. 289-291.
100. R. te Slaa & E. Klijn, *De NSB. Ontstaan en opkomst van de Nationaal-Socialistische Beweging, 1931-1935*, Amsterdam: Boom 2009, pp. 323-324, p. 369 ff. (p. 375).

> The NSDAP theories about 'Blut und Boden' are contrary to any concept of law. How such ideas can be espoused by a people, the ostensible bearers of high 'Kultur', is beyond me.[101]

The professors in the Nijmegen law faculty also took an active stance. As early as 1928, Van der Grinten opposed the 'false' state doctrine of the fascists, which centred on the dictatorship of a 'great man', a 'Caesar', "It is dangerous because of its basic premise and its consequences", the 'permanent revolution'. The notion of power prevailed over that of justice, the politics of the deed replaced the politics of the word. The fact that Van der Grinten opposed fascism and its 'great man' and 'dictator' Mussolini drew the attention of a host of (Catholic) newspapers.[102]

Van der Heijden also openly opposed the National Socialist doctrine. At a Roman Catholic State Party (RKSP) retreat on 29-30 July 1933 in Amersfoort, he spoke about the meaning of the rule of law (*rechtsstaat*) in the light of the authority emanating from God. His reflections would result in a sixteen-page booklet, entitled *Gezag en Vrijheid* [Authority and Freedom]. He regarded the fight against National Socialism as a fight against liberalism, fascism, social democracy, and communism at one and the same time. All these movements were based on a factual order and lacked any form of transcendental philosophy. According to the views of these movements, the *rechtsstaat* was a product of the government alone and therefore nothing more than a state of power (*machtstaat*) in disguise. The only thing that distinguished these movements was the nature of the factual foundation. "The philosophy of all of them ends (...) in power and facts." According to them, the law began first with the state. In Catholic teaching, however, the law was the foundation of the *rechtsstaat*. Rightly, of course, Van der Heijden was not referring to positive law, but to "the law that has been revealed to us and has been laid down in the nature of things." The *rechtsstaat* presupposed a legal order that was more deeply founded than in a specific figure of state. Thus there was a deep gulf between a *rechtsstaat* and a *machtstaat*.

> Must we, in need of strong authority, throw ourselves into the arms of the new *machtsstaat*, abandon all thought of freedom? We answer with conviction: no.

---

101. H.A. Poels, in: 'Jodenvervolging en katholieken', *De Tijd* 31 January 1936, front page. On Brandma's opposition to National Socialism: A. Jacobs, *Kroniek van de Karmel in Nederland 1840-1970*, Hilversum: Verloren 2017, p. 72 ff.
102. J. van der Grinten, 'De gezagsleer van het Fascisme', *De Tijd* 28 November 1923, front page; J. van der Grinten, 'Het parlementarisme' (1927/1928), in: *Verspreide Opstellen van Prof. Mr. Dr. J.H.P.M. van der Grinten*, p. 115 ff. Cf. 'Het fascisme. Een stem uit Nijmegen', *De Tijd* 19 January 1928, Derde blad, p. 9 and 'Het fascisme en wij', *De Maasbode* 18 January 1928, front page.

As long as Fascism and National Socialism do not demonstrate that they have made the principles of law the foundation of their State, they cannot therefore be our party. The *rechtsstaat* is sacred to us above all else.[103]

Van der Heijden believed that in his day there was every reason to reflect on the Ten Commandments. "The Soviet people have become mere ciphers. The fascist hierarchy builds from top to bottom: the will of the head is the last law. In National Socialism, it is not the State, but race that is paramount. (...) Mussolini is a dictator by his own right. Nor does Hitler stand on the ground of God's will. (...) Will the world that disregards the Ten Commandments perish? We do not know. What is to come will be borne by God's will."[104]

In an address for *Sanctus Augustinus*, the Leiden student association, Kamphuisen expressed similar thoughts to those of Van der Heijden. He discussed the distinction between church and state in liberalism and National Socialism. He rejected both political movements from the point of view of the Catholic doctrine of the state. Liberalism was based too much on individualistic principles, National Socialism too much on the interests of the state. It was completely wrong for the state to intervene in spiritual life, "as we see, for example, in Germany at present." If the interest of the state was 'paramount', "as in Germany", then it was inevitable that the church would become subordinate to the state. Kamphuisen was therefore sceptical about the ideas of the NSB.[105]

Prompted by Kamphuisen's discussion of *Brochure nr. 4. Actueele Vragen. Antwoord van het Nederlandsche Nationaal-Socialisme (Fascisme) op een tiental Nederlandsche Vragen* [Pamphlet no. 4. Current questions. Response of Dutch National-Socialism (fascism) to ten Dutch questions] (1934)[106] in the *Nieuwe Venlosche Courant*, a fierce argument arose between Kamphuisen and the *Limburger Koerier*. He had agreed with some of the constitutional principles outlined in the NSB pamphlet, for example, that the Dutch state should profess God as the driving force of national moral life. Religion should indeed remain a matter for the churches, which was

---

103. E.J.J. van der Heijden, *Gezag en Vrijheid*. Publication of the secretariat of the Roman Catholic State Party. The Hague 1933. 'De dreiging van overspannen Nationalisme', *De Zuidwillemsvaart* 4 July 1933, front page (in anticipation of the retreat in Amersfoort) and 'Doelbewust werk. De R.K. Staatspartij verstaat de teekenen des tijds', *Nieuwe Venlosche Courant* 4 July 1933, front page. He also touched on the theme during the Ninth Limburg Social Study Week in Rolduc from 6 to 8 August 1933. Cf. 'Het katholicisme en de moderne Wereldcrisis. Gezag en vrijheid, democratie en dictatuur', *Nieuwe Venlosche Courant* 9 August 1933, front page: 'Lenin, Hitler, Mussolini have no legal principles for their power. We must not participate in a state of power for the sake of principle.' See the reproduction of Van der Heijden's words in: 'Na den landdag der N.S.B. Nationaal-socialisme en Demo-liberalisme stoelen op denzelfden wortel', *Limburger Koerier* 17 October 1935, front page; 'Beginsel en stelsel. Nationaal-socialisme en Demo-liberalisme', *Limburger Koerier* 29 October 1935, front page.
104. *De Zuidwillemsvaart* 8 August 1934, p. 3.
105. 'Kerk en Staat. Een voordracht van prof. Kamphuisen over de liberale en de christelijke opvatting', *De Tijd* 30 January 1934, p. 2.
106. On this pamphlet: Te Slaa & Klijn, *De NSB*, p. 407 ff.

entitled to the support and protection of the state. Kamphuisen noted that the NSB distanced itself here from the racial doctrines of the Nazis in Germany.[107]

In a contribution to the *Nieuwe Venlosche Courant* more than a year later, Kamphuisen – referring to his earlier argument in that same newspaper – explained the difference between the liberal and the National Socialist state doctrine and the objections to both views. He felt that the *Limburger Koerier* had lumped liberalism and National Socialism too much together in an editorial, whereas there was a big difference between the two movements. The liberal doctrine, as he had argued earlier, placed too much emphasis on the importance of the individual, while National Socialism placed too much on the value of the state. The Catholic view made a stand against both doctrines: "neither pushing the individual excessively to the fore, nor defending the doctrine of the absolute value of the state."[108]

The *Limburger Koerier* responded with irritation: "Principle and system. Comments of an absent-minded professor." The paper accused Kamphuisen of agreeing with the NSB views expressed in *Pamphlet no.4*. National socialism (the NSB) and liberalism did indeed have in common the notion of the state of power – a state based solely on facts and not on law, as Van der Heijden had demonstrated in his pamphlet *Gezag en Vrijheid*. There was almost no difference between social democratic, communist or fascist political views on the state.

> The philosophy of all of them ends, no differently from that of liberalism, in power and facts. Their state is also not supported by a legal foundation. Only the factual foundation is different, the power is shifted. All salvation is now expected to come, not from freedom, but from coercion.[109]

Kamphuisen agreed with Van der Heijden's analysis. Indeed, liberalism had never succeeded in finding a correct theory as to why the law bound the liberal state, "a phenomenon which we firmly believe can only be understood in Thomist philosophy." However, he continued to oppose the *Limburger Koerier*'s view that liberalism was based on a state of power. He did nonetheless agree with the newspaper's editor that a National Socialist state would in practice also mean a

---

107. P.W, Kamphuisen, 'Staatkundige Notities. XXIV', *Nieuwe Venlosche Courant* 30 March 1934, front page.
108. P.W. Kamphuisen, 'Staatkundige Notities. CXXX', *Nieuwe Venlosche Courant* 23 October 1935, front page.
109. 'Beginsel en stelsel. Opmerkingen van een verstrooiden professor. Nationaal-socialisme en demo-liberalisme', *Limburger Koerier* 29 October 1935, front page. An echo of this view in the *Limburger Koerier* could be found in a response from an (anonymous) student in the Nijmegen student newspaper *Vox Carolina*. Kamphuisen felt obliged to state in a subsequent issue that he had a principled aversion to the NSB's doctrine of the state. See Brabers, *De Faculteit der Rechtsgeleerdheid van de Katholieke Universiteit Nijmegen 1923-1982*, p. 129 (note 120).

state of power in the Netherlands.[110] The *Limburger Koerier* saw this last sentence as a 'genuflection' on Kamphuisen's part: "Prof. Kamphuisen is slowly coming to a more correct understanding." The newspaper reiterated once again that the NSB did not support its politics "on a positive principle, which was based on God's law. For [the NSB], law was what the leader decreed. The dictatorship of the Leader is the constitution of its politics. For National Socialism, the subjective insight and independent will of the leader are the sources of all law."[111] It was a mystery to Kamphuisen how the *Limburger Koerier* could think that he had expressed agreement with the NSB's doctrine of the state. Right from the start in 1934, he had been sceptical about the views of the NSB.[112] He had also argued in *Vox Carolina* that he had no political aspirations for himself and no wish to engage in politics more than was necessary for his position as professor.[113]

In his doctoral thesis Brabers pointed out that, in their teaching and in the activities that they organised for students, the professors did not keep aloof from the political developments of the 1930s, especially in Germany. Van der Heijden in particular had demonstrated a special responsibility. In 1935 he had established a 'political club of Nijmegen students'. At his request, they wrote short political reports on subjects such as National Socialism's understanding of the law, German racial theory, the idea of social regulation, the papal encyclical *Mit brennender Sorge* (1937) and the history of National Socialism. These reports were debated during discussion evenings at Van der Heijden's home. Brabers reports that the students also took part in political role-plays on these evenings, with Van der Heijden ensuring first and foremost that they presented an intellectual challenge – in terms of substance – to the totalitarian ideologies.[114]

At the end of the 1930s, the Roman Catholic State Party (RKSP) saw the NSB as its biggest electoral rival in the south of the country. In 1937, almost all the law professors at the Nijmegen faculty (Van der Heijden, Hoogveld, Kamphuisen, Raaijmakers, Russel and Van Welie) supported the Catholic newspapers' call to vote for the RKSP. "The RKSP, the most socially engaged and progressive party in the Netherlands, offers the best guarantees that neither the Nazis of the NSB nor

---

110. P.W. Kamphuisen, 'Staatkundige Notities. CXXXII', *Nieuwe Venlosche Courant* 2 November 1935, front page.
111. 'Zonderlinge volksvoorlichting. Prof. Kamphuisen komt langzaam tot juister inzicht. De Machtsstaat der N.S.B.', *Limburger Koerier* 7 November 1935, front page and p. 2. The newspaper turned Kamphuisen's 'genuflection' into a drama in four acts.
112. P.W. Kamphuisen, 'Staatkundige Notities. CXXXV', *Nieuwe Venlosche Courant* 19 November 1935, front page.
113. As can be read in 'De student in de politiek?', *Nieuwe Venlosche Courant* 9 March 1934, p. 2, tweede blad.
114. Brabers, *De Faculteit der Rechtsgeleerdheid van de Katholieke Universiteit Nijmegen 1923-1982*, p. 129 and Appendix 2 (p. 503). *Mit brennender Sorge*, which had been deliberately published in German, discussed the position of the Roman Catholic Church in Nazi Germany. The encyclical contained a condemnation of National Socialism and racism, as well as a rejection of the totalitarian state whenever it placed itself above natural law.

the Communists will ever run this country. The stronger our party, the more insignificant the chance of dictatorship."[115] Thus the pre-war image of the Nijmegen law faculty was one of aversion to Nazi ideology and racial theory.

6   THE LAW STUDY ASSOCIATIONS

On Van der Heijden's initiative, law students from Nijmegen had founded the Contardo Ferrini legal debating society on 26 February 1924. Ferrini (1859-1902) had been professor of Roman and Byzantine law in Pavia. Known for his 'mystical' piety, he was beatified in 1947. The aim of Contardo Ferrini was to organise lectures on legal, social and political topics. Pompe, Van der Heijden, Duynstee, Jurgens, Petit and Van der Grinten assumed successive responsibility for the academic quality of the lecture content and the subsequent debate. The debates probably faded away in the late 1960s or early 1970s.

The Law Faculty of Nijmegen students was founded on 24 February 1927 and was renamed the Law Faculty Association (JFV) in 1938. It formed part of Carolus Magnus, the Roman Catholic Student Association, but these ties were severed in the mid-1960s. The JFV also aimed to organise lectures, as well as conferences. In addition, it was a means by which students could express their views on curriculum design and lecture and exam content to the professors. At the end of the 1960s, the JFV took part in the – sometimes heated – discussions about the 'democratisation' of the university. *Morgen Meester*, the newspaper for Nijmegen law students that was founded in 1967, had strong links with the JFV. The first issue appeared on 14 December 1967. Later, the JFV came up with its own association magazine. The JFV continues to this day.[116]

7   CONCLUSION

The professors and lectors of the Nijmegen law faculty showed themselves to be socially engaged and committed Catholics.[117] They soon formed a close-knit group, which succeeded in building a good reputation within the academic world. After his departure for Utrecht, Pompe continued to be involved in the affairs of the faculty. After some time he complained: "The rivers appear to form a large gulf

---

115. 'Laatste Advies' and 'Oproep', *Nieuwe Venlosche Courant* 25 May 1937, front page and p. 8 and 'Oproep', *De Tijd* 25 May 1937, p. 6. It is not clear to me why Duynstee's name was missing.

116. Brabers, *De Faculteit der Rechtsgeleerdheid van de Katholieke Universiteit Nijmegen 1923-1982*, pp. 78-79, pp. 106-107, p. 438. J The JFV website features a description of its history.

117. In 1939, all professors in the faculty (Bellefroid, Duynstee, Van der Heijden, Hoogveld, Kamphuisen, Raaijmakers, Russel and Van Welie) supported the call for 'spiritual' and 'material' support for Colonial Mission Week. They believed that the Kingdom of the Netherlands in Europe had a duty to let people in the overseas territories share in the wealth, civilisation and the gospel of the Netherlands. See 'Koloniale Missieweek', *De Tijd* 22 May 1939, Avondblad, p. 4; 'Koloniale Missie-week. Een oproep van de Katholieke professoren', *De Maasbode* 22 May 1939, Avondblad, p. 5.

between Nijmegen and the region above Moerdijk (...) Is this destiny, this alienation?"[118] Van der Heijden and Van der Grinten became scholars with a formidable reputation. The same was true of Duynstee and Kamphuisen and, after the war, Hermesdorf. The Nijmegen professors shared many principles when it came to their approach to law: (neo-Thomist) natural law as the foundation of positive law,[119] dogmatics as the core of academic practice, viewing legalism in perspective (not all law could be found in legislation), the interaction between theory and practice, legal principles as the foundation of the rule of law, the link with the RKSP (with the exception of Van der Heijden, most professors took no active part in politics) and an abhorrence of fascism, National Socialism and communism. They publicly demonstrated their antipathy in Catholic newspapers, sometimes with the help of those newspapers. They were convinced that holding additional posts added value to their academic practice. They collected such posts by the dozen, and not just in the Catholic world. From the moment that the university opened its doors, the law professors struggled with the influence of the bishops, preferring to keep them at arm's length. More than we know of today, they wrote on a wide spectrum of current topics in the many Catholic newspapers and journals of the time, thereby helping to give shape and content to Catholic culture.

The number of law students rose steadily. Sixty-six students enrolled in the first academic year (1923-1924) and by 1927-1928 there were already 145.[120] They had to work hard. Lecture hours ran from Monday morning to Saturday afternoon. Most professors taught several days a week, with Bellefroid teaching on Mondays, Wednesdays, Thursdays, Fridays and Saturday mornings! Van der Heijden taught Legal History and Civil Law on Tuesdays, Civil Law and Commercial Law on Thursdays and Legal History and Commercial Law on Fridays. Looking back on the first decades of the Nijmegen law faculty, we can justifiably conclude that the professors and lectors succeeded in achieving the university's mission – to become the crowning glory of Catholic emancipation.[121]

---

118. KDC, Brom Archive (68), BROG-1018: letter from Pompe to Brom, 16 April 1936. He clearly still had regular contact with Duynstee and Van der Grinten.
119. In his farewell address in 1961, Russel reminded his listeners of the fact that Thomas Aquinas regarded a law as unjust if it did not distribute the burden evenly among the citizens. Such laws could not bind them in conscience. He railed that as soon as party politics were involved, the teachings of Aquinus, 'the Prince of Scholastics', were replaced by 'the teachings of Lieftinck-Van der Kieft-Hofstra'. Lieftinck (1902-1989), Van der Kieft (1884-1970) and Hofstra (1904-1999) were successive ministers of finance in 1945-1952, 1952-1956 and 1956-1958 respectively. See G.M.G.H. Russel, *Confiscatoire belastingtarieven en misbruik van strafwetgeving*, Utrecht: Dekker & Van der Vegt 1961, p. 5.
120. Brabers, *De Faculteit der Rechtsgeleerdheid van de Katholieke Universiteit Nijmegen 1923-1982*, p. 73.
121. Timetable of teaching hours in the Faculty of Law, 1923-1924 (property of Dr A. Steneker).

The Nijmegen Faculty of Law in the Second World War (1940-1945)

1   Introduction

The commander-in-chief of the Dutch land and sea forces, General Henri Winkelman (1876-1952), called on his troops to abandon the fight on 10 May 1940. On 15 May he signed the capitulation. On 18 May 1940, Adolf Hitler (1889-1945) placed the Netherlands under the authority of a Reich commissioner, by the name of Arthur Seyss-Inquart (1892-1946). In an appeal to the Dutch people on 25 May 1940, Seyss-Inquart declared his intention that the law that currently applied should remain in force. He added that he wished to maintain the independence of the judiciary. "On the other hand, I expect that all Dutch judges, public officials and civil servants in active service will strictly comply with my decrees issued for this purpose and that the Dutch people will follow this lead with reason and composure."[1] At 12 noon on 29 May 1940 in the Ridderzaal in The Hague, Seyss-Inquart accepted civil authority over the Netherlands. The decree that underpinned his exercise of the government's powers in the Netherlands stated once again that Dutch law would remain in force, insofar as this was compatible with the occupation, and that the administration of justice would remain independent.[2] These words were met with relief by the Dutch legal sector. An anonymous contribution appeared in the *Nederlands Juristenblad* [Dutch Law Journal] of 15 June 1940, stating that Dutch lawyers could appreciate this position on the part of the occupying power.[3]

The Roman Catholic University soon faced the greatest crisis of its young life. Although Seyss-Inquart's reassuring words seemed to augur well, Catholic criticism of National Socialism and Dutch support for German religious figures had not escaped the notice of the occupying power. Seyss-Inquart moved quickly,

---

1.   Decree 2/1940. See also Article 5.1 of Decree 1/1940: 'The law in force up to now shall remain in force, insofar as it is compatible with the occupation.'
2.   Decree 3/1940.
3.   'De Regeeringsbevoegdheden in Nederland t.a.v. de rechtspraak', *NJB* 1940, p. 505.

arresting four professors, including two from the law faculty, for their 'anti-German stance'.[4]

2   THE ARRESTS OF REGOUT AND HOOGVELD

Before the war, law professors in Nijmegen had expressed criticism of National Socialism (Van der Heijden, Kamphuisen and Regout) or aspects of National Socialist doctrine (Duynstee). As men of religion, Raaijmakers and Hoogveld were opposed to the threat that National Socialism posed to the Catholic faith. They rejected the 'dictatorship' of communism, fascism, liberalism, socialism *and* National Socialism. The papal encyclical *Mit brennender Sorge* (1937) was their benchmark. One of the best-known German opponents of the Nazis was the Jesuit Friedrich Muckermann (1883-1946), a friend of Henri Poels, priest and leader of the Catholic labour movement in Limburg and an early opponent of National Socialism. Muckermann had fled to Oldenzaal in 1934, where he continued his fight against Nazism in his publication *Der Deutsche Weg*. In the same year he gave a number of lectures in the Netherlands on 'National Socialism as a new faith'. These included an address on 21 October to the Roman Catholic Workers' Union in Heerlen and a few days later in Amsterdam on the foundation day of Sanctus Thomas Aquinas, the Catholic student association. On both occasions, Muckermann roundly condemned the racial theory of the Nazis. There was, he said, no such thing as an Aryan or a Jewish race. What, he asked, was at the heart of Nazi doctrine?

> The faith in the new doctrine is concentrated in the faith of the Führer, which is very strong in itself, but which, as a precaution, is reinforced with the slogan that everything must be done to keep the blood pure and free of alien taints.

A 'new Reformation' had taken place in the 'third German Reich', a complete reversal, a change in nature. Muckermann denounced the 'bringing into line' in German university education, whereby all criticism was suppressed. "But what remains is the Catholic soul, which is soft as a Hymn to Mary in a Praise, but which can be hard as a diamond, which can be harder than an iron chancellor, when faith

---

4.   On the history of the Roman Catholic University during the war, see: J. Bosmans et al., *Tot hier en niet verder! De RK Universiteit in oorlogstijd*, Katholieke Universiteit Nijmegen 70 jaar: Nijmegen 1993; Brabers, *De Faculteit der Rechtsgeleerdheid van de Katholieke Universiteit Nijmegen 1923-1982*, p. 126 ff.; J. Brabers, 'Studeren in bezet Nijmegen', *Vox* 05/2018, p. 6 ff.; J. Brabers and L. Savenije, 'Radboud bevrijd. Afstuderen in een frontstad', in: *Impressie. Nieuwsbrief van het KDC* 2019, p. 4 ff.

is touched."[5] Articles in *Der Deutsche Weg* on a host of Nazi utterances and acts against Catholicism (such as searches carried out at German monasteries) also made it into the Dutch press.[6] In 1938, Muckermann left for Paris to continue his fight against the Nazis.

Despite the fact that, by May 1940, Muckermann had been gone from the Netherlands for two years, the German secret police went hunting for "Muckermann's network of friends and supporters" in Nijmegen soon after Seyss-Inquart assumed power in June 1940.[7] They arrested Hoogveld on 18 June 1940. On 29 June they stood at Regout's door and that of the Jesuit Muckermann. Regout, who was staying in The Hague at that time, reported to the German secret police on his return home. Brom and Alphonsus Mulders (1893-1981), professor of fundamental theology, missiology and Eastern theology, were also arrested.[8] They were imprisoned in Arnhem's panopticon prison for being 'anti-German'. Brom and Mulders were released after a time: there was no network around Muckermann. For Hoogveld, however, release was delayed for six months, following a period of detention in a cell in Emmerik. He was a broken man on his release and his death on 23 July 1942 is attributed to the hardships he experienced as a prisoner of the Germans. J.J.A. Ellis, an alumnus of the Nijmegen university who was attorney general in the Netherlands Antilles after the war, wrote in the *Amigoe di Curaçao*: "(...) Hoogveld went to a concentration camp, only to return later to Nijmegen, a dying man (...)."[9] Regout was sent to Berlin. The German police were aware of his publications and his anti-Nazi sentiments. He was transferred to Dachau concentration camp in July 1941, where he died on

---

5.   'Pater Muckermann te Heerlen. Het nieuwe geloof: Nationaal-Socialisme. – Het staat vierkant tegenover het Christendom', *Limburger Koerier* 22 October 1934, p. 6; 'Het Duitsche Nationaal-Socialisme een nieuw geloof', *De Limburger* 22 October 1934, p. 2; 'Het Nationaal-Socialisme in religieus opzicht', *Nieuwe Venlosche Courant* 23 October 1934; 'Pater Muckermann over het Nat.-Socialisme', *Overijselsch Dagblad* 24 October 1934, p. 6; 'Sint Thomas Aquinas. Pater Muckermann over nat.-socialisme', *Algemeen Handelsblad* 27 October 1934, Avondblad, p. 13. The iron chancellor is a reference to Chancellor Bismarck and the 'Kulturkampf'.

6.   'Antikatholicisme in Duitschland. Relaas uit een r.k. blad te Oldenzaal', *Nieuwe Tilburgsche Courant* 4 April 1935, p. 10.

7.   Brabers, *De Faculteit der Rechtsgeleerdheid van de Katholieke Universiteit Nijmegen 1923-1982*, p. 135; L. Savenije, *Nijmegen, collaboratie en verzet. Een stad in oorlogstijd*, Vantilt: Nijmegen 2018, pp. 152-154.

8.   A report of their arrest appeared in a newspaper in the Dutch East Indies: 'Professoren in de Gevangenis', *Bataviaasch Nieuwsblad* 30 September 1940, p. 2. The German secret police probably thought that Hoogveld and Mulders were also Jesuits. The newspaper corrected a report from London to this effect.

9.   J.J.A. Ellis, 'Bij het vierde lustrum van de R.K. Universiteit te Nijmegen', *Amigoe di Curaçao* 13 October 1943, p. 2. In memoriams about Hoogveld appeared in Dutch newspapers: 'Mgr. Prof. dr. J. Hoogveld overleden. Leidende figuur in het kath. beschavingsleven', *De Tijd* 23 July 1942, front page and 'Gevoelig verlies voor de R.K. Universiteit te Nijmegen', *Limburger Koerier* 24 July 1942, front page. Neither newspaper mentioned the circumstances in which Hoogveld had died.

29 December 1942, exhausted by the many beatings and degradations.[10] His death was a bombshell for students. Almost all of them knew him: for many years he had been their beloved spiritual counsellor.[11]

For the Nijmegen law faculty, Regout's death at the end of 1942 meant the loss of its third professor in a short space of time. Earlier, in 1941, Van der Heijden had succumbed to a debilitating illness that had first struck in 1938/1939, and in 1942 the faculty was affected by the loss of Hoogveld. Duynstee had taken over the teaching of Hoogveld's philosophy of law. International law was not taught. Kamphuisen wanted to succeed Van der Heijden in civil law, but he was unpopular with the bishops, as had been evident in 1939. Originally a company lawyer and still working as a legal advisor for AKU, Kamphuisen had stated at the time that he wished to combine commercial law from Van der Heijden's teaching remit and private international law from that of Bellefroid. The faculty supported his plan, but the bishops did not: they felt that he had treated them with contempt. Kamphuisen had continued to live in Velp, near Arnhem. He rented a room in a Nijmegen hotel on a permanent basis and arranged his university affairs from there. The bishops had observed all this with disgust. Kamphuisen therefore did not 'get' commercial and international private law. After Van der Heijden's death, Kamphuisen had expressed an understandable wish to become a professor of civil law. He was an expert *par excellence* in the field and had published a great deal on civil law. Once again, he came away empty-handed from the board and the bishops. The St Radboud Foundation permitted him only to 'fill in' in civil law.[12] In 1944 (I'm now jumping ahead in time), Louwers, the virtually invisible lector in matrimonial property and inheritance law, died. His position had been debated since 1939, when Van der Heijden began to focus on civil law and had divested himself of commercial law. Louwers' lectorate thus became redundant. He had achieved nothing on the academic front.[13] With Louwers' death, the faculty had lost half of its academic staff.

3   THE NIJMEGEN FACULTY OF LAW UP TO APRIL 1943

For the first few months after May 1940, the occupying forces had left university education in peace. The St Radboud Foundation had decided not to seek approval from the Department of Education, Science and Cultural Protection for the appointment of new professors. From 25 November 1940, the secretary-general of that department was Jan van Dam (1896-1979), a former professor at the

---

10.   A. Haverkamp, 'Ode aan gemartelde studentenvriend Robert Regout', *Vox* 09/2015, p. 30 ff.
11.   Titus Brandsma arrived in Dachau on 19 June 1942 and died on 26 July. He spent June and July 1942 in the infirmary. It cannot be ruled out that Regout and Brandsma saw and spoke to one another there.
12.   Brabers, *De Faculteit der Rechtsgeleerdheid van de Katholieke Universiteit Nijmegen 1923-1982*, pp. 90-91, pp. 140-142.
13.   Brabers, *De Faculteit der Rechtsgeleerdheid van de Katholieke Universiteit Nijmegen 1923-1982*, p. 89.

University of Amsterdam and a member of the NSB.[14] As a consequence of the St Radboud Foundation board's decision, no appointments could be made to the Roman Catholic University after 1 December 1940. Thus Kamphuisen's plan to succeed Van der Heijden in civil law never had any chance of success.

From October 1940, the occupying power tightened its grip on Dutch academic life. Forms were sent to all staff at Dutch universities and colleges. This form, based on a decree of 13 September 1940 by Reich Commissioner Seyss-Inquart, came to be called the Aryan Declaration. The decree, which violated Article 5 of the then Constitution, made it possible for the legal position of officials and other public servants and, in particular, the conditions under which they could be appointed or dismissed, to be subject to a regulation that derogated from the law in force up to that time.[15] In early October 1940, all civil servants were sent a form on which they had to state whether they had Jewish parents or grandparents and/or whether they were married or engaged to a Jewish partner. Apparently, the Nijmegen professors and lectors also came under this regulation, although they were not civil servants and the university received no government subsidies. At the behest of the Board of Governors, the then board of the university, they filled in and sent off the declaration.[16]

Professors who had indicated on their form that they were of Jewish origin were suspended from the exercise of their duties in November 1940. Among law professors, the most famous victim of this measure was Eduard Meijers (1880-1954), professor of civil law and private international law in Leiden. His *promotus* and colleague Rudolph Cleveringa (1894-1980) seized on his suspension and that of Martin David (1898-1986) to deliver a protest speech on 26 November 1940 in the Grand Auditorium at Leiden University. This speech has become the defining symbol of university resistance to the occupying power's anti-Semitic measures during the Second World War. Following this first concrete sign of academic protest, Seyss-Inquart had Cleveringa and Telders arrested. He also

---

14.   On Van Dam: P.J. Knegtmans, 'Onderwijspacificatie in de Nieuwe Orde Jan van Dam (1896-1979)', in: P.J. Knegtmans, P. Schulten, J. Vogel, *Collaborateurs van niveau. Opkomst en val van de hoogleraren Schrieke, Snijder en Van Dam*, Amsterdam: Vossiuspers AUP 1996, p. 223 ff.

15.   Decree 137/1940. It related to Decree 108/1940, which gave Seyss-Inquart the authority to dismiss officials. Article 4 of Decree 189/1940 determined who was Jewish.

16.   Brabers, *De Faculteit der Rechtsgeleerdheid van de Katholieke Universiteit Nijmegen 1923-1982*, p. 139. In Nijmegen, only one professor had Jewish origins: J.A.A.M. Kors O.P. (1885-1966), professor of moral theology, mysticism and general sociology. B.M.P.E. Vidos (1902-1987), a lector in Italian and Spanish, was also Jewish. Vidos was fired in 1941.

ended teaching at Leiden University.[17] On Monday, 25 November 1940, a day before Cleveringa gave his speech, Victor Koningsberger (1895-1966), professor of botany in Utrecht, had condemned the suspension of all his Jewish colleagues. His speech in the Utrecht Academy Building was short and sharp:

> With profound sorrow and disappointment, my conscience compels me to commemorate the removal from the exercise of their duties of a number of Dutch colleagues, for reasons of origin and religion. While my deep sympathy goes out to them, I feel that we all share in the insult that has been done to them. After all, since 1579, the year in which the Union of Utrecht was signed in what is now the Great Auditorium of our university, it was always the highest Dutch ideal that no one should be persecuted for their race or religion.[18]

There was a new stand-off between the Nijmegen law professors and the occupying power in the course of 1941. The conflict centred on a letter from Mgr De Jong, which had been read from the pulpit by all pastors and chaplains on 26 January 1941. It was directed against the NSB. De Jong stated that the NSB threatened to obstruct the Church in the free exercise of its duty and posed a serious danger to the Christian view of life. Members of the NSB should therefore be denied all sacraments, such as baptism, communion and the consecration of marriage. Seyss-Inquart was enraged by the letter.[19] He wanted to remove all clergy from teaching posts. On 23 February 1941, Van Dam announced in a radio broadcast that clergy were not permitted to head institutions of (higher) education.[20] The rector magnificus of the Roman Catholic University at that time was Father Duynstee. An order from secretary-general Van Dam on 21 February 1941 required him to resign his rectorship on 1 May. The 'headstrong' Kamphuisen became his successor on 3 June. In the summer of 1941, he riled the Germans by refusing to hand over the addresses of students. He arranged for the file to disappear into a safe in the archbishop's palace in Utrecht. It should come as no surprise that Kamphuisen's rectorship lasted a mere four months. The St

---

17.   See K. Schuyt, *R.P. Cleveringa. Recht, onrecht en de vlam der gerechtigheid*, Amsterdam: Boom 2019, p. 179 ff.; M. Schwegman, 'Cleveringa en Meijers. Een weerbarstige geschiedenis van getuigen en overleven', Cleveringarede 27 November 2017, available online; W. Otterspeer, *Het horzelnest. De Leidse universiteit in oorlogstijd*, Amsterdam: Prometheus 2019, p. 109 ff. Cleveringa was not the only lawyer who protested against the expulsion of his Jewish colleagues. In Amsterdam, P. Scholten (1875-1946), H.R. Hoetink (1900-1963) and I. Kisch (1905-1980) did so too. The *OVT* radio programme declared Cleveringa's speech on 25 January 2015 to be the most important public address of the twentieth century in the Netherlands. See Schuyt, *R.P. Cleveringa*, p. 474. On the speech: C.J.H. Jansen and W. Rijnenberg, 'Slechts de "principieele" houding lijkt mij in dezen "doelmatig". Review of Kees Schuyt's *R.P. Cleveringa. Recht, onrecht en de vlam der gerechtigheid'*, *Ars Aequi* 2019/11, p. 919 ff.
18.   Excerpted from F. Broeyer, *Het Utrechtse universitaire verzet, 1940-1945. 'Heb je Kafka gelezen?'*, Utrecht: Stichting Matrijs 2014 (hereafter referred to as Broeyer 2014), p. 50.
19.   See A. van Liempt, *Aan de Maliebaan. De kerk, het verzet, de NSB en de SS op een strekkende kilometer*, Amsterdam: Balans 2015, p. 52 ff.
20.   Knegtmans, 'Onderwijspacificatie in de Nieuwe Orde', p. 257 ff.

Radboud Foundation had to find a new rector for the 1941-1942 academic year.[21] In his rectoral address, Kamphuisen no doubt provoked the ire of the occupying power by praising Robert Regout – since arrested – as the originator of a plan to allow students at the Roman Catholic University to play more sports, making the university "the first in the Netherlands" to do so.[22]

From the beginning of 1941, the Germans took measures against Jewish students. On 11 February 1941, secretary-general Van Dam proclaimed a *numerus clausus* whereby only a limited number of Jewish students – it was rumoured that this should not exceed three percent of all students – could continue their studies, and young Jews who were not yet studying couldn't begin their studies. A protest against this measure in the Nijmegen student newspaper *Vox Carolina* promptly led to a ban on its publication. The law faculty had a single Jewish student, Fritz Polak. He was murdered in Auschwitz in 1943.[23] There was little in the way of clashes between students and the occupying power in the first years of the war. Jo Cals (1914-1971) had spent four weeks in jail in 1940 as *praeses* of Carolus Magnus (a position he held as a graduate in the first year of the war at the request of student pastor Father Regout). His imprisonment was because of a brawl at the student association building involving a German student who refused to sing the *Wilhelmus*, the Dutch national anthem. From 1940 onwards, Cals and his wife Trees, the daughter of professor Van der Heijden, operated a law practice together in their house at Wilhelminasingel 3 in Nijmegen. They frequently gave shelter to people in hiding and members of the underground also met at their home. Cals became head of the local Criminal Investigation Department (POD) at the end of 1944.[24]

Students increasingly ran into the heavy hand of the German occupying forces. They themselves closed the student association building in March 1942, after their senate – with Archbishop De Jong's support – had decided not to put up a 'No Jews allowed' sign. The decision not to display the sign was one of principle as no Jewish students were members of Carolus Magnus. The closure marked the end of student association life in Nijmegen. There was a coda to the senate's decision: on

21.   Brabers, *De Faculteit der Rechtsgeleerdheid van de Katholieke Universiteit Nijmegen 1923-1982*, p. 145. Kamphuisen also ignored a request from Van Dam to adapt constitutional law "to the current circumstances". He refused to preach doctrines that were contrary to the Catholic doctrine of faith (see Brabers, *De Faculteit der Rechtsgeleerdheid*, p. 147). The new rector was the physician F.J.Th. Rutten (1899-1980).

22.   'De katholieke universiteit. Rede van den aftredenden rector-magnificus', *De Tijd* 15 September 1941, front page. See Brabers, *Een zoet juk*, pp. 52-53.

23.   Brabers, *Een kleine geschiedenis van de Radboud Universiteit*, p. 19.

24.   J. Meihuizen, *Smalle marges. De Nederlandse advocatuur in de Tweede Wereldoorlog*, Amsterdam: Boom 2010, p. 147, p. 398.

16 June 1942, the Germans dissolved the Nijmegen Student Society as an association.[25]

In the autumn of 1942, there were growing rumours about forced labour for several tens of thousands of Dutch men, who were required to take the place of German workers fighting at the front. On 8 December 1942, Van Dam had sent a letter to university rectors, including the Nijmegen rector, Kamphuisen once more, who was filling in that position. The letter contained a communication from Seyss-Inquart to the effect that some seven to eight thousand Dutch students would have to work in Germany for twelve months as part of the *Arbeidsinzet* (forced labour). Like the other Dutch rectors, Kamphuisen refused to cooperate with implementing this measure. As a result, the Germans, in the hope of being rid of troublemaker Kamphuisen, agreed to the appointment of the unassuming Hermesdorf as the new rector magnificus of the Catholic University on 16 December 1942. However, they were mistaken about Hermesdorf's resolve.[26] In the meantime, the *Arbeidsinzet* threatened to end in failure.

Van Dam's announcement sparked great unrest among Dutch students. In some cities, they 'went on strike'. Law student Jozef van Hövell van Wezeveld en Westerflier (1919-1945) was the 'driving force' behind the student protest in Nijmegen. He was *praeses* of Carolus Magnus, which was banned at the time, and in that capacity the Nijmegen representative on the Council of Nine, the consultative committee of the Dutch student resistance. He succeeded in ensuring that Nijmegen students no longer came to lectures.[27] In December 1942, the illegal press published calls for others to follow the example of students in Utrecht, Nijmegen, Wageningen and, from 8 December, the University of Amsterdam (then the Municipal University) and to go on strike. For students, the danger of deportation had become very real. The professors were also asked to stop teaching.[28] In January and February 1943, raids were carried out in various university cities.

On 5 February 1943, General Seyffardt (1872-1943), an NSB member and figurehead of the Dutch Legion, was attacked. Drawing his last breath, he managed to say that two of his attackers looked like students. Raids on university buildings in Amsterdam and Utrecht followed on 6 and 9 February. The boards of all the universities met in great urgency. On 10 February 1943, the Nijmegen board decided that no more lectures should be held (lectures had only just got off to a

25.   According to Charles Rutten, the *praeses* of Carolus Magnus at that time, in an interview: 'Studeren in Nijmegen voor, in en na de oorlog', in: C.D.J. Bulten, L.J.T.M. Hermans-Brand and C.J.H. Jansen (eds), *Meesterlijk Nijmegen*, The Hague: Boom juridische uitgevers 2008, pp. 59-60.
26.   Brabers, *De Faculteit der Rechtsgeleerdheid van de Katholieke Universiteit Nijmegen 1923-1982*, p. 149.
27.   L. Savenije, 'In de voetsporen van Jozef van Hövell', *Vox* 05/2018, p. 16 ff. Savenije, *Nijmegen, Collaboratie en verzet. Een stad in oorlogstijd*, p. 267, p. 288, p. 290, p. 293, p. 314 (photo).
28.   'Nederlandse Studenten!', *De Vrije Katheder* December 1942; 'De staking van de studenten. Een voorbeeld voor eensgezind nationaal verzet' and 'Nederlandse Studenten!', *De Waarheid* 16 January 1943, pp. 3-4.

halting start once again). Tests and exams could still take place. There would also be no more teaching in other university cities. The rectors of Amsterdam and Utrecht requested the release of students who had been arrested. An impasse threatened. Seyss-Inquart then came up with the declaration of loyalty, which he sent to the universities on 13 March 1943. It read as follows:

> The under-signed ... solemnly declares that he shall comply in good conscience with the laws, decrees and other provisions in force in the occupied Dutch territories and shall refrain from any act directed against the German Reich, the German Wehrmacht, or the Dutch authorities, including acts or conduct which endanger public order in the institutions of higher education, given the prevailing conditions.

Students who refused to sign the declaration were sent to Germany to work for an indefinite period. The Council of Nine launched a nationwide appeal to not sign the declaration.[29] How did the Roman Catholic University react to the declaration of loyalty?

4   The Nijmegen Faculty of Law from 11 April 1943 to 1945

In early March 1943, Van Dam had informed the St Radboud Foundation in 'a confidential discussion' of every student's obligation to sign a declaration of loyalty. Archbishop De Jong was of the view that Catholic students could not in all conscience sign such a pledge. He consulted Hermesdorf on 8 March. On 13 March 1943, he convened a meeting of the Nijmegen professors. All but one were opposed to students signing. The Senate therefore unconditionally rejected cooperation on the part of the university with the declaration. On 7 April, the board of the St Radboud Foundation met in the presence of the Board of Governors (the board of the university), the rector magnificus (Hermesdorf) and Joannes Cornelissen (1893-1947), professor of Dutch and general history and secretary of the Senate of professors. They unanimously took the decisions of principle to cease university activities and not to send the declaration of loyalty to students. On Friday 9 April, the Senate of Nijmegen professors convened an emergency meeting. "It was the shortest Senate meeting ever held in Nijmegen: it lasted just a few minutes. At my [Hermesdorf's] question as to whether they could approve the decision of 7 April, all but one of the members of the Senate expressed their support." On Saturday 10 April, the decision was displayed in the hall of the university's main building on Keizer Karelplein, "with the message that in Nijmegen no opportunity would be given to sign."

---

29.   J. Bosmans, 'De academie in bezettingstijd', in: Bosmans et al., *Tot hier en niet verder! De RK Universiteit in bezettingstijd*, pp. 15-18; Brabers, *De Faculteit der Rechtsgeleerdheid van de Katholieke Universiteit Nijmegen 1923-1982*, p. 148 ff.; Broeyer, *Het Utrechtse universitaire verzet, 1940-1945. 'Heb je Kafka gelezen?'*, p. 143 ff.

Proclamation

The Board of the St Radboud Foundation, of the opinion that the Roman Catholic University cannot cooperate on grounds of principle with the implementation of Art. 2 of the Decision of the Secretary-General of the Department of Education, Science and Cultural Protection of 10 March 1943 (no. 28), has stipulated that the 'declaration' forms on behalf of the University will not be sent to the students, nor can signed forms be submitted to the rector.

Furthermore, since the 'declaration' has not been amended, the Board has felt compelled, on grounds of principle, to order – entirely in accordance with the feelings of the Senate – that no lectures be given, that no tests or exams be administered and that no PhD conferral ceremonies be held from 11 April until further notice.

Nijmegen, 9 April 1943

The Rector Magnificus[30]

On 10 April, the building was still humming with students sitting tests and exams. On 11 April 1943, the Roman Catholic University closed its doors.[31]

Hermesdorf was always modest about his role in closing the Roman Catholic University. He was not one to sing his own praises. Although he expected to be arrested by the Germans, this never happened. A search of his house was carried out on 7 July 1944 but didn't lead to his arrest. Hanns Rauter (1895-1946), the highest-ranking German police chief in the Netherlands, left Hermesdorf in peace. He was happy for the denominational educational institutions to close their doors because he wanted nothing to do with church-led education.[32] Hermesdorf was therefore able to maintain contacts with students (either in hiding or put to work in Germany), together with Jesuit father Van Ogtrop (1915-1975), another Bernard, who had replaced Regout as spiritual counsellor (père). Things would end badly with the courageous Joseph van Hövell. Neither Hermesdorf nor Van Ogtrop were able to do anything for him. Van Hövell had begun to play a leading role in the National Resistance Committee. He was apprehended by chance in The Hague on 27 March 1944 and transported to Germany on 5 September. Exhausted by hard labour, he died in January 1945 at the Neuengamme concentration camp near Hamburg.[33]

---

30. Excerpted from Bosmans et al., *Tot hier en niet verder! De RK Universiteit in oorlogstijd*, p. 37.
31. B.H.D. Hermesdorf, 'Uit de Geschiedenis onzer Universiteit gedurende de jaren 1942-43, 1943-44 en 1944-45', *Vox Carolina* 2 June 1945, Bevrijdingsnummer; KDC, B.H.D. Hermesdorf Archive (160), inv. nos 111 and 334 (quotes from a letter from Hermesdorf to L. de Jong, 12-4-1963). The dissenting vote was cast by Th.L.J.A.M. Baader (1888-1959), a German and professor of Germanic language and literature, who, after the German invasion, proved to be a Nazi. Brabers, *De Faculteit der Rechtsgeleerdheid van de Katholieke Universiteit Nijmegen 1923-1982*, p. 151 ff.
32. The Tilburg Hogeschool also closed its doors. See T. Gerritse, *Rauter. Himmlers vuist in Nederland*, Amsterdam: Boom 2018, pp. 382-383.
33. Savenije, 'In de voetsporen van Jozef van Hövell', p. 23.

The students in hiding did the best they could to continue their studies and sit their exams. Before the war, the professors' teaching hadn't been critical for students to succeed in their studies as the professors never covered the entire course material in an academic year, but would instead often focus on a particular topic in depth. They continued this practice during the war years. Kamphuisen, for example, dealt only with force majeure in his lectures on civil law in 1941/1942 and with torts the following year.[34] Students relied on coaches (*repetitoren*), who had access to the professors' full lecture notes. Students prepared for tests and exams on the basis of these notes and the help of the *repetitoren*. The two most important *repetitoren* in Nijmegen were the lawyers J.H.P.M. Kuijpers and L.F.T. Keyzer.[35] During the war they had made agreements about taking tests. Students who passed a test with the aid of a *repetitor* were granted an exemption from the later exam, according to a letter from Kuijpers to rector Hermesdorf dated 10 November 1944.

> In consultation with Messrs Professors, we informed the students and guaranteed that if a student had passed a test with us, he would then be exempt from the exam for that course (...). With this exemption, the student had passed the course in question, but he still had to take a formal exam and receive in advance a *caput* (a part) for it from the professor in question, about which he would then be asked in the exam, but which he had in practice already passed.[36]

On 17 September 1944, Hermesdorf recorded in his notes that the battle for the liberation of Nijmegen had begun. On 20 September, the city was regarded as liberated, but it would continue to be bombed for months to come. Nothing remained of the university's main building on the Keizer Karelplein. Jan Bluyssen (1926-2013), the later bishop of Den Bosch, who was staying with his parents on the Fretstraat in the Hazenkamp neighbourhood, wrote in his diary on Thursday 21 September: "All private houses on the Keizer Karelplein have burned down as far as the Bisschopstraat, including the University."[37] The same was true of a number of institutes and the psychological laboratory. Professors' homes had been razed to the ground. The bronze statue of Thomas Aquinas, however, stood

---

34. He had published an in-depth article on force majeure in *WPNR* 1940/3695 and 3696. This publication presumably formed the basis of his teaching.
35. Kuijpers also taught state systems at the Catholic training institute (RK Leergangen) in Tilburg. Kuijpers and Keyzer coached students for the *kandidaats* (undergraduate) and *doctoraal* exam. Students could also go to Dr F. Reinach for these exams. In addition, C.C.C. van de Bult coached students in economics and tax law, while H.C.C.M. Tromp, also a lawyer, coached students in Heerlen (see letters from Tromp in KDC, Hermesdorf Archive (160), inv. no. 114). Tromp worked mainly with Duynstee.
36. KDC, B.H.D. Hermesdorf Archive (160), inv. no. 334. See also J. Brabers, 'Studeren in bezet Nijmegen', *Vox* 05/2018, p. 6 ff.
37. J. Bluyssen, *Oorlogsdagboek, Nijmegen september t/m december 1944*, edited by P. Kriele, 's-Hertogenbosch: Uitgeverij Bastion Oranje 2013, p. 17.

unscathed in front of the completely destroyed main building, as a "symbol of the incorruptibility of Catholic culture and scholarship."[38]

Despite the personal and material misery, university life got underway again remarkably quickly. On 25 October 1944, Cornelis de Kat was the first to complete his law studies at the liberated university. Van Eck, Duynstee and Jurgens were the examiners. The graduation was probably held at the home of one of the professors.[39] The first official meeting of the Senate of Nijmegen professors took place on 28 October 1944. They were particularly annoyed about the wayward action of the three lawyers from Nijmegen. Hermesdorf recorded in his notes that the first exams weren't held until 1 November 1944, in icy student rooms. Uri Nooteboom (1903-1945), the editor-in-chief of *De Gelderlander* and a former student of the Roman Catholic University, called on the 'Carolina' to reflect on its task as the first liberated university of the Netherlands. He felt that the university was called on:

> To help build and restore our homeland by giving students a profound religious and true
> national conviction. We often speak in these times of the sacrifices that have been made and are
> yet to be made. Sacrifice, however, finds its very reason in religion, which demands of people
> subjugation before God. The idea of the omnipotence of science and scholarship, the delusion
> that the evolution of peoples, the development of the mind, would lead humanity to happiness,
> has had its day. (...) In this light, may the Carolina help build the restoration of the
> Netherlands, the shaping of the heart and spirit of Dutch youth, through a confident Catholic
> scholarship.[40]

While the Netherlands had not yet been liberated, the Nijmegen professors resumed their classes, partly at the request of Gerrit Bolkestein (1871-1956), the Minister of Education, Arts and Sciences. They did so in two rooms at Oranjesingel 72 or in their homes. The first doctorate in law was conferred in the Aula on the Wilhelminasingel on 13 July 1945.[41] The Supreme Court – relocated from The Hague to Nijmegen by the occupying power in 1943[42] – had not yet completely vacated the building (this wouldn't happen until August 1945) but had made space available. The official opening of the academic year took place at all Dutch

---

38. 'Alma Mater te Nijmegen heropend', *Het Binnenhof* 18 September 1945, front page.
39. 'Afstuderen in oorlogstijd: over de eerste afstudeerder in bevrijd gebied' (date reported on the Radboud University website 8 October 2019). See also Brabers and Savenije, 'Radboud bevrijd. Afstuderen in een frontstad', p. 8.
40. U. Nooteboom, 'De Nijmeegsche universiteit en de oorlog', *De Gelderlander. Provinciaal Dagblad* 7 November 1944, front page. Nooteboom was hit by a German 'sniper' in Zutphen on 15 April 1945, while seated in a jeep. The sniper shot from the opposite bank of the IJssel, which was occupied by the 'Germans'.
41. W.B. Helmich, *De theorie van het rechtsmisbruik in het Romeinsche, Fransche en Nederlandsche recht*. Promotor was Kamphuisen.
42. C.J.H. Jansen, *De Hoge Raad en de Tweede Wereldoorlog. Recht en rechtsbeoefening in de jaren 1930-1950*, with the cooperation of D. Venema, Amsterdam: Boom 2011, pp. 102-104, p. 109 ff.

universities on 18 September. *De Volkskrant* ran the headline: 'Roman Catholic University begins with renewed courage.'[43]

5   CONCLUSION

Compared with their counterparts at other Dutch universities, the Nijmegen Faculty of Law was hit hard in the early years of the war. Two professors, Hoogveld and Regout, were snatched from their midst. They died in 1942 from their sufferings – one at home, the other in a concentration camp. Van der Heijden (1941) and Louwers (1944) also died. In those same early years of the war, Kamphuisen, as (acting) rector, proved to be a thorn in the side of the Germans. Unlike in Leiden, Utrecht and Amsterdam, the Aryan declaration (1940) didn't trigger protests among Nijmegen's professors or students. It seemed remote to them in many ways because there were almost no Jews studying or working at the university. Nijmegen professors, such as Brandsma, Brom, Van der Heijden, Kamphuisen and Regout, had already opposed anti-Semitism and National Socialism before the war.[44] Faith kept them on a steady course. During the war too, they took an anti-National Socialist stance. Carolus Magnus refused to display the 'No Jews allowed' sign. The declaration of loyalty hit the Nijmegen professors and students head-on. Under the leadership of rector magnificus Hermesdorf and with the support of Archbishop De Jong and spiritual counsellor Van Ogtrop, the Roman Catholic University bared its teeth. They refused to cooperate in sending or receiving the declaration of loyalty, an extraordinarily courageous decision at a time when the Germans were stepping up their actions. Hermesdorf, who played a leading role in the matter of the pledge of loyalty, deserves to be mentioned in the same breath as university law professors and resistance heroes Koningsberger, Cleveringa and Telders.[45]

---

43.   *De Volkskrant. Katholiek Dagblad voor Nederland* 18 September 1945, p. 2. After the war, there were grumblings among students about Duynstee and Kamphuisen. They were accused of caring little about the fate of students. Kamphuisen, who lived in Velp, was probably unreachable from September 1944 onwards. However, his stance before and during the war was irreproachable. See Brabers, *De Faculteit der Rechtsgeleerdheid van de Katholieke Universiteit Nijmegen 1923-1982*, pp. 160-161.
44.   I refer the reader to *Beginselen der Nederlandsche Politieke Partijen* (1935) by the Nijmegen librarian A.J.M. Cornelissen (1902-1977), in which he denounced the state doctrine of the NSB. De *Limburger Koerier* of 28 November 1935 ran the headline: 'Goede voorlichting uit Nijmegen' [Good information from Nijmegen].
45.   C.J.H. Jansen, 'Het Nederlandse universitaire verzet in de Tweede Wereldoorlog', *RMThemis* 2020/2, p. 57 ff.

Development and expansion of the Nijmegen Faculty of Law (1945-1970)

1 Introduction

The Nijmegen law faculty was in a parlous state when it held its first post-war meeting on 28 May 1945. It had survived the war, but don't ask how. Apart from the wretched state of the faculty in material terms, Van der Heijden, Regout, Hoogveld and Louwers had died. Raaijmakers had turned 70 in 1941 and reached his retirement. Vacancies had thus arisen for civil law, international law, philosophy of law and economics. Van Eck, who had been appointed lector in criminal procedural law and criminology in 1939, still didn't have a PhD and therefore didn't attend the professorial meeting on 28 May. Absent too was Russel. That will come as no surprise; he was never there and – true to form – stayed in Amsterdam. Seated at the table were Willem Duynstee, Hermesdorf, Jurgens and Kamphuisen. Raaijmakers was also present.

Hermesdorf had amassed considerable prestige in the outside world through his actions as rector magnificus. He remained a modest man, however. Jan Leijten (1926-2014), who had been taught by Hermesdorf, wrote of him: "He was a withdrawn, lonely man, stiff, almost humourless (...). In short, no one would imagine a real hero to be like that." He ranked low in the faculty hierarchy and – according to Leijten – it was mainly his younger colleagues who showed him the admiration that he deserved.[1] Kamphuisen was in fact the *primus inter pares.* Students said of him: "Kamphuisen was a man of the world. He behaved differently, he was a great guy." And "(...) compared to Kamphuisen, most of them – with the exception of Van der Heijden – were incredibly provincial."[2] As chair of the faculty, it was Kamphuisen and not rector Hermesdorf who took the lead in deliberations about the faculty's future at that meeting on 28 May. Kamphuisen was keen to acquire the chair in civil law, a position he had held

1. J. Leijten, 'Een juridische broedplaats', *NRC Handelsblad*, Boeken 3 November 1994, p. 3. See the words of praise of G.C.J.J. van den Bergh, 'Het wetenschappelijk werk van prof. mr. B.H.D. Hermesdorf. Zijn eigen plaats onder de Nederlandse rechtshistorici', *De Tijd-Maasbode* 5 July 1965, p. 5.
2. Bulten, Hermans-Brand, Jansen, 'Studeren in Nijmegen voor, in en na de oorlog', in: Bulten, Hermans-Brand, Jansen (eds), *Meesterlijk Nijmegen*, p. 56.

temporarily for four years. This would create a vacancy in constitutional and administrative law. The meeting decided to split the constitutional and administrative law position into two parts: 1) constitutional law (minus municipal law) and international law, and 2) administrative law, municipal law and employment law. They were of the opinion, quite rightly, that the command economy and planned incomes policy would spark a surge of interest in employment law after the Second World War. The meeting had an alumnus in mind for the latter position: Louis Beel (1902-1977), who obtained his doctorate in 1935 under Kamphuisen with a thesis entitled *Zelfbestuur of afhankelijke decentralisatie?* [Self-government or dependent decentralisation?]. He had resigned as Eindhoven town clerk in 1942 when a member of the NSB was made mayor of the city. No-one could therefore object to Beel's appointment. There was only one hesitation: he was still Minister of the Interior in the Gerbrandy III cabinet (the Dutch government in exile).[3]

Little came of all these plans of the faculty and of Kamphuisen in particular. Kamphuisen himself would soon disappear from the scene and Beel was not appointed extraordinary professor until 1949. As outlined in the previous chapter, the Board of Governors (the board of the university) and the bishops had developed a hearty dislike of the proud, headstrong Kamphuisen. They threatened to investigate him for his insufficient involvement with students during the war. This threat from the university administration must have offended him, especially given his firm stance during the occupation. Kamphuisen took matters to their logical conclusion and resigned.[4]

Like Van der Heijden and Van der Grinten in the period from 1923 to 1940, the major players in the faculty at this time would once again be a private law and a public law specialist: Willem van der Grinten (1913-1994), son of the professor of constitutional law Jos van der Grinten, who died at a fairly young age, and Frans Duynstee (1914-1981), a nephew of the professor of criminal law, Willem Duynstee, who was thereafter referred to as 'old Duyn'. They were both alumni of the Nijmegen faculty. Something else they had in common was that neither was appointed in a field in which he had obtained his PhD (criminal law and commercial law respectively). Supervised by Willem Duynstee, Van der Grinten wrote his doctoral thesis on the legality of the death penalty (1937), while Frans Duynstee obtained his PhD under Van der Heijden with a book entitled *Commanditaire Vraagstukken* [Issues of limited partnerships] (1940). Like the previous generation, the professors appointed during this period were characterised by the pursuit of the foundation of positive law in natural law. Willem Duynstee in particular influenced their views on natural law.

---

3.   Brabers, *De Faculteit der Rechtsgeleerdheid van de Katholieke Universiteit Nijmegen 1923-1982*, p. 186 ff.
4.   Brabers, *De Faculteit der Rechtsgeleerdheid van de Katholieke Universiteit Nijmegen 1923-1982*, p. 188 ff.

I have chosen the year 1970 as the end date for this chapter because the University Administration (Reform) Act of 9 December 1970 (*Staatsblad* 601) put an end to the governance structure that had characterised the Roman Catholic University since its foundation in 1923. In addition, the student protests that began in 1968 did not leave Nijmegen unscathed. The era of the 'critical university' (*kritiese Universiteit*) had arrived. Students wanted the university to train them as critical intellectuals rather than 'narrow specialists'. The new generation of students could no longer afford the luxury of a *repetitor* to help them prepare for their tests and exams. Professors had to do the work themselves. The upshot was that the number of academic staff – a phenomenon that had made its appearance in Nijmegen in the 1950s – would rise rapidly in the 1960s. The practice of opening lectures with a prayer was also discontinued in about 1970. In short, that year seems to me to be an appropriate one with which to end this chapter.

2   ADMINISTRATIVE AND ORGANISATIONAL CHANGES

Before and during the war, the St Radboud Foundation had exerted a major influence on the day-to-day running of the law faculty. Archbishop De Jong was given less and less time for intensive involvement with the university and its faculties. This was especially true after he was appointed cardinal in 1945, which meant having to spend more time at the Vatican. An Executive Board was established in 1947, which would operate until 1961. From 1945, however, the main administrative body was the Board of Governors. It continued to exist alongside the Executive Board and was responsible for day-to-day operations. In 1961, the two governing bodies were merged into a single entity, which continued under the name of Board of Governors. The president-curator was Reinier Post (1894-1968), priest and professor of ecclesiastical history, general history, and national history in the Middle Ages. He had been rector magnificus in the 1947-1948 academic year.[5] As an administrator, he was one of those responsible for expanding the Roman Catholic University: a medical faculty was added in 1951 and a science faculty in 1957. In the early 1960s, the Catholic University Foundation took over responsibility for the university from the St Radboud Foundation.

Since its foundation, the Roman Catholic University was funded by the Catholic world itself, in the form of voluntary contributions from the faithful. That too changed after the war. From 1948, the university received a government grant that covered 65% of its operating costs. It was only the costs of the theological faculty that were not reimbursed: as a special institution, the university had to pay for this itself. By 1948, the 'dubbeltje' (10 cents) requested in 1923 from believers was no longer enough to pay for the university. Carl Romme (1896-1980), parliamentary

---

5.   Looking back at the history of Nijmegen University, he wrote in 1947 that the future looked rosy: "increase in funds, new buildings, better ratio of teachers to students (...)." See *Nijmeegsche Studenten-Almanak* 1947, p. 60.

leader of the Catholic People's Party (KVP) in the House of Representatives from 1946 to 1961, reminded southern Catholics that they needed to contribute more to the university. Catholics in the provinces of Groningen, Friesland, Drenthe and Overijssel gave the most financial support, although they 'benefited' from the university the least. The overwhelming majority of students came from the South.

> Where they form a small minority, Catholics seem to be more aware of the importance of finding Catholics for prominent positions requiring academic training, and of how important it is that there be Catholic lawyers, Catholic doctors, both in view of the demands of daily life and to enhance and confirm the prestige of the Catholic part of the population, of the Catholic worldview, of Catholic understanding.[6]

The government grant would eventually increase from 95% in 1957 to 100% a few years later.

Cals, an alumnus of the university and Minister of Education, Arts and Sciences from 1953 to 1963, was responsible for introducing the University Education Act of 1960 (*Staatsblad* 559)[7] and the Academic Statute of 1963. These regulations meant that the Nijmegen faculty – along with other Dutch faculties of law – had to make fairly radical changes to the way in which they taught law. Universities retained some freedom of choice. In 1965, *kandidaats* education (roughly equivalent to today's Bachelor's degrees) was restructured in Nijmegen, with a transitional arrangement until 1968. In 1968, a new structure was introduced for the *doctoraal* years (roughly equivalent to a Master's programme). To use modern terminology, the aim was to make the programme 'more doable'. In the *kandidaats* stage, students were introduced to private law (a course that Nijmegen had added in 1958), constitutional law and criminal law. Canon law also became a compulsory part of the *kandidaats* examination in Nijmegen. The *doctoraal* year was split into a general component (containing philosophy of law, transferred from the *kandidaats*) and a specialisation component in one of the major areas of law. The entire programme would take five years.[8] In his history of the Groningen Faculty of Law, Lokin described the changes:

---

6. 'Kath. Wetenschap onmisbaar. Zuiden schiet tekort bij de geldelijke steunverlening', *Limburgsch Dagblad* 16 September 1948, front page.
7. This Act replaced the Higher Education Act of 1876 (*Staatsblad* 102)!
8. Brabers, *De Faculteit der Rechtsgeleerdheid van de Katholieke Universiteit Nijmegen 1923-1982*, p. 175.

Before 1970, parents who had studied law could easily recognise their own education in their child's study programme; in the study programme after 1970, they recognised nothing.[9]

There were also organisational changes on the academic front. The phenomenon of 'research institute' made its appearance. In 1965, the Centre for Criminal Law, Criminology and Penology was established, which would eventually die a quiet death. The same cannot be said of the Van der Heijden Institute, founded in 1966 by Willem van der Grinten and J.M.M. (Sjef) Maeijer (1932-2018) as a study centre for legal persons and company law. The Institute celebrated its 50th anniversary in 2016.[10]

3   THE POST-WAR GENERATION OF LAW PROFESSORS

The professors who came to prominence after 1945 were of a calmer and more modest disposition than the great 'helmsmen' of the years 1923-1940. Jurgens was appointed to commercial law, civil procedural law and private international law in December 1939. The first subject came from the teaching remit of Van der Heijden, who was ill, the latter two from that of Bellefroid, who had retired. In 1945, Charles Petit (1896-1978) succeeded the deceased Van der Heijden in civil law. Frans Duynstee was appointed professor of constitutional law in that same year. Raaijmakers' successor in economics was Jan van den Brink (1915-2006), who held the post for just a short time. He became Minister of Economic Affairs in 1948, the youngest minister in Dutch parliamentary history.[11] If he had been appointed professor in 1941 (which the Nijmegen faculty had intended but which couldn't go ahead because the St Radboud Foundation had not wanted – on principle – to seek permission from the occupying forces), he would – at 26 – have also been the youngest professor in Nijmegen. As the successor of the deceased Regout, Father Leo Beaufort OFM (1890-1965) was made professor of international law by special appointment in 1946. The extraordinary professor of employment law Joop van der

---

9.   Lokin, *De Groninger Faculteit der Rechtsgeleerdheid (1596-1970)*, p. 6. Also, from 1968 onwards, a *gymnasium* education was no longer a prerequisite for a law degree. Until 1972 (Royal Decree/KB of 27 September 1972), students had to take a compulsory entrance exam in Latin with the professor of Roman law. See F.F.X. Cerutti, 'Tentamen Latijn voor HBS-ers', *Morgen Meester* 1969/8, p. 3 ff. Cf. W.J. Zwalve, 'De klassieke propedeuse van de jurist', *Groninger Opmerkingen en Mededelingen (GrOM)* 1986, p. 1 ff. and 'The cultivation of incompetence", *GrOM* 2003, p. 1 ff. and Lokin, *De Groninger Faculteit der Rechtsgeleerdheid (1596-1970)*, p. 535 ff. His wife, P.E.M.S. Lokin-Sassen, paints a picture of the Nijmegen law school from 1964 to 1971: Bulten, Hermans-Brand, Jansen, 'Kind van mijn tijd. Interview met mw. mr. Pia E.M.S. Lokin-Sassen', in: Hermans-Brand and Jansen (eds), *Recht in Nijmegen*, p. 99 ff.
10. *50 jaar Van der Heijden 1966-2016*, Serie vanwege het Van der Heijden Instituut Deel 148 (2017).
11. Van den Brink was succeeded by G.W. Groneveld (1909-1987), who was professor of general economics, public finance and the economic cycle until 1976.

Ven (1907-1988) took up his position in 1947.[12] Van Eck obtained his PhD in 1947, with Duynstee as his supervisor. In that same year he became professor of criminal law, criminal procedural law and criminology. Both Van Eck and Van der Ven were 'home-grown' appointees.

Nijmegen law professors as of 1946

Employment law: J.J.M. van der Ven

Tax law: G.M.G.H. Russel

Civil procedural law, commercial law, private international law: J.W.G.P. Jurgens

Civil law: Ch.J.J.M. Petit

Canon law: F.A.M. van Welie

Economics: J.R.M. van den Brink

Constitutional law and (from 1948) administrative law: F.J.F.M. Duynstee

Criminal law and introduction to jurisprudence: W.J.A.J. Duynstee

Criminal procedural law and criminology: Van Eck (lector)

International law: L.J.C. Beaufort

The Nijmegen professors were all staunch Catholics. Some – like Van den Brink, Beaufort, Duynstee and Jurgens – were active in the Roman Catholic State Party (abbreviation in Dutch: RKSP), which later became the Catholic People's Party (abbreviation in Dutch: KVP). Van den Brink, Duynstee and Jurgens were part of the national leadership of the Centre for Political Education (abbreviation in Dutch: CSV), a think tank initiated by and affiliated with the RKSP/KVP, which was tasked with "reflecting together on current political issues".[13] Although active in the CSV, Petit was somewhat of an outsider: as a Catholic, he described himself as "fairly sceptical and independent". He lectured on subjects that devout Catholics found painful, such as divorce. He didn't care for the RKSP/KVP.[14] On occasions, the professors acted in unison. In 1959, via the Catholic newspapers and in their capacity as Nijmegen law professors (Petit had already left by then), they

---

12. Van der Ven would soon leave Nijmegen. He was succeeded as extraordinary professor in 1952 by Frans van der Ven (1907-1999), a namesake but no relation. Frans van der Ven is mainly associated with the Tilburg University of Applied Sciences, where he was full professor of employment law and twice rector magnificus. I therefore do not discuss his work in this book.

13. 'Centrum voor Staatkundige Vorming. Ook niet-leden der Staatspartij kunnen toegelaten worden. Gemeenschappelijke bezinning', *De Tijd* 25 August 1945, front page; 'Centrum voor Staatkundige Vorming', *de Volkskrant* 27 August 1945, front page. Willem van der Grinten was also part of the national leadership. Jurgens was an advisory member of the KVP party council on behalf of the Senate of Nijmegen professors, a nebulous position that caused misunderstandings at times because – as Frans Duynstee wrote – the "Roman Catholic University stands outside politics; as a university, it has no judgment of its own in politics." See 'Nijmegen in de Partijraad', *De Tijd* 18 February 1952, front page.

14. J.M. van Dunné, P. Boeles, A.J. Heerma van Voss, *Acht civilisten in burger*, Zwolle: W.E.J. Tjeenk Willink 1977 (Interview with Petit), p. 176 (right-hand column). Petit also published on other topics sensitive to Catholics, such as abortion. See Ch.J.J.M. Petit, 'De belanghebbenden bij een beslissing over abortus', *NJB* 1972, p. 484 ff.

called on voters in South and North Holland, Zeeland and Utrecht to vote for Karel van Rijckevorsel (1913-1999), who had fulfilled the role of Catholic law scholar 'in excellent fashion' in the House of Representatives. He was in danger of not being re-elected because he was ranked nineteenth place on the list.[15]

In this section I will discuss the persona and work of Jurgens, Petit, Van der Ven and Van Eck. But first I will mention Syward baron van Wijnbergen (1913-2006), full professor of provincial law, municipal law, water management law, administrative law and public administration from 1954 to 1984. He published relatively little and was rector magnificus from 1968 to 1969. He had to deal with the student revolt, although his fellow professors felt that he hadn't taken a decisive enough stand. Student tempers regularly boiled over, resulting in occupations and uproar in lecture theatres. Van Wijnbergen's perceived tolerance towards students earned him the nickname of 'Red Baron'. He lost the confidence of some of the Nijmegen professors, especially those in the medical faculty, who feared too far-reaching a 'democratisation' of university relationships. He resigned as rector on 16 June 1969. According to Willem van der Grinten, Frans Duynstee had persuaded Van Wijnbergen to resign. Good relations were never restored between the two men.[16]

3.1   Joop Jurgens

Jurgens' professorial appointment was announced in the newspapers in late January 1940.[17] His name had been put forward by Van der Heijden. As Jurgens didn't have a PhD, there was clearly a limited number of suitable Catholic candidates for the position of professor in the late 1930s.[18] What's more, he had only a few publications to his name.[19] An article on commercial law had been published in 1939; dealing with public limited companies, it was the sixth part of

---

15.   'Oproep Katholieke Hoogleraren. "Kies mr. Van Rijckevorsel'", *De Maasbode* 5 March 1959, front page; 'Oproep Kath. Hoogleraren. Brengt uw stem uit op mr. Van Rijckevorsel', *De Tijd* 5 March 1959, p. 3. The appeal, also supported by other Catholics, was successful. Van Rijckevorsel received 91,000 preferential votes. The campaign was organised by the Jewish entrepreneur Jacques Levi Lassen (1884-1962).

16.   J.M. van Dunné, *Ex tunc, ex nunc. Twee generaties juristen aan het woord over de ontwikkeling van het recht*, Zwolle; W.E.J. Tjeenk Willink 1990 (Interview with W.C.L. van der Grinten), pp. 199-200; Brabers, *Een zoet juk*, pp. 108-109.

17.   E.g. 'Prof. Mr. J. Jurgens', *De Maasbode* 24 January 1940, p. 11; 'Prof. Mr. J. Jurgens', *Provinciale Noordbrabantsche en 's-Hertogenbossche Courant* 25 January 1940, Tweede blad, p. 1.

18.   Remarkably, he would act as PhD supervisor on twelve occasions. This number put him head and shoulders above his contemporaries.

19.   E.g. J. Jurgens, 'Koop en verkoop van eens anders goed: art. 1507 B.W.', *WPNR* 1927/3017-3020 and J. Jurgens, 'De vereenigingen van de Crisis-Varkenswetgeving', *Themis* 1934, p. 1 ff.

Schermer's *Ontwerpen van Notarieele Akten* [Drafting notarial deeds].[20] Even after his appointment, his output was modest.

When the South of the Netherlands was liberated in 1944, Jurgens was given an important post. Pending the establishment of the Raad voor het Rechtsherstel [Council for the Rehabilitation of Civil Rights] and the Nederlands Beheersinstituut [Netherlands Property Administration Institute],[21] the Dutch Military Authority was responsible for implementing the Besluit Herstel Rechtsverkeer [Restitution of Civil Rights Decree] (*Staatsblad* E 100) and the Besluit Vijandelijk Vermogen [Enemy Appropriation Decree] (*Staatsblad* E 133). In December 1944, Hendrik Kruls (1902-1975), the Chief of the Military Authority Staff, founded the Military Commissariat for the Rehabilitation of Civil Rights and for the Administration of Enemy Property, which exercised the powers of the Council for the Rehabilitation of Civil Rights (then being set up) in liberated areas. One of the tasks of the Military Commissariat was to prevent transactions involving Jewish property and to place under management the property of NSB members, Germans, Japanese, Italians, traitors and internees. There were four military commissioners: Jannes Eggens (1891-1964) from 8 December 1944 to 1 March 1945, Emilius Gimbrère (1891-1949), professor of banking and law at the Catholic Business School (*RK Handelshoogeschool*) in Tilburg, from 1 March 1945 to August 1945 (both holding the rank of reserve lieutenant colonel), Petrus van Berkum (1901-1977), professor of "business theory, in particular company finance" at the RK Handelshoogeschool, from 8 December 1944 to August 1945, and Jurgens (the latter two holding the rank of reserve major). Van Berkum and Jurgens were mainly tasked with leading the legal redress work of the military commissioners in the liberated districts and provinces.[22]

> Jurgens (1895-1963) came from Oss in Brabant. He had studied law in Utrecht, where he was
> known as a student of Johannes Suijling (1869-1962), professor of civil law from 1911 to 1929.
> Suijling was a legalist in every respect: the authority of the law was paramount. In their
> dealings with one another, people had to be able to build on certainty in law as though on a
> rock. If there were ambiguous provisions in the law, judges couldn't simply make judgements

---

20.   Full title: J.W.P. Schermer, *Ontwerpen van Notarieele Akten, volgens de aanteekeningen en mededeeling van rechtspraak en literatuur*, re-edited and supplemented under the editorship of G.J.H. Kuijk (1891-1958), 4th edition, W.E.J. Tjeenk Willink, Zwolle 1939.

21.   See W. Veraart, *Ontrechting en rechtsherstel in Nederland en Frankrijk in de jaren van bezetting en wederopbouw*, Deventer: Sanders Instituut/Kluwer 2005, p. 58 ff. (on the role of Eggens) and p. 66 ff. (on the Council for Legal Redress).

22.   'Rechtsherstel en Beheer', *Oost-Brabant. Dagblad voor Midden- en Oost-Brabant* 28 February 1945, front page; 'Tweede Persconferentie te Eindhoven', *Vrije Stemmen. Dagblad voor Zeeland* 28 February 1945, front page; 'Kapt. Cikot over Rechtsherstel en Beheer', *Trouw* 18 May 1945, front page. The archives of the Military Commissariat for Legal Redress are held in the National Archives in The Hague.

at their own discretion. Judges continued to be bound by the law even if society 'suffered'.[23] Molengraaff therefore called his colleague Suijling a 'legist à outrance'.[24] According to the newspapers that reported Jurgens' appointment, Suijling influenced Jurgens' views on civil law. After completing his studies in 1921, Jurgens remained in Utrecht for some time as a *repetitor* for civil law. In 1928 he became registrar of the district court in Zuidbroek. In 1933 he was appointed judge at the Roermond district court. His inaugural address on 16 May 1941 (one and a half years after his appointment!) bore the title: *De processueele werking der verjaring* [The processual effect of prescription]. Another publication was his speech on the foundations of private international law, to mark the 25th anniversary of the Roman Catholic University. Jurgens was rector magnificus in the 1948-1949 academic year. He was known as a friend of students. To his delight, he was made an honorary member of Carolus Magnus, the Nijmegen student association, in 1949. Dries van Agt (b. 1931), the later professor of criminal law and prime minister of the Netherlands, resided at the Jurgens family home at Sint Annastraat 170 during his first years as a student.[25]

Suijling's legalistic influence meant that Jurgens was one of the few Nijmegen professors of his time who had no affinity with natural law. His farewell speech was to have been on legalism and the foundations of positive law but he died before he could deliver it. The speech would have presented "a detailed theory of how he saw his legalism and why he saw it that way". He found it pretentious for lawyers to explain positive law with the aid of arguments derived from 'an absolute order'. Positive private law had no natural law as a foundation. In his obituary for Jurgens, Frans Duynstee wrote "Colleague Jurgens was humble, not only as a human being, but also as a lawyer, and that was his constant yardstick."[26] Maeijer, Jurgens' successor, had little time for his legalistic method. He related how "[Jurgens] took an article of law and talked for months about that one provision. In my *doctoraal* exam he asked me a question about limited partnerships, which was regulated in the then Art. 19 of the Commercial Code. He asked how many partnerships there were. I said what the theory was: you have limited partnerships and general partnerships. He then shouted 'academic waffle! How many are there? One!' Because art. 19(2) said: a company may at the same time be a general partnership, etc. An indefinite article was thus elevated to a numeral during the exam."[27]

---

23. C.J.H. Jansen, 'J.Ph. Suijling (1869-1962)', in: Jansen, Smits, Winkel (eds), *16 juristen en hun filosofische inspiratie*, p. 29 ff.
24. *Rechtsgeleerd Magazijn* 1919, p. 539.
25. 'Huis Jurgens', Uit Huis van de Nijmeegse Geschiedenis (available online).
26. F. Duynstee, 'In memoriam prof. mr. J.W.G.P. Jurgens', *De Tijd-Maasbode* 14 February 1963, p. 5.
27. C.D.J. Bulten, L.J.T.M. Hermans-Brand, C.J.H. Jansen, '"Het leven is goed." Interview met prof. J.M.M. Maeijer', in: Hermans-Brand and Jansen (eds), *Recht in Nijmegen*, pp. 87-88.

3.2   Charles Petit[28]

Petit was somewhat older when he was appointed professor. He had excellent academic credentials. He had studied in Leiden and obtained his PhD in 1920 with a thesis on agreements contrary to morality, supervised by the renowned Leiden professor Eduard Meijers.[29] 'Morality' had become highly topical as a legal concept because of the Dutch Supreme Court's ruling in Lindenbaum v Cohen in 1919.[30] 'Our' Supreme Court regarded as unlawful not only an act or omission that violated the rights of others or that was contrary to the legal obligations of the perpetrator, but also an act or omission that was contrary to morality or to the due care considered acceptable in society. According to Petit, Meijers was very enthusiastic about the ruling: "You see, the Supreme Court has come round." The judgment breathed new life into Petit: "after January 1919, all manner of acts could be unlawful, just as all manner of agreements could be contrary to morality. This ran parallel, also with regard to transgressions in marriage (...)."[31] Morality in human relations had continued to fascinate Petit since his doctoral thesis. In his work he focused particularly on the individual, whom he saw as the central figure in civil law. "I think people are much more important than the things they fight about."[32] His inaugural address at the university, *Het beeld van den mensch in de burgerlijke wetgeving* (1947) [The image of the individual in civil law], focused on the picture that the legislator of the Civil Code had in mind. That wasn't always clear. What was clear was that the legislator focused too often on a person's wealth ('economic assets').

> (...) in the titles of marriage, of parental authority, of minority and guardianship, there is scarcely any mention of the duty of the woman to obedience, of the child and minors to deference and reverence, without the legal editor fleeing these personal matters and going to the more familiar asset management (...).[33]

In keeping with Petit's notion of the centrality of the individual in law, he also regarded the person behind the student as important. He gave *privatissima* (small, 'active' tutorials) at home on a wide range of subjects as this gave him an

---

28.   J.M.M. Maeijer, 'Charles Jean Joseph Marie Petit (1896-1978)', in: Hermans-Brand and Jansen (eds), *Recht in Nijmegen*, pp. 65-67.
29.   At the editors' invitation, Petit wrote an article in *De Tijd* in 1950 about Meijers' significance on his farewell to Leiden University: Ch. Petit, 'Groot rechtsgeleerde neemt afscheid', *De Tijd* 16 September 1950, front page and p. 7.
30.   HR 31 January 1919, *NJ* 1919, p. 1; *W.* 1919/10365 with comment from Molengraaff.
31.   Van Dunné et al., *Acht civilisten in burger*, p. 168.
32.   Van Dunné et al., *Acht civilisten in burger*, p. 178.
33.   Ch.J.J.M. Petit, *Het beeld van den mensch in de burgerlijke wetgeving*, Nijmegen-Utrecht: Dekker & Van de Vegt 1947, p. 7.

opportunity to train students more 'directly'. "Students really appreciate the personal contact that this gives rise to."[34]

> Petit (1896-1978) was born in Teteringen in West Brabant. He married a Frenchwoman and would cherish a great fondness for France throughout his life. He was the spiritual father of the close academic contact between the Nijmegen faculty and that of Poitiers from 1950 on. His Poitevin counterpart was René Savatier (1892-1984), a renowned professor of civil law and a politician.[35] Petit was awarded an honorary doctorate from Poitiers in 1954. His honorary supervisor was Savatier, who described the event as a 'French-Dutch celebration'.[36] In 1958, Savatier was awarded an honorary doctorate from Nijmegen, with Willem van der Grinten as his honorary supervisor. After his doctorate, Petit worked as a lawyer in Rotterdam from 1920 to 1935. Then, from 1935 to 1945, he was a judge at the Court of Maastricht. He continued to publish during this period. His best-known book was *De burgerlijke rechtstoestand van de gehuwde vrouw* [The civil law status of married women] (1930). During the Second World War he demonstrated that he was made of the right stuff. Reich Commissioner Seyss-Inquart dismissed him on 1 May 1942, when he refused to shake hands with a justice of the peace who was a member of the NSB.[37] Petit was rector magnificus of the Roman Catholic University in the 1952-1953 academic year. In 1956 he became the first chair of the Dutch Central Adoption Council.[38] He was appointed judge in the Supreme Court in 1957. His departure was seen as a loss for Nijmegen.[39] In 1960, Petit caused a stir by adopting a position as a 'civil' lawyer against canon law in matters of matrimonial law. He felt that canon law lawyers were too inclined to base their judgements on predetermined notions, using a dogmatics that Meijers had already rejected. "Whatever a canonist wants, he attributes to a deus ex machina, which he brings down like stone tablets on Mt Sinai, and that lower Sinai, which is called natural law, is therefore closely connected to the heavenly Jerusalem (...)."[40] This argument of Petit's marked his definitive departure from the Nijmegen law faculty tradition.

At the 29th anniversary of the founding of the Roman Catholic University in 1952, Petit spoke as rector magnificus about the person in property law. His address was typical of his academic practice. It featured copious examples, from both legal

---

34. 'Prof. mr. Ch. Petit zestig jaar. Het hoogleraarsgewaad na de advocaten- en rechterstoga. Onbevooroordeeld wetenschapsbeoefenaar', *De Tijd* 12 May 1956, p. 3.
35. See Ch. Petit, 'Prof. R. Savatier. Een der meest vermaarde rechts-auteurs uit het Franse taalgebied', *De Maasbode* 8 November 1958 (rubriek week in – week uit).
36. 'Erepromotie van prof. Ch. Petit. "Een Frans-Nederlands feest"', *De Tijd* 3 May 1954, p. 3.
37. D. Venema, *Rechters in oorlogstijd. De confrontatie van de Nederlandse rechterlijke macht met nationaal-socialisme en bezetting*, The Hague: Boom Juridische uitgevers 2007, p. 271.
38. 'Prof. mr. Ch.J.J.M. Petit: Kinderen vóór adoptie over hun afkomst voorlichten', *De Tijd* 21 November 1959, p. 7. On the establishment of this Council, see: Besluit Centrale Adoptieraad van 1 augustus 1956, *Staatsblad* 431. The Council was abolished in 1973.
39. 'Verlies voor Nijmegen', *De Tijd* 19 February 1957, p. 3. The students described him as "an amiable man, who was there for them day and night." He was not known as a gifted teacher or writer. See Maeijer, 'Charles Jean Joseph Marie Petit (1896-1978)', pp. 66-67.
40. 'Civiele juristen bespreken canoniek huwelijksrecht', *De Tijd-Maasbode* 29 February 1960, p. 7.

history (invoking Roman law) and comparative law (invoking French legal literature). The opening sentence encapsulated his scholarly interest: "It is the task of all law to serve humankind, and this service is due to them as individuals, that they may realise their destiny as individuals."[41] Although property law had become increasingly commercialised over time, it still contained a personal element to a greater or lesser degree.[42]

3.3   *Joop van der Ven*

When the Second World War ended, the Dutch government was especially active regarding issues of employment law and social security. The Schermerhorn/Drees cabinet took office on 25 June 1945. Willem Schermerhorn (1894-1977) was the leader of the Nederlandse Volksbeweging (NVB). The idea was to break with the 'old', pre-war political landscape. Recovery and renewal was the party's motto. In late May/early June 1945, the NVB issued an appeal, together with an outline of its programme. In social terms, a radical reform of national life meant "the elevation of labour in a well-ordered socioeconomic system", "co-determination in business and cultural organisations" and exercising justice when laying the foundations for new economic and social relationships.[43] Van der Ven was attracted to these ideas, as was Petit. Much post-war writing on labour law was explicitly concerned with achieving social justice.[44] A corollary of such justice was that Dutch citizens would have security of livelihood, even if they were unable to work. In his inaugural speech in Nijmegen, Van der Ven regarded not only wage labour as the object of employment law. He focused his attention on all labour in society, on human labour in its social sense. "This now brings together again as employment law that which also belongs together as a right regarding work: the right of both apprentice and master, the right of those who work for an employer and for themselves, the right of civil servants and of 'workers', the right of officials and of casual employees."[45]

---

41.   Ch.J.J.M. Petit, *De persoon in het vermogensrecht*, Nijmegen-Utrecht: Dekker & Van de Vegt 1952, p. 5.
42.   Petit, *De persoon in het vermogensrecht*, p. 19.
43.   'Oproep van de Nederlandsche Volksbeweging', *De Typhoon* 19 May 1945, p. 2; 'Nederlandsche Volksbeweging: Radicale vernieuwing van ons volksleven noodzakelijk', *Het Parool* 23 May 1945, front page; 'De Nederlandsche Volksbeweging', *Het Nieuwsblad voor het Zuiden* 30 May 1945, front page; 'Oproep van de Nederlandsche Volksbeweging. Radicale vernieuwing van ons volksleven noodzakelijk', *Gelders-Overijsselse Courant* 5 June 1945, front page.
44.   Not only in the writings of Catholic jurists who pointed to the encyclicals *Rerum Novarum* of 15 May 1891 and *Quadragesimo Anno* of 15 May 1931. Both encyclicals spoke of social justice and the importance of a fair wage in bringing about this justice (nos 34-35 and no. 63 ff. respectively).
45.   J.J.M. van der Ven, 'De eenheid van het arbeidsrecht' (1947), in: *Van sociale politiek naar sociaal recht. Een bundel arbeidsrechtelijke oraties*, Alphen aan den Rijn: Samsom 1966, p. 263.

Joop van der Ven (1907-1988) studied in Nijmegen. He was influenced by Willem Duynstee and Van der Heijden throughout his life.[46] He worked as a lawyer in Den Bosch from 1932 to 1934 and in Arnhem from 1934 to 1936. From 1936 to 1947 he was deputy registrar of the Centrale Raad van Beroep [The Administrative High Court] in Utrecht. In 1945 he was chair of the Tribunal in the context of special justice (trying defendants accused of treason and war crimes). Van der Ven wrote his doctoral thesis on the standard of care developed by the Supreme Court in its case law concerning Art. 1401 of the Old Civil Code. Van der Ven's intended supervisor, Van der Heijden, wrote to him that his book should take as its point of departure the finding that the legislator displayed a growing preference for norms that lacked material positivity, for natural norms. This enabled judges to come near to *iustum* in their rulings. Van der Heijden advised Van der Ven to classify all the elaborations of standard of care found in case law according to scope and considerations. He had to work objectively: "In that way, you codify the content of the modern concept of unlawfulness. Determine the content of this particular natural standard. Moral standards (*verkeers-moraliteit*) then turn out not to be a matter of irrational feeling, but of reasonable standards (*verkeers-redelijkheid*)."[47] Van der Heijden died seven weeks before Van der Ven's PhD was conferred, on 4 July 1941, with Kamphuisen as supervisor.[48]

Like Van der Grinten, Van der Ven published frequently on the employment legislation introduced by the occupying forces. The private law rules governing employment contracts continued to apply, but public law severely restricted the freedom of employees and employers. Van der Ven saw the occupation regulations as "an example of the intrusion of public law into the private law sphere of civil contracts".[49] Before the war, he had regularly published articles on employment law issues in the journal *De Naamlooze Vennootschap*.[50] It was no wonder that a number of universities wanted him after the war. Both judge and legislator were interested in employment law. In 1947, Van der Ven became extraordinary professor in Utrecht and Nijmegen. He left his *alma mater* in 1950, when his extraordinary professorship at Utrecht became a full professorship. His teaching remit in Utrecht was also extended to include philosophy of law and sociology of law, two fields that were dear to his heart. Van der Ven continued to give lectures in Nijmegen until 1952. In his time in Utrecht, he built up a

---

46.   J.J.M. van der Ven, 'Willem Duynstee, de juridisch-wijsgerige denker', in: Struyker Boudier et al., *De "oude Duyn herdacht"*, p. 30 ff.

47.   KDC Nijmegen, J.J.M. van der Ven Archive (407), inv. no. 1: letter from E.J.J. van der Heijden to J.J.M. van der Ven 7 March 1938. See also the letter from Van der Heijden to Van der Ven 16 March 1938.

48.   J.J.M. van der Ven, *De zorgvuldigheidsnorm krachtens art. 1401 B.W. toegepast door den Hoogen Raad* (1941).

49.   J.J.M. van der Ven, 'Overzicht van de nieuwste sociale wetgeving', *De Naamlooze Vennootschap* (*De NV*), I, 1941/1942, p. 282 ff.; p. 283, p. 284 ("public law is here rushing headlong into the private law relationship between employers and employees"); J.J.M. van der Ven, 'Overzicht van de nieuwste sociale wetgeving', II, *De NV* 1942, p. 8.

50.   E.g. J.J.M. van der Ven, 'De directeur der n.v. als gevaarsobject der sociale verzekering', *De NV* 1936/1937, p. 353 ff. and J.J.M. van der Ven, 'De rechtspositie van den directeur-aandeelhouder eener naamlooze vennootschap', *De NV* 1940/1941, p. 65 ff.

formidable reputation at home and abroad as a philosopher of law. He maintained many contacts with German lawyers. He remained a Roman Catholic until his death.[51]

Van der Ven never abandoned the philosophical views that he had acquired in Nijmegen, although he did become less of a neo-Thomist in his work. He continued to see justice as a foundation and critical standard for positive law. Recourse to natural law was an inspiration for legal thinking. People had to be there for one another.[52] Private law thinking underwent the same influences as law and law-making in a turbulent society: "flexibility, mobility, adaptation to idealistic wishes and values and to real interests and forces."[53]

3.4   Dirk van Eck[54]

Dirk (Dick) van Eck came from a large Catholic family. At the age of 12, he went to the Redemptorist Fathers' seminary in Wittem, where Willem Duynstee had also trained for the priesthood. Van Eck and Duynstee met in Nijmegen, where Van Eck had studied law after the failure of his priestly vocation. Like Duynstee, Van Eck was captivated by neo-Thomism. Van Agt wrote: "Exploring the philosophical legacy of Thomas Aquinas – but thoroughly thinking through the propositions contained therein – Van Eck gradually arrived at a certain identification of law and ethics. He came to the mature conviction, which he expressed in speech and in writing, that the task of the state and of criminal law is not only to protect citizens from infringements of their rights, but also to promote morality, for morality is essential to human society and human dignity."[55] In his rectoral address on the position that the criminal court should adopt on conscientious objectors, Van Eck pointed out the dilemma that the punishment of conscientious objectors was morally unjustified on the one hand, but that positive law demanded punishment on the other. He felt, as a result, that the issue touched at the heart of the relationship between law and morality. Van Eck regarded the legal order and moral order as synonymous "in the deepest sense of the word". 'Retribution' assumed the presence of moral guilt. Someone who could not be accused of moral

---

51. He was given a *liber amicorum* (or Festschrift): *Recht als instrument van behoud en verandering. Opstellen aangeboden aan Prof. mr. J.J.M. van der Ven*, Kluwer: Deventer 1972.
52. See e.g. J.J.M. van der Ven, *Existentie en recht* (1969), W. Luijpen, *Fenomenologie van het Natuurrecht* (1976) and W. Luijpen, *Rechtvaardigheid*, 2nd edition (1979)
53. J.J.M. van der Ven, 'De beoefening van het privaatrecht als discipline van juridisch denken', in: *Van Opstall-Bundel. Opstellen aangeboden aan Prof. Mr. S.N. van Opstall*, Deventer: Kluwer 1972, p. 196.
54. A.A.M. van Agt, 'Dick van Eck (1911-1968)', in: Hermans-Brand and Jansen (eds), *Recht in Nijmegen*, p. 69 ff.; J. Brabers, 'Eck, Dirk van (1911-1968)', Biografisch Woordenboek van Nederland (available online).
55. Van Agt, 'Dick van Eck (1911-1968)', p. 70. See also *Recht en ethiek. Geschriften van Prof. mr. D. van Eck*, Deventer: Kluwer 1971. Van Eck's lecture notes on criminal procedural law, criminal law and philosophy of law are held at the KDC, D. van Eck Archive (664), inv. nos 15-18.

guilt should not be subject to retributive punishment. Van Eck was of the view that a conscientious objector did not necessarily lack moral guilt.[56]
When Van Eck succeeded Willem Duynstee in 1947, he was the third neo-Thomist to occupy the chair of criminal law. Pompe's views on criminal law had also been inspired by Aquinas' teachings. Van Eck had a great admiration for Pompe and praised his complete mastery of legal dogmatics. "But anyone who saw Pompe as only a criminal law dogmatist would do him an injustice and seriously misrepresent who he was." From his time in Nijmegen, Pompe had always been concerned about people and had felt compassion for offenders. Pompe's view of criminal law was characterised not only by his mastery of the foundations of criminal law, but also his "pure sense of the concrete, of the *ius in causa positum*". This is because the focus of the law was on application. Pompe therefore had no hesitation in becoming involved as a judge and in all manner of civil society organisations in a legal capacity. He had been hugely important in the process of Catholic emancipation in the Netherlands, both academically and in societal terms.[57] Pompe's view appealed to Van Eck, who was also – as the words of Van Agt show[58] – a criminal law dogmatist of some stature. Van Eck too, was involved in many community activities – in the field of probation, like Pompe, but also in child protection and youth care. He was also a judge in numerous judicial tribunals.

> Van Eck (1911-1969) graduated *cum laude* in Nijmegen in 1938 after a four-year law degree. On the recommendation of Willem Duynstee, he was appointed lector in criminal procedural law and criminology in 1939. Pompe and Willem Duynstee were very interested in the causes of criminal behaviour among Catholics and therefore recognised the importance of criminology as a discipline. Van Eck accepted his lectorship in 1940 with a speech on the value of criminal statistics. When teaching came to a standstill in Nijmegen during the war, Van Eck registered as a barrister and solicitor in Nijmegen. He acted as an appeals lawyer for the Nijmegen-based Supreme Court and also pleaded for pardons for several police officers sentenced to death by the occupying forces. From October 1944 to May 1945 he headed the Political Investigation Department (POD) in Nijmegen (Cals would succeed him in that post). In 1945, Van Eck was appointed judge at the Bijzonder Gerechtshof in Arnhem. His first major post-war publication was *Het misdrijf van hulp aan den vijand in verband met de bepalingen van het Besluit Buitengewoon Strafrecht* [The crime of aiding the enemy in connection with the provisions of the Decree on Extraordinary Criminal Law] (1945, with a foreword by Willem Duynstee). The book became a standard reference work and exerted considerable influence on the way in which suspected

---

56.   D. van Eck, *De strafrechter tegenover het gewetensbezwaar*, Nijmegen-Utrecht: Dekker & Van de Vegt 1956. 'Prof. Van Eck over strafrecht en gewetensbezwaar', *Algemeen Handelsblad* 18 October 1956, p. 11.
57.   D. van Eck, 'Prof. mr. W.P.J. Pompe 65 jaar. Zijn betekenis als strafrechtsgeleerde. "Het recht is eerst volledig in zijn toepassing"', *De Tijd* 10 March 1958, p. 4.
58.   Van Agt, 'Dick van Eck (1911-1968)', p. 69.

Dutch collaborators were tried. With Willem Duynstee as supervisor, Van Eck obtained his doctorate *cum laude* on 2 July 1947 with the first part of the two-volume work *Causaliteit en aansprakelijkheid voor gevolgen in het strafrecht* [Causality and liability for consequences in criminal law]. Several months later he was appointed professor of criminal and criminal procedural law and criminology. When Willem Duynstee retired in 1956, Van Eck took over philosophy of law from him. From 1952, he was deputy judge in the Arnhem Court of Appeal as well as in the Arnhem, Almelo and Zwolle district courts. He was also – and this is just a small selection of the positions he held – president of the Roman Catholic Probation Association, a member of the Central Advisory Council for Prisons, vice-president of the Catholic Union for Child Protection, a member of the Child Care and Protection Board in Arnhem and chair of the board of the St Maartenskliniek in Nijmegen. His life came to an abrupt end on 6 May 1968: he was just 57 years old.

Van Eck had received in-depth training in philosophy and theology from the Redemptorists in Wittem, where natural law was a standard component of the philosophical and theological repertoire. Wim Jonkers SCJ (1923-1986),[59] lector in criminology in Nijmegen from 1962 and therefore a close colleague of Van Eck, wrote in his obituary that Van Eck didn't talk much about his time with the Redemptorists but throughout his academic career had adhered, with considerable intellectual strength, to "the foundations that he had learned to see there as correct".[60] Van Eck considered some criminal law principles to be 'essential by nature' (*natuur-noodzakelijk*). He wondered if this also applied to the principle of *nulla poena*. The exceptional circumstances of the occupation seemed to show that the principle had only a relative significance. Van Eck, however, wanted to make a sharp distinction "between the diverse principles that are set out in Art. 1 of the Dutch Criminal Code. This was especially necessary in times of social upheaval." He wrote:

> At such a time it will be important to separate these relative principles from those absolute rules of law, which derive their application from immutable relations and objectives, and which are therefore not affected by changes in the social constellation, however abruptly and however revolutionary these may be.[61]

---

59. On him: Y. Buruma (ed.), *100 jaar strafrecht. Klassieke teksten van de twintigste eeuw*, Amsterdam: Amsterdam University Press 1999, p. 25, p. 163 ff.
60. W.H.A. Jonkers, 'Het abrupte afscheid van prof. D. van Eck', *De Volkskrant* 8 May 1968, p. 13. See also 'Prof. D. van Eck overleden', *De Tijd* 8 May 1968, p. 4.
61. D. van Eck, 'Enkele beschouwingen omtrent het nulla-poena-beginsel', in: *Opstellen over recht, wet en samenleving op 1 October 1948 door vrienden en leerlingen aangeboden aan Prof. Mr. W.P.J. Pompe*, Nijmegen-Utrecht: Dekker & Van de Vegt 1948, p. 71.

4   FRANS DUYNSTEE AND WILLEM VAN DER GRINTEN: MAINSTAYS OF THE
         NIJMEGEN FACULTY OF LAW

Many of the professors in the law faculty were generalists. They were knowledgeable about several areas of law or had a thorough and comprehensive mastery of a particular area of law, such as private law. I will cite some examples. Van der Heijden wrote about civil law, commercial law, constitutional law and the history of law, Bellefroid about civil law, civil procedural law, international law, private international law and general legal theory, Kamphuisen about the history of law, civil law, commercial law, philosophy of law, general constitutional and legal theory and constitutional law, and Willem Duynstee about civil law, philosophy of law, criminal law, criminal procedural law and criminology. Frans Duynstee and Willem van de Grinten were also generalists. Duynstee had already made a name for himself as a commercial lawyer[62] when he began to focus on criminal and constitutional law, immigration law, international law, general constitutional theory and parliamentary history. Willem van der Grinten published on employment law, socioeconomic law, civil law, commercial law, general legal theory (collectivism in private law, morality and good faith), insolvency law and administrative law. These two generalists dominated the Nijmegen law faculty for many decades and they are the focus of this section.

4.1   Frans Duynstee[63]

After graduating in 1936, Duynstee began work as a lawyer, first in his hometown of Maastricht and then in Enschede. At the outbreak of the Second World War he was employed at Department 6 (Legislation) of the Ministry of Justice. When the occupying forces submitted the Aryan Declaration (stating whether or not you were of Jewish origin) to the department's officials in October 1940, the officials told Secretary-General Jan Tenkink (1899-1986) that they could not in all conscience sign the declaration. It took Jan Donner (1891-1981), a member of the Supreme Court and Tenkink's counsel, to convince them to sign. They eventually did sign when Donner pointed out that a refusal could have an adverse effect on

---

62.   Before 1945 he published regularly in *De NV*. See F.J.F.M. Duynstee, 'De bescherming van den Franschen aandeelhouder, speciaal bij de uitgifte van aandeelen', *De NV* 1938-1939, p. 301 ff.; F.J.F.M. Duynstee, 'De civielrechtelijke verantwoordelijkheid der Administrateurs', *De NV* 1939-1940, p. 129 ff., p. 179 ff. and F.J.F.M. Duynstee, 'Aansprakelijkheid van den ondernemer', *De NV* 1940-1941, p. 194 ff. He co-authored the book *Vennootschapsrecht* [Company law] (1942) with H.P.J.M. Coebergh.

63.   M.D. Bogaarts, 'Duijnstee, Frans Jozef Ferdinand Marie (1914-1981)', *Biografisch Woordenboek van Nederland* (available online); C.A.J.M. Kortmann, 'Frans Joseph Ferdinand Marie Duynstee (1914-1981)', in: Hermans-Brand and Jansen (eds), *Recht in Nijmegen*, p. 73 ff. See *Politiek, Parlement, Democratie. Opstellen voor Prof. mr. F.J.F.M. Duynstee*, Deventer: Kluwer 1975.

Lucy Schönfeld-Polano, a civil servant who was Jewish.[64] Duynstee worked for the underground Catholic newspaper *Christofoor* during the war.[65] After liberation, from 1 June to 1 August 1945, he was legal advisor to the Political Investigation Department (POD) in The Hague. His experiences convinced him that what was being done to investigate and prosecute collaborators was the wrong course of action.

> If you sit quietly at home and talk about NSB members and people who lent assistance in any way to the enemy, you tend to forget that the people involved are people. Political offences have the peculiar characteristic that people who can be good people outside their political views are branded criminals. We are mistaken if we think that being a member of the NSB implies criminality.[66]

Duynstee asked that a distinction be made between 'minor' and 'serious' cases.

> But in no case are we ourselves Nazis. We would have to be Nazis ourselves to apply or wish to apply Nazi practices, or even to imagine that they are enforceable in our society. We must build our community on the principle of humanity, which underpins everything. Humanity and true justice are mutually inclusive.[67]

NSB leaders or voluntary collaborators deserved the death penalty or life-long exile. "Humanity, however, demands leniency towards those who have gone astray." Duynstee advocated the conditional release or conditional non-prosecution of the weak and the misled. The Dutch government heard his plea and asked him to draft a regulation making it possible to exempt 'minor' cases of collaboration from prosecution. The resulting regulation would become known as the Political Offenders Decree, promulgated on 26 October 1945 (*Staatsblad* F 244). Together with Jaap le Poole (1914-1993), former secretary of the Board of Confidential Advisors and temporary secretary-general at the Ministry of the Interior, and F. Hollander (1903-1982), tax attorney at the Special Court of Justice in The Hague, he established the Foundation for the Supervision of Political Offenders, of which he became president and le Poole secretary. The Foundation oversaw and arranged probation for 'minor' collaborators who had been released. In June 1946, le Poole and Duynstee attended the trial of Seyss-Inquart at the International Military Tribunal in Nuremberg. They were accompanied by Pompe

64. M. Verburg, *Geschiedenis van het Ministerie van Justitie 1940-1945. Een departement in oorlogstijd*, Amsterdam: Boom 2016, p. 201. Duynstee was the last to sign the Aryan Declaration on 30 October (p. 211, p. 431, note 29). On this subject: R. Bakker, *Boekhouders van de Holocaust. Nederlandse ambtenaren en de collaboratie*, Hilversum: Uitgeverij Verbum 2020.
65. On this newspaper: Von Benda-Beckmann, Rapport verkennend onderzoek 'De rooms-katholieke kerk en de grenzen van verzet in Nederland tijdens de Tweede Wereldoorlog', p. 25 ff.
66. F.J.F.M. Duynstee, 'De politieke arrestaties', *Het Binnenhof* 4 August 1945, front page.
67. Duynstee, 'De politieke arrestaties', *Het Binnenhof* 4 August 1945, p. 2.

and Jan Verzijl (1888-1987), both of whom were judges in the Special Court of Appeals.[68] Whether his presence at Nuremberg helped Verzijl as a judge is open to question. Kees Wijckerheld Bisdom (1908-1995), a well-known lawyer from The Hague, had his doubts. He wrote about Verzijl as a judge at the Special Court of Appeals:

> At that time, for me at least, he gave the impression that he had already made up his mind before the hearing, and he demonstrated that too. He interrupted lawyers who defended positions – I admit that they were often not very sound – in order to silence them. I think that his straightforwardness, which you also point out, played a role in this.[69]

Frans Duynstee was deeply impressed by what he saw and heard in ravaged Germany.[70]

> Duynstee (1914-1981) was appointed professor in September 1945. He was a prolific publicist. His well-known speeches include *Over de beteekenis van de onderscheiding tusschen de begrippen staat in formeelen en in materiëelen zin* [On the significance of the distinction between the concepts of state in a formal and material sense] (inaugural lecture, 1946) and *Het zedelijk karakter der rechtswetenschap* [The moral character of legal science] (rectoral address, 1950). He wrote about the 1953 constitutional reform. Later, he immersed himself in the study of parliamentary history. Here I will mention only *De kabinetsformaties* 1946-1965 [Government formations 1946-1965] (1966) and *Het kabinet Schermerhorn-Drees 24 juni 1945-3 juli 1946* [The Schermerhorn-Drees Cabinet 24 June 1945-3 July 1946] (I, 1977), co-authored with J.M.J Bosmans (b. 1945). In 1970 he founded the Centre for Parliamentary History.
>
> From 1947 to 1950 Duynstee acted as political editor and writer for *De Gelderlander*. In subsequent years he addressed current constitutional and political issues (as a political writer) in *De Maasbode* (1951 to 1959), *De Tijd* (1959-1966) and *De Telegraaf* (1966-1981). He was well

---

68.   'Seyss-Inquart over zijn daden in Nederland', *De Maasbode* 11 June 1946, p. 3; 'Het proces te Neurenberg. Seyss in den getuigenstoel. "Mijn politiek in Nederland is mislukt"', *Limburgsch Dagblad* 11 June 1946, front page; 'Seyss-Inquart, advocaat en anti-semiet', *Het Vrije Volk* 11 June 1946, front page.

69.   Letter from C.R.C. Wijckerheld Bisdom, Domburg 25-1-1988. See also a letter from G.E. Langemeijer, Bloemendaal 28-02-1988, to the same effect: "He sometimes irritated people in the Special Court of Appeal as well. Some of us – and I'll admit that I was one of them – felt that he often made too little distinction between a suspect and his lawyer." Letters belonging to P.J.M. von Schmidt auf Altenstadt. Wijckerheld Bisdom is known from a poem about a judicial review case in 1942: "The Supreme Court says, because it has to, that you can't test the right of occupation. But the Court of Time and Diligence foresees a time soon when we will wipe our bottoms with it." Meihuizen, *Smalle marges*, p. 92. J. Meihuizen, *Richard Fiebig en de uitbuiting van de Nederlandse industrie 1940-1945*, Amsterdam: Boom 2018, p. 327 described as inappropriate the way in which Verzijl gave Fiebig's lawyer the opportunity to unduly influence the appeals process.

70.   See also: KDC, Brom Archive (68), BROG-1018: letter from Pompe to Brom, 19 June 1946. "The process was moving, at times heartbreaking. Most cities destroyed, the population generally desperate."

established in the political circles surrounding the KVP and was involved behind the scenes in the formation of the first Van Agt cabinet in 1977. Duynstee survived as a university administrator during the turbulent 1960s. He didn't shy away from engaging in debate with students. He loved the 'political game'. He was rector magnificus from 1972 to 1976.[71]

There are many testimonies about Duynstee as a teacher. This is what Constantijn Kortmann (1944-2016), who succeeded him as professor in 1981, had to say: "But you couldn't rely on his lectures, in terms of either content or whether he would turn up. I have some of his lecture notes in my office, in large, broad script. They begin with a classic exposition on 'the state'. Some twenty pages later, you suddenly hear about how the Carthaginians organised their army. Students stayed away in increasing numbers, as – eventually – did Duynstee himself, and the lecture notes are yet another unfinished set. Duynstee didn't appear to have a problem with it. Exams, all of them oral, were an extraordinary experience. The subject matter was constitutional law, *all* constitutional law. You couldn't predict where the discussion would lead, nor whether you would pass or fail. The best thing was to enter into a debate, but who dared?"[72]

In his early constitutional work, Frans Duynstee showed himself to be a sincere believer in and an uncompromising proponent of natural law. He proceeded from the notion of human freedom. However, there was an order in the nature of humankind that bound human freedom. God – Duynstee believed – had placed this order in his Creation. The realisation of this order was how people honoured God. There was more:

> Through Christ, humankind's orientation to the meaning of their lives has acquired a supernatural perspective and a supernatural foundation, into which supernatural order humankind has been integrated by God's grace. Thus, the guidance of life in the divine dimension has also been taken from humankind's self-disposing power and entrusted to the power ordained by God for this purpose.[73]

In Duynstee's view, the central government had the task – as part of maintaining the legal order of society – of monitoring and maintaining religious orientation. Respect for this orientation was at the heart of upholding morality. In order to maintain the social legal order, the government also had to uphold morality, despite the lurking danger that the government would thereby infiltrate people's spiritual sphere.[74] Many people were horrified by Duynstee's ideas. Julius van

---

71. Brabers, *De Faculteit der Rechtsgeleerdheid van de Katholieke Universiteit Nijmegen 1923-1982*, p. 349 ff.
72. C. Kortmann, 'Frans Joseph Ferdinand Marie Duynstee (1914-1981)', p. 73. Cf. the *Nijmeegsche Studenten-Almanak* 1947, p. 210: "Late announcement for the reading public: Prof. F.J.F.M.D. will probably arrive ... hours and ... minutes late."
73. F.J.F.M. Duynstee, 'Is het gewenst wijziging te brengen in de bestaande bepalingen in grondwet en wet betreffende de vrijheid van meningsuiting door middel van drukpers, toneel, film, en radio, zo ja, in welke zin?', *HNJV* 1949-I (tweede stuk), p. 19, pp. 38-39.
74. Duynstee, *HNJV* 1949-I, p. 98.

Photographic materials

Photo 1

Photo 2

Photo 3

Photo 4

Photo 5

Photo 6

Photo 7

Photo 8

Photo 9

Photo 10

Photo 11

Photo 12

Photo 13

Photo 14

Photo 15

Photo 16

Photo 17

Photo 18

Photo 19

PHOTO CREDITS

1. Cover.
Celebration of the Silver Priest Feast of Prof. Ch.A.M. Raaijmakers; f.l.t.r.:
Prof. Mr. Ch.A.M. Raaijmakers, Prof. E.J.J. van der Heijden, Prof. W.P.J. Pompe,
Prof. J.H.P.M. van der Grinten and Prof. J.H.P. Bellefroid (1927)
Source: Catholic Documentation Center Nijmegen/AFBK-6A515.*

2. RC University main building, Keizer Karelplein 11, Nijmegen (1924)
Source: Catholic Documentation Center Nijmegen/AFBK-1A1398.

3. Auditorium RC University, Wilhelminasingel 13 Nijmegen
Source: J.M. Moerkerk, Catholic Documentation Center Nijmegen/AFBK-1A22646.

4. The destroyed main building of RC University
Source: Nijmegen Regional Archives.

5. Funeral procession Prof. J.H.P.M. van der Grinten (1932)
Source: Catholic Documentation Center Nijmegen/AFBK-2A3338.

6. Funeral procession Prof. E.J.J. van der Heijden (1941)
Source: Catholic Documentation Center Nijmegen/AFBK-2A19755.*

7. Stairs Auditorium RC University, Wilhelminasingel 13 Nijmegen, with portraits
of Prof. J.H.P.M. van der Grinten, Prof. W.J.A.J. Duynstee and Prof. E.J.J. van der
Heijden (1973)
Source: J. van Teeffelen, Catholic Documentation Center Nijmegen/AFBK-1A526.

8. Prof. mr. B.H.D. Hermesdorf
Source: Fotopersbureau Gelderland/J. Trum, Catholic Documentation Center
Nijmegen/AFBK-1B11403.

9. Prof. mr. W.J.A.J. Duynstee
Source: Fotopersbureau Gelderland/J. Trum, Catholic Documentation Center
Nijmegen/AFBK 2A2635.

10. Prof. mr. J.W.G.P. Jurgens
Source: Catholic Documentation Center Nijmegen/AFBK-2A4757.*

11. Prof. mr. F.J.F.M. Duynstee (1975)
Source: J. van Teeffelen, Catholic Documentation Center Nijmegen/AFBK-2A2621.

12. Prof. mr. D. van Eck
Source: Catholic Documentation Center Nijmegen/AFBK-2A2670.*

13. Prof. mr. Ch.J.J.M. Petit
Source: J.M. van Moerkerk, Catholic Documentation Center Nijmegen/
AFBK-2A7311.

14. Prof. mr. W.C.L. van der Grinten (1994)
Source: F. Franssen, Catholic Documentation Center Nijmegen/AFBK-6B1776.

15. Prof. mr. S.F.L. van Wijnbergen (1969)
Source: Ge van der Werff, ANP Historical Archive (Image number 315385984).

16. Prof. mr. A.V.M. Struycken (left) and prof. mr. G.C.J.J. van den Bergh in
discussion with students (1968) on the role of professional knowledge and the
knowledge of the social impact of law in legal education.
Source: Taken from Morgen Meester of 30 October 1968 (volume 2, number 2).*

17. Prof. mr. M.J.A. van Mourik in discussion with students (1968).
Photo: Taken from Morgen Meester of 30 October 1968 (volume 2, number 2).*

18. Building of the Nijmegen Faculty of Law (1982-2014), Thomas van Aquinostraat 6, Nijmegen.
Photo: Dick van Aalst (Corporate Communication, Radboud University).

19. Grotius Building. Building of the Nijmegen law faculty since 2014.
Photo: Dick van Aalst (Corporate Communication, Radboud University).

* The author has tried to trace the copyright holder of the photo. Any rights holder
can report to the Faculty of Law, Radboud University.

Oven (1881-1963), professor of Roman law in Leiden, abhorred the vision of the future in Duynstee's reflections: a dictatorship to rival that of the Soviet Union or Nazi Germany: "in his world you won't be allowed to write what you want, see films, read books (...)."[75] Duynstee, unsurprisingly, saw things differently. He was opposed to all forms of totalitarianism and believed that the totalitarian lie should not be allowed to continue. He was therefore (with some inherent contradiction) in favour of banning the Communist Party of the Netherlands (CPN). If only the NSB had been banned in the 1930s, he thought.

> One united world has proved a utopia, a 'cold war' is raging everywhere and we have to adjust to a conflict situation so on edge that it is impossible to continue to use the methodology of a strict democracy.

Democracy had to stand up for the principles on which it was founded, principles that were not set out in a party manifesto but which had evolved historically.

> But when we now experience how the CPN has continued to negate all Christian and humanist principles, we must recognise that democracy cannot leave unlimited freedom to those who seek the destruction of democracy itself and of its foundations.[76]

4.2   *Willem van der Grinten*[77]

Willem van der Grinten was still a student when he lost his father – Prof. Jos van der Grinten – to pneumonia in 1932. He had experienced little of his father's professorship, having only attended two or three of his lectures. Van der Heijden was a regular visitor to the Van der Grinten family home. Willem's sister was in the same class as Van der Heijden's daughter. There were personal ties: "Van der Heijden was a giant of a man", "The most important figure for me, especially after my father died, was Van der Heijden." In 1934/1935, Van der Heijden had asked Van der Grinten to assist with the third edition of his textbook on public limited

---

75.   J.C. van Oven, 'Interventie', *HNJV* 1949-II, pp. 61-62.
76.   'Moet men de C.P.N. verbieden? Prof. F. Duynstee: De totalitaire leugen mag niet blijven voortbestaan. Prof. W. Pompe: Wij zouden door verbod de C.P.N. een aureool verlenen. Een zaak van de rechter, niet der regering', *De Tijd* 11 March 1948, front page.
77.   See *Goed en trouw. Opstellen aangeboden aan Prof. mr. W.C.L. van der Grinten ter gelegenheid van zijn afscheid als hoogleraar aan de Katholieke Universiteit Nijmegen*, Zwolle: W.E.J. Tjeenk Willink 1984; J.M.M. Maeijer, 'Willem Christiaan Leonard van der Grinten 7 september 1913 – 1 juni 1994', *Levensberichten en herinneringen* (Koninklijk Nederlandse Akademie van Wetenschappen) 1994, p. 43 ff.; G.H.A. Schut, 'W.C.L. van der Grinten – Een pragmatisch realist', in: *Juristenportretten*, Zutphen: Uitgeverij Paris 2014, p. 59 ff.; C.J.H. Jansen, S.C.J.J. Kortmann, G. van Solinge, 'Willem Leonard Christiaan van der Grinten (1913-1994)', in: C.J.H. Jansen, S.C.J.J. Kortmann, G. van Solinge (eds), *Verspreide geschriften van W.C.L. van der Grinten*, Deventer: Kluwer 2004, p. XVII ff. and S.C.J.J. Kortmann, 'Willem Christiaan Leonard van der Grinten (1913-1994)', in: Hermans-Brand and Jansen (eds), *Recht in Nijmegen*, p. 77 ff.

companies. In 1940 Van der Heijden asked him to join the editorial board of the *Naamlooze Vennootschap*. Van der Grinten became editor a year later. That is how Van der Grinten came to company law. He described Van der Heijden's greatest achievement in that field as the fact that "he connected company law with civil law; more so than others at that time."[78] Van der Grinten would also embrace this view: he had a remarkable knowledge of civil and company law. And like Van der Heijden, he recognised the added value of general clauses, such as good faith and fairness. "Reasonableness and good faith help determine the contractual relationship. They are normative for parties, not because they wished this, but because the law entails it."[79]

In a 1953 speech, *Recht en rechtsgemeenschap* [Law and community], Van der Grinten adopted a position in the debate of his day about the relationship between judges and the law. He argued that the civil law of his time could not be known from legislation alone. Applicable law could be deduced from case law, which had been established in and by the community based on the law, made up of the general public in their societal interactions. The judge legitimised this law and was literally the 'law finder' (*rechtsvinder*).[80] A guiding principle in the court's interpretation of the law was the notion that what was generally accepted in society should also apply in law. Societal reality and community based on law were not separate entities. What was deemed acceptable in society should be given legal recognition. In Van der Grinten's view, another guiding principle for the creation of non-statutory law was that the law should adapt to the needs of society. Prime examples of ensuring that civil law was kept up to date were the Supreme Court's rulings on the transfer of ownership as security.[81] The *law* must not be allowed to become outdated, but *legislation* alone could never prevent this. Good law tended towards justice and had to be rooted in the legal awareness of citizens. Equating law and legislation affected an essential feature of the law: the legal awareness of the general public. Insisting on legal certainty alone entailed a major risk:

---

78.   Van Dunné, *Ex tunc, ex nunc*, pp. 194-195. Molengraaff, Van der Heijden's teacher, held the same view.
79.   W.C.L. van der Grinten, 'Redelijkheid en billijkheid in het overeenkomstenrecht'(Mededelingen van de KNAW 1978), in: *Verspreide geschriften van W.C.L. van der Grinten*, p. 105. See also Maeijer, 'Willem Christiaan Leonard van der Grinten 7 september 1913 – 1 juni 1994', p. 47.
80.   W.C.L. van der Grinten, 'Recht en rechtsgemeenschap' (1953), in: *Verspreide geschriften van W.C.L. van der Grinten*, pp. 24-25. Van der Grinten received support from Langemeijer for his plea "for the freer interpretation of the law that has been so much contested in recent years": G.E. Langemeijer, '[Bespr. van:] W.C.L. van der Grinten, Recht en rechtsgemeenschap', *NJB* 1954, pp. 263-265. See also W.C.L. van der Grinten, 'Moraal en billijkheid als bron van verbintenis', *Donum Lustrale*, Nijmegen-Utrecht: Dekker & Van de Vegt 1949, p. 435 ff.
81.   Van der Grinten, 'Recht en rechtsgemeenschap' (1953), p. 28 ff. and p. 31 ff.

> This certainty is undoubtedly a great good, but it must also be a certainty of *law*. In our
> imperfect society, equating law and legislation can only provide a certainty of injustice.[82]

Van der Grinten believed that a democratic society should have a balance between
the demands of justice and those of legal certainty, bearing in mind the political
and economic foundations of the legal system. By his own account, his position sat
between that of Scholten and Meijers. He thought that Scholten underestimated the
importance of legislation. Like Meijers, Van der Grinten was in favour of
legislation with open standards.[83] In 1976 he wrote an article in the *Nederlands
Juristenblad*, in which he endorsed the aims of the Draft Civil Code to achieve a
balanced division of roles between legislator and judge. There could be different
views on whether the draft of the code had succeeded in its intentions. Van der
Grinten regarded the statement of objections in Book 6 of the Dutch Civil Code as a
comprehensive treatise on the *ius constituendum*, a textbook of 'eminent' value, in
part because of the wealth of information it contained on comparative law. He
pointed out that there were major disadvantages of recodification in the short term:
it brought legal uncertainty, landmark rulings of the Supreme Court would lose
their value and manuals would need to be rewritten. In the longer term, however,
a new civil code offered significant benefits. Legal certainty would be enhanced by
statutory regulations that were in line with the contemporary situation in society.
Moreover, after more than 150 years, it was time to 'rethink' the private law rules
and system. Van der Grinten felt that the best course of action was to complete the
codification of civil law.[84] And that is what happened. He was still alive to see the
introduction of the most important books of the Dutch Civil Code in 1992.

> As the eldest of the nine children, Van der Grinten (1913-1994) took on some of the
> responsibility for supporting his family following the death of his father. He was a lawyer in
> Arnhem from 1934 to 1936. In 1936 he left for Rotterdam to become a corporate lawyer at
> Unilever. He became head of the Rotterdam office of the Netherlands Property Administration
> Institute (NBI) in 1945. At the same time, he played an active role in the RKSP/KVP. In 1947,
> Van der Grinten became president of the party's think tank, the CPV, where he met Van den
> Brink, professor of economics at the Nijmegen Faculty of Law. When Van den Brink was made
> Minister of Economic Affairs in the Drees-Van Schaik cabinet in 1948, he asked Van der Grinten

---

82.   Van der Grinten, 'Recht en rechtsgemeenschap' (1953), p. 34. Van der Grinten borrowed this
      formulation from his teacher Van der Heijden., 'Natuurlijke normen in het positieve recht' (1933),
      in: *Verspreide Geschriften van E.J.J. van der Heijden*, p. 246. For this passage, see: C.J.H. Jansen, *De
      wetenschappelijke beoefening van het burgerlijke recht tussen 1940 en 1992*, Deventer: Wolters Kluwer
      2016, pp. 60-62.
83.   Van Dunné, *Ex tunc, ex nunc*, p. 201, p. 204. Also Maeijer, 'Willem Leonard Christiaan van der
      Grinten 7 september 1913 – 1 juni 1994', p. 47.
84.   W.C.L. van der Grinten, 'Boek 6 van het nieuwe BW', *NJB* 1976, p. 1189 ff., p. 1201. See also
      W.C.L. van der Grinten, 'Handelen te goeder trouw', in: *Opstellen over recht en rechtsgeschiedenis
      aangeboden aan prof. mr. B.H.D. Hermesdorf*, Deventer: Kluwer 1965, p. 157.

to be state secretary. Van der Grinten's greatest achievement was the introduction of the Wet op de Publiekrechtelijke Organisatie [Industrial Organisation Act] (Act of 27 January 1950, *Staatsblad* K 22). The Act established commodity boards, industry boards and the Social and Economic Council of the Netherlands (SER). As chairman of a Commission named after him, he was jointly responsible for a bill that aimed to provide legal protection against decisions and acts of the 'bodies' established under the Act. The bill became the Administrative Justice (Trade and Industrial Bodies) Act (1954).

Following his ventures into politics, Van der Grinten was appointed professor of civil law and commercial law in the economics faculty of the Katholieke Hogeschool in Tilburg. In 1957 he succeeded Petit as professor of civil law in Nijmegen, a position that he held until 1984. During his Nijmegen tenure, Van der Grinten held many additional positions as arbitrator, commissioner and advisor. His main 'roles' were as a member of the SER (from 1952) and later of its executive board (from 1957 to 1984). From 1968 to 1992 he was chair of the Company Law Committee. In that capacity, he left his mark on corporate law during those years. He also authored the first draft of Title 7 of Book 7 of the Dutch Civil Code (contract for services, which entered into force on 1 September 1993) and Title 13 of Book 7 of the Dutch Civil Code (companies; this bill was not passed into law). Van der Grinten was dean of the Faculty of Law for more than 10 years (1972-1982). He and two others held the rectorship of the university in Nijmegen between 1969 and 1972. Lastly, Van der Grinten supervised the PhDs of an entire generation of Nijmegen professors: Maeijer, Emile Luijten, Hubert Hennekens, Antoon Struycken and Bas Kortman. By the end of his life, he had supervised a grand total of 28 PhD theses.

Goed en Trouw contains Van der Grinten's publications up to 1984.[85] I will confine myself here to three major works: an adaptation of Van der Heijden's *Handboek voor de naamlooze vennootschap naar Nederlandsch recht* [Handbook of public limited companies under Dutch law] (fourth edition 1949 through to twelfth edition 1992), *Arbeidsovereenkomstenrecht* [Employment contract law] (first edition 1943) and the volume on *Vertegenwoordiging en Rechtspersoon* [Representation and legal persons] (third edition 1959 through to sixth edition 1985/1986) in the Asser series. Van der Grinten wrote numerous annotations, in the *NJ* and *Ars Aequi*. He was instrumental in ensuring that the institutional conception of legal person, an approach aimed at companies and their affiliated enterprises, became the dominant one in corporate law.[86] He was a member of the Royal Netherlands Academy of Arts and Sciences from 1969. In 1966, together with Maeijer, he founded the Van der Heijden Institute, which has been in existence for over 50 years. With company law in a state of flux, they wanted to make it a subject of systematic study.[87]

Van der Grinten was the *informateur* for the Van Agt-Wiegel cabinet, which would serve a full four-year term (1977-1981). Political whim had stood in the way of his appointment as Minister

---

85. Van der Grinten was given a second collection of essays in 1991 when he retired as a guest lecturer from the University of the Netherlands Antilles, *Uní Ku UNA*. It contains his publications up to 1991.

86. See M.W. den Boogert, in *Ondernemingsrecht* 2001-1/2, pp. 12-13; see also Schut, 'W.C.L. van der Grinten – Een pragmatisch realist', p. 63.

87. G. van Solinge, 'Vijftig jaren Nijmeegs vennootschapsrecht', in: *50 jaar Van der Heijden Instituut 1966-2016*, Deventer: Wolters Kluwer 2017, p. 1.

of Justice in 1959, while in 1973 he himself turned down an appointment as Queen's Commissioner in North Brabant.

Much has been written about Van der Grinten's style. Maeijer described his writing as short and succinct. Almost invariably, he expressed his own viewpoint in adamant fashion. "He rarely appears to doubt and if that is the case, you often encounter the phrase: it can be argued that etc."[88] He was known to work quickly, to be decisive, straightforward, pragmatic, austere and a deeply religious Catholic.[89] He never lost sight of the human dimension.

Collectivisation in private law was one of the key developments in social and legal relations after the Second World War. Van der Grinten could not conceive of a modern society without collective legal entities (e.g. legal persons, collective labour agreements or insurance). He therefore believed that private law should not be individualistic but should reflect the essence of what it is to be human: with a focus on fellow human beings. This would prevent private law from degenerating into legal technique.[90] According to Van der Grinten, the basic rule of all private law was that people – the general public – should act reasonably and fairly in their interactions with one another. Many rules of conduct and legal institutions had developed from this basic rule, and these were laid down in statutory regulations. The legislator could not stipulate which rules of conduct entailed reasonableness and fairness in practical terms, as that depended on the circumstances of the case. This was an important task for the judge. Judges always ruled on a historical situation, whereas the future was the concern of the legislator.[91]

5   NIJMEGEN PROFESSORS AND NATURAL LAW

There was a growing interest in natural law after the Second World War, not just among German lawyers, but in the Netherlands too. This was mainly due to judgments by the German *Bundesverfassungsgericht* and *Bundesgerichtshof* (BGH). The civil chamber (*Zivilsenat*) of the BGH considered in a ruling from 1951:

> The law reaches its limit where it goes against the generally accepted rules of international law or natural law, or where the positive law's inconsistency with justice reaches such an intolerable level that the law must give way to justice as an 'incorrect law'.[92]

---

88. Maeijer, 'Willem Leonard Christiaan van der Grinten 7 september 1913 – 1 juni 1994', p. 48.
89. Jansen, S. Kortmann, Van Solinge, 'Willem Leonard Christiaan van der Grinten (1913-1994)', p. XXIII.
90. W.C.L. van der Grinten, 'Collectivering in het privaatrecht' (1957), in: *Verspreide geschriften van W.C.L. van der Grinten*, p. 37 ff.
91. Van der Grinten, 'Handelen te goeder trouw', p. 157, p. 159, p. 171. Van der Grinten referred in this article to Roman law and to German and French law, something that he rarely did.
92. *BGHZ* 3, p. 94 ff. See the contribution of the President of the BGH: H. Weinkauff, 'Der Naturrechtsgedanke in der Rechtsprechung des Bundesgerichtshofes', *Neue Juristische Wochenschrift* 1960, 2. Halbband, 1691 ff.

This deliberation from the BGH seems to have been greatly influenced by a 1946 newspaper article on legal injustice and non-statutory law by legal philosopher Gustav Radbruch (1878-1948).[93] Radbruch believed that natural law should function as a supra-legal positivist benchmark, by which Nazi law could be declared invalid.[94] In an interview with Van Dunné, Van der Grinten had this to say on the subject: "After the war you saw the reappearance of natural law, which before the war seemed to be somewhat on the decline."[95]

The 'revival of natural law' in Germany after the Second World War was independent of the Catholic tradition of natural law, influenced mainly by Thomas Aquinas, which could be found among the Nijmegen professors.[96] The chief representative of this Thomism-inspired natural law was Willem Duynstee, who influenced Kamphuisen (who left as professor after 1945), Frans Duynstee, Willem van der Grinten, Van Eck and Van der Ven. Van Eck, for example, wrote in a 1965 contribution on international criminal law that there were norms whose content was of a universal human nature without further positivisation. These norms included the prohibition on committing murder and rape. In Van Eck's opinion, the source of authority for these norms was natural law, "which has its foundation in binding human individuals to their human good and therefore in the authority of God as the foundation of human nature and human existence."[97]

Van der Grinten said in 1990 that he hadn't been aware of Thomas Aquinas' influence on his views on the principle of good faith.[98] The wording of his early work, however, clearly reveals a foundation in Catholic natural law. In 1949 he articulated the basic rule of non-statutory law as follows: "Thou shalt act in society towards your fellow human beings as befits a reasonable person." [99] He called this basic rule the general standard of reasonableness. Following Van der Heijden, Van der Grinten qualified this standard as a natural – or supra-legal positivist – norm. It

---

93.   G. Radbruch, 'Gesetzliches Unrecht und übergesetzliches Recht', *Süddeutsche Juristenzeitung* 1946, S. 105-108. Cf. T. Mertens, 'Rechtspositivisme, nazisme en Radbruchs these van het wettelijk onrecht', in: Y. Buruma et al. (eds), *Recht door de eeuw. Opstellen ter gelegenheid van het 75-jarig jubileum van de Faculteit der Rechtsgeleerdheid van de Katholieke Universiteit Nijmegen*, Deventer: Kluwer 1998, p. 263 ff.; T. Mertens, *Mens & Mensenrechten. Basisboek Rechtsfilosofie*, Amsterdam: Boom 2012, p. 63 ff.

94.   H.J. Hommes, *Een nieuwe herleving van het natuurrecht*, Zwolle: W.E.J. Tjeenk Willink 1961, p. 149 ff.

95.   Van Dunné, *Ex tunc, ex nunc*, p. 217. Cf. C.M. Scheuren-Brandes, *Der Weg von nationalsozialistischen Rechtslehren zur Radbruchsen Formel. Untersuchungen zur Geschichte der Idee vom "Unrichtigen Recht"*, F. Schöning: Paderborn [etc.] 2006.

96.   See Hommes, *Een nieuwe herleving van het natuurrecht*, p. 95 ff. (Roman Catholic views on natural law in West Germany), p. 159 ff. (Roman Catholic views on natural law in the Netherlands and elsewhere after the Second World War).

97.   D. van Eck, 'Het universele karakter van het strafrecht', *Opstellen over recht en rechtsgeschiedenis aangeboden aan prof. Mr. B.H.D. Hermesdorf*, Deventer: Kluwer 1965, pp. 139-141 (quotation).

98.   Van Dunné, *Ex tunc, ex nunc*, pp. 203-204.

99.   W.C.L. van der Grinten, 'Moraal en billijkheid als bron van verbintenis' (1949), in: *Verspreide geschriften van prof. mr. W.C.L. van der Grinten*, p. 3.

inevitably led to legal uncertainty. "Not because there is no objective reasonableness. To act reasonably is to act in accordance with God-created human nature, to act reasonably is to act morally. For a Catholic, there can be no doubt that objective reasonableness exists."[100] As already mentioned, Van der Grinten emphasised in his inaugural address at Nijmegen, *Collectivering in het privaatrecht* [Collectivism in private law] (1957), that private law was not primarily a legal technique. "It is law because it touches people as moral beings. It could be said that private law incorporates morality into natural relationships that are bound to matter."[101] Lastly, there can be little doubt that the early work of Frans Duynstee proceeded from the assumption that natural law was the foundation of positive law. "The law (lex), which could be natural law, customary law, written law, is the standard of law ... but it is so in very different ways; there are laws that impose on people as such in very general terms something that needs to be further specified (laws that establish certain natural law relationships), (...).''[102]

This interest in natural law would subside in the course of the 1950s. In their later work, Frans Duynstee and Willem van de Grinten no longer talked about natural norms and about natural law as a touchstone for positive law. Van der Grinten in particular gained a reputation as an exceptionally gifted legal positivist. The same was true of Frans Duynstee, although he went on in his later work to distinguish himself in the field of parliamentary history. During his academic career, Van Eck did not 'abandon' natural law. However, a new trend – more noticeable in some areas of law than in others – gradually emerged within jurisprudence. This was a more functional approach to law. Societal expectations, the law as an instrument of change in the life of society (modification) and the organising role of the law in society assumed a central place in the thinking of lawyers, including those in Nijmegen.[103]

---

100. Van der Grinten, 'Moraal en billijkheid als bron van verbintenis' (1949), *Verspreide geschriften van prof. mr. W.C.L. van der Grinten*, p. 17. In footnote 38 on this page, he also made explicit reference to Van der Heijden.

101. W.C.L. van der Grinten, 'Collectivering in het privaatrecht' (1957), in: *Verspreide Geschriften van prof. mr. W.C.L. van der Grinten*, p. 53. Cf. also his 'Handelen te goeder trouw', in: *Opstellen over recht en rechtsgeschiedenis* (1965), p. 155 ff. In his farewell lecture to students in 1984, Van der Grinten said that justice and fairness were values for life and should serve as guide in all our dealings. "Why should this be so? Why shouldn't we be solely mindful of our own benefit, our own gain?" These questions touched on the meaning of life. "Faith, especially the Catholic faith, the Christian faith, provides an answer. We were created by a personal God, in his image and likeness." According to Van der Grinten, 'DI-Afscheidscollege' (1984), in: *Verspreide geschriften van prof. mr. W.C.L. van der Grinten*, pp. 121-122.

102. F. Duynstee, *HNJV* 1949-I (tweede stuk), p. 30.

103. See e.g. W.C.L. van der Grinten, 'Sociaal-economische wetgeving en de civiele rechtsorde', in: *Verspreide geschriften van W.C.L. van der Grinten*, p. 635 ff.; T. Koopmans, 'De rol van de wetgever' (1970), in: T. Koopmans, *Juridisch stippelwerk*, Deventer: Kluwer 1991, p. 151 ff.; Y. Buruma, *Wat is een goede rechter? Een mentaliteitsgeschiedenis (1900-2020)*, Nijmegen: CPO, Radboud University 2016, pp. 28-29.

6   Canon law in the Nijmegen law curriculum

In keeping with the wishes of the founders of the Roman Catholic University, the law faculty's curriculum had a particular focus on canon law. The first professor of canon law in Nijmegen was Frans van Welie (1886-1968). He was a professor in both the theology and law faculties. His specialism was ecclesiastical marriage law and his lectures often dealt with the insolubility of marriage. Van Welie had few academic aspirations. In 1946, some of his lectures appeared in print: *Hoofdstukken van Canoniek Huwelijksrecht* [Chapters on canonical marriage law], which was subtitled *Algemeene Begrippen omtrent het Huwelijk, de Toestemming in het Huwelijk, de Scheiding van de Echtgenooten* [General concepts concerning marriage, consent within marriage, divorce of spouses] (Nijmegen-Utrecht: Dekker & Van de Vegt). His full lecture notes, *Canoniek Huwelijksrecht* [Canonical marriage law] (Nijmegen-Utrecht: Dekker & Van de Vegt), were published in 1954. He retired three years later. Van Welie's teaching, and his exams, had a reputation for being easy. In *Met recht meer meester*, a collection marking the 25th anniversary of the Centre for Professional Legal Education (CPO), Herman van Run (1918-2012) – a well-known journalist and radio producer in his day and the last editor-in-chief of the Catholic newspaper *De Tijd* – recounted how the highlight of Van Welie's lecture cycle was his treatment of the 'marital act', which all the students were sure to attend.

> As soon as the moment had come, Van Welie would bend his head over the textbook in front of him to avoid any eye contact with his audience, would abandon Dutch and switch to Latin because he saw two advantages in this: precision of formulation and drawing a veil over the awful reality. And he would read: "penetratio membri virilis in vaginam mulieris..."[104]

Jo van der Hoeven (1916-2001), who was appointed professor of constitutional law at the University of Amsterdam in 1960, reported that students preferred to take electives that they could easily pass, which is why some Catholic students opted for canon law in Nijmegen.

> No one failed that exam in Nijmegen because Prof. Van Welie, a priest, felt so bad for the students who had come all the way from Amsterdam to take an exam with him. If a student who had studied the subject on the train to Nijmegen made too big a blunder, Van Welie would content himself with saying: "Nou, lulde" ("you are talking bullshit"), but the candidate would pass.[105]

---

104. H. van Run, 'Van Welie en de Daad', in: *Met recht meer meester*, CPO, Radboud University 2004, p. 68.
105. J. van Dunné, *Ex tunc, ex nunc*, p. 283.

Van Welie had studied Roman law and canon law at the Pontifical Gregorian University. He obtained his doctorate in 1915 with a thesis entitled *Ecclesiae jurisdictio in negotia temporalia et politica* [Ecclesiastical jurisdiction in secular and political affairs]. He was held in high esteem by dignitaries of the church.

> Van Welie (1886-1968) was born in Dreumel in Gelderland. He was ordained a priest in the St John's Cathedral in Den Bosch in 1912. In 1916 he was appointed professor of moral theology at the Groot-Seminarie in Haaren (North Brabant). From 1926 he was rector of the Pius *convict*, a home for secular clergy from the Dutch dioceses who studied at the Roman Catholic University. On the 10th anniversary of the *convict*, the Pope appointed Van Welie as one of his 'secret chamberlains'. In 1952 he received the honorary title of 'house prelate' to the Pope. Van Welie was rector magnificus in the 1935-1936 academic year.[106]

Like his colleagues Van der Heijden, Jos van der Grinten, Pompe, Willem Duynstee, Kamphuisen and Van Eck, Van Welie worked in legal practice. Jacobus Nieskens (1924-2010), a student of Willem Duynstee and for a short time temporary lector in the introduction to jurisprudence (1955/1956-1958) at the Roman Catholic University, spoke of a "very fruitful interaction between academia and the practice of law". Van Welie, for example, presided over the diocesan court in Den Bosch (where parties could litigate in matrimonial matters) and was chair of the diocesan Committee on Marriage as well as of its Nijmegen branch.[107] And, like his colleagues, Van Welie was viewed as a stalwart of the RKSP. In 1937 he supported the call by a large number of Dutch Catholics to vote for the RKSP and to take the wind out of the sails of the 'Nazis of the NSB' and the 'Communists'.[108] When Van Welie retired in 1957, the university and faculty had difficulties finding a successor. Professor Willy Onclin (1903-1989), whose job since 1958 had been to teach the history of canon law at the theological faculty at Leuven, taught canon law in both faculties for two years (1959-1960). He was succeeded in 1960 by the redemptorist Engelbertus Eijkemans (1904-1964), who – like Van Welie – was a specialist in church marriage law. He too had studied in Rome. His sudden early death four years later created a vacancy once again. The Nijmegen theologians and jurists found the Dutch Jesuit Petrus Huizing (1911-1995) in Rome. He was an alumnus of the Nijmegen law faculty and professor of canon law at the Gregoriana. He was not immediately available and couldn't be appointed professor of canon law and mission law until 1965. Huizing, like Van Welie and

---

106. 'Jubileum Prof. F. van Welie', *De Telegraaf* 1 June 1937, p. 6; 'Prof. F. van Welie overleden', *De Tijd* 26 January 1968, p. 5. Brabers, *Een zoet juk*, p. 42 describes how Van Welie was a loyal and obedient priest of the old school and that he was often the object of ridicule among students.
107. J.J.H. Nieskens, 'Mgr. Prof. Dr. F.A.M. van Welie verlaat de universiteit. Kennis van canoniek recht in wetenschap en zielzorg', *De Tijd*, 10 August 1957, p. 11. Nieskens said that Van Welie devoted considerable attention in his lectures not only to marriage law but also to the relationship between church and state.
108. 'Laatste advies' and 'Oproep', *Nieuwe Venlosche Courant* 29 May 1937.

others, was a specialist in marriage law, a field of law that had become highly topical in the 1960s because of the rising number of divorces. In a 1968 article in the journal *Concilium*, Huizing dared to raise the issue of the absolute insolubility of marriage under ecclesiastical law. *Osservatore Romano*, the Vatican newspaper, attacked him head-on. There was only one correct position: baptism had sealed the evangelical insolubility of marriage between baptised people and made it irrevocable.[109]

The stories about Huizing's teaching resemble those about Van Welie. It was easy to complete the canon law course with a good grade. The most important thing for exam candidates was to take due note of Huizing's inaugural address, *De Trentse huwelijksvorm* [The Trent Marriage Form] (1966).[110]

In 1971, when Huizing accepted a two-year visiting professorship at an American university, the curtain came down on canon law as part of the faculty curriculum. Almost none of the Nijmegen professors believed that canon law or the history of canon law offered any added value for future lawyers. Moreover, the Roman Catholic Church had come under heavy attack in the late 1960s. Even Van der Grinten resigned himself to canon law's disappearance from law teaching at Nijmegen. The history of canon law was given a second life after 1976. Along with Roman law and national customary laws, canon law was one of the legal systems that has influenced the content of our modern (private) law.[111]

7   THE BEGINNINGS OF NIJMEGEN'S NOTARY TRAINING AS AN ACADEMIC
           STUDY

Civil-law notaries had a low status in the legal world during the 19th and much of the 20th century. Willem Zwalve (b. 1949), professor of history of law at Leiden, has sketched a picture of the social divide separating the notarial profession on the one hand the legal profession and the judiciary on the other in the Groningen town of Winschoten at the end of the 19th century.[112] Adriaan Pitlo (1901-1987), the first professor of notarial law in the Netherlands, and Amsterdam legal historian Theo Veen (1943-2005) wrote that the most important contribution made by civil-law

---

109. 'Prof. Huizing aangevallen. Osservatore keert zich tegen Nederlander. Mogelijkheid echtscheiding gevoelig punt', *De Volkskrant* 22 November 1968, p. 7; 'Aanval Osservatore op Nijmeegs hoogleraar', *De Tijd* 21 november 1968, p. 6.
110. F.W.H.M. Kusters, 'Ach toen, ja', in: W. Gitmans et al. (eds), *Te Recht in Nijmegen*, Deventer: Kluwer 2003, pp. 125-126.
111. Brabers, *De Faculteit der Rechtsgeleerdheid van de Katholieke Universiteit Nijmegen 1923-1982*, pp. 409-411. P.L. Néve (b. 1933) in particular, professor of Roman law from 1975, has made a strong case for this discipline. Three professors have taught this course since 1976: A.J. de Groot (1915-1996), G. Dolezalek (b. 1943) and E.C. Coppens. See C.J.H. Jansen, 'De Nijmeegse traditie van de Geschiedenis van het Canoniek Recht', in: E.C. Coppens (ed.), *Secundum Ius. Opstellen aangeboden aan prof. mr. P.L. Nève*, Nijmegen: GNI 2005, p. IX ff.
112. W.J. Zwalve, 'Luijten's plaats in de rechtsgeschiedenis', in: *Luijten en Kleijn nader bekeken*, Deventer: Kluwer 2001, p. 3 ff.

notaries to private law jurisprudence in the 19th century was to establish and maintain authoritative journals, to which not they, but notable civil-law experts contributed: "The non-notary lawyers filled at least ninety percent of the column inches."[113] Notary training lacked the academic quality that characterised legal training. The literature on matrimonial property and inheritance law was frequently written by professors with a knowledge of contract and property law. The most famous notarial writer of the 19th century was Jacobus Sprenger van Eyk (1842-1907), who provided an article-by-article commentary on the Dutch Law on Notaries (Act of 9 July 1842, *Staatsblad* 20).[114] Perhaps the clearest indication of lack of academic status in the first half of the 20th century was the absence of a commentary on the development of notarial law in the authoritative *Gedenkboek Burgerlijk Wetboek 1838-1938* [Civil Code Memorial Book 1838-1938], which supposedly covered all legal disciplines. Although Libourel, president of the Notary Fraternity of the Netherlands from 1932 to 1949, plugged this gap with a detailed and thorough article on the link between the Civil Code of 1838 and the notarial profession from 1838 to 1939, the absence of notarial law from the *Gedenkboek* remained a sore point.[115] A bright spot was the publication of *Huwelijksgoederen- en erfrecht: handleiding bij studie en practijk* [Matrimonial property and inheritance law: guide to study and practice] (first edition, Arnhem: Gouda Quint 1904), by junior civil-law notary J.G. Klaassen. The fifth (1931/1933) and subsequent editions were edited by Eggens, who was appointed professor in the 'Dutch East Indies' in 1935 and, after the war, professor at the University of Amsterdam.

The notarial profession was firmly convinced that the elevation of notary training to an academic programme of study would boost the quality of professional practice. The training of civil-law notaries was carried out by the notaries themselves. They were often affiliated with universities as private lecturers, as was the case with the aforementioned Pitlo (Amsterdam) and Eggens (Utrecht). In 1956, Van Oven, Minister of Justice and for many years editor of the *WPNR* and professor of Roman law in Leiden, created security of livelihood for civil-law notaries by making a notarial deed mandatory for the supply of immovable property and the establishment of limited immovable-property rights (Art. 671a

---

113. A. Pitlo, *De geschiedenis der notariële wetenschap*, Geschiedenis der Nederlandsche Rechtswetenschap, part V, no. 2, Amsterdam: Noord-Hollandsche Uitgevers Mij 1956, p. 283; T.J. Veen, 'Inleiding', in: T.J. Veen and P.C. Kop (eds), *Zestig juristen. Bijdragen tot een beeld van de geschiedenis der Nederlandse rechtswetenschap*, Zwolle: W.E.J. Tjeenk Willink 1987, p. 71.

114. *De wet op het notarisambt*, first edition (1861; sixth and last edition 1928, prepared by Ph.B. Libourel (1878-1954)).

115. P. Scholten and E.M. Meijers (eds), *Gedenkboek Burgerlijk Wetboek 1838-1938*, Zwolle: W.E.J. Tjeenk Willink 1938. It was a sore point because the *Gedenkboek* did contain commentary on the Civil Code and administrative law (P.S. Gerbrandy), the Civil Code and tax law (P.J.A. Adriani) and the Civil Code and criminal law (L.C. Besier). See Ph.B. Libourel, 'Ons honderdjarige Burgerlijk Recht en het Notariaat', *Correspondentie-blad van de Broederschap der Notarissen in Nederland* 1938/11, p. 281 ff.

Old Dutch Civil Code; see Art. 3:89(1) Dutch Civil Code and Art. 3:89(4) in conjunction with Art. 3:98 Dutch Civil Code).[116] This law created a monopoly for civil-law notaries, thereby ensuring a steady source of income. Two years later, following years of discussion (Jimmy Polak (1922-2014) even spoke of an '80-year war'), notary training became an academic programme under the Law of 30 October 1958 (*Staatsblad* 494), with effect from the 1959-1960 academic year.[117]Arthur Begheyn (1916-2009) had been private lecturer for the notarial profession in Nijmegen since 1946. He had a tax office in the city and, from 1953, was leader of the KVP on the city council. The faculty wished to reward him for his years of loyal service and proposed him as extraordinary professor of notarial law.[118] Van der Grinten was against the appointment, saying that Begheyn did not have a good reputation in the tax world. The Board of the University eventually vetoed his coming.[119] Number two on the shortlist was Laurent Nouwen (1903-1997), a lawyer in The Hague. In 1959 he was appointed extraordinary professor of notarial practice. His inaugural address was entitled *Aan de wieg van de notariële meester in de rechten* [*The inception of the Master of notarial law*] (Nijmegen: Dekker & Van de Vegt 1959). In 1961, Nouwen took over tax law from Russel, who retired as the longest-serving professor at the Catholic University. Nouwen remained in that position until 1973.[120] In 1974 he made the headlines with his statement that the Dutch tax system was contrary to the sense of justice.[121]

As extraordinary professor of notarial law, Nouwen had been supported by Emile Luijten (1919-2016), a junior civil-law notary in Nieuwenhagen since 1947. In 1959, Luijten was appointed lector in matrimonial property and inheritance law. Shortly before his appointment as lector, he had published an excellent article entitled *De gemeenschap van vruchten en inkomsten in het licht der emancipatie* [Community of benefits and incomes in the light of emancipation] (*WPNR* 1957/4481) and an important preliminary opinion for the Notary Fraternity of the Netherlands, entitled *De ouderlijke boedelverdeling van de artt. 1167 e.v. BW* [The division of the

116. Act of 28 June 1956, *Staatsblad* 1956, 376, which took effect on 15 August 1956; see J.S.L.A.W.B. Roes, *De zaakwaarnemer. Een notarieel-historische terugblik*, Ars Notariatus 157, Deventer: Kluwer 2014, p. 231 ff.

117. See F.W.J.M. Schols and B. Snijder-Kuijpers, 'De academische juridische opleiding; verleden, heden en vooral de toekomst', in: C.J.H. Jansen and J.S.L.A.W.B. Roes (eds), *175 jaar KNB*, The Hague: Sdu 2018, p. 65 ff. (quote from Polak on p. 67). See also J.H.A. Lokin, *De Groninger Faculteit der Rechtsgeleerdheid (1596-1970)*, The Hague: Boom juridisch 2019, p. 529 ff.

118. Begheyn obtained his PhD in 1947, with Petit as his supervisor.

119. Brabers, *De Faculteit der Rechtsgeleerdheid van de Katholieke Universiteit Nijmegen 1923-1982*, pp. 237-238.

120. Nouwen criticised the design of the notarial programme. For example, he disagreed with the fact that criminal law was not part of the curriculum. His criticism reached the newspapers. 'Kritiek op universitaire opleiding tot notaris', *Het Parool* 20 November 1959, p. 7. See P.L. Nève, 'Een surnumerair in toga: Laurent Nouwen (1903-1997)', *Pro Memorie* 8.1 (2006), p. 115 ff. Nouwen had an affinity with natural law.

121. 'Belastingstelsel is in strijd met het rechtsgevoel', *Limburgs Dagblad* 1974, p. 29; 'Belastingstelsel valt niet samen met rechtsgevoel', *Nieuwsblad van het Noorden* 29 April 1974, p. 13.

parental estate of art. 1167 et seq. Dutch Civil Code] (1958). Luijten described in detail how his appointment as lector at the Roman Catholic University had come about.[122] Wednesday became notarial day and was known as 'suit day', with all the students coming to lectures neatly attired in suits. Luijten shared his office at the Law Institute with Van Eck, his criminal law colleague "whose views on neo-Thomism I fully shared".[123] Thus it was no coincidence that Luijten continued to open his lectures with a prayer. After obtaining his doctorate *cum laude* in 1962 with *Het nieuwe huwelijksvermogensrecht* [The new matrimonial property law], supervised by Van der Grinten, nothing stood in the way of his appointment as extraordinary professor of notarial law in 1963. He occupied that chair until 1987. As well as a focus on the history of law and comparative law, Luijten's approach was characterised by a comparison with general property law. With this generalist approach to his field, he aligned himself with the tradition of Van der Heijden and Van der Grinten. In 1964, Luijten published his first adaptation of Klaassen's *Huwelijksgoederen- en erfrecht* [Matrimonial property and inheritance law].[124]

8   THE MAELSTROM OF TIME: DEPILLARISATION AND DEMOCRATISATION

Starting in the 1960s, the faculty underwent major changes. It was swept along in the maelstrom of time as 'depillarisation' (*ontzuiling*) and secularisation tightened their grip on society. In 1966, the university set up a committee headed by the theologian and professor Edward Schillebeeckx (1914-2009), which was tasked with publishing a report on the university's Catholic character. The report didn't appear until 1971. Its conclusion was reassuring: secularisation hadn't changed the primary task of the university, which remained the practice of scholarship and the provision of academic education. That same year, the board of the Nijmegen Faculty of Law set up its own committee to advise on the catholicity of the university and faculty. The majority of the committee proposed breaking with catholicity as an essential point of reference. "I have never before encountered a report," wrote committee member Leijten, "that was so absolutely and completely buried following its release."[125] Nevertheless, around 1970, typical Catholic elements such as canon law and opening lectures with a prayer (except for Luijten) disappeared as 'compulsory' electives from the curriculum. In 1971, the first non-Catholic professor, Salomon (Sam) van der Kwast (1927-1982), was appointed to the faculty for forensic psychiatry. The second non-Catholic followed a short time later: Catharina Irma Dessaur (1931-2002), who enjoyed fame as a writer under the

---

122. E.A.A. Luijten, 'De notariële studierichting aan de KU Nijmegen in retrospectief', in: Gitmans et al. (eds), *Te Recht in Nijmegen*, p. 103 ff. Luijten was appointed civil-law notary in Heerlen in 1964.
123. Luijten, 'De notariële studierichting aan de KU Nijmegen in retrospectief', p. 107.
124. A.J.M. Nuytinck and A.H.N. Stollenwerck, 'In memoriam prof. mr. E.A.A. Luijten', *WPNR* 2016/7130. See also A.J.M. Nuytinck, 'Luijten en het algemene vermogensrecht', *Luijten en Kleijn nader bekeken*, p. 15 ff.
125. J. Leijten, 'Een juridische broedplaats', *NRC Handelsblad*, Boeken 3 November 1994, p. 3.

pseudonym Andreas Burnier. She became a lector in criminology in 1971 and a full professor in that field in 1973.[126]

Around 1970, the Nijmegen university and the Faculty of Law were engulfed by the 'wave of democratisation' that swept through Dutch universities. The student protests in Berlin and Paris were positively received by some Dutch students, including those in Nijmegen. Many still remember the famous occupation of the Maagdenhuis, the main administrative building of the University of Amsterdam, in 1969. The Roman Catholic University had experienced a large influx of young people in the preceding years, partly as a result of the post-war baby boom. Scholarships also encouraged more young people to study. The elite nature of university education was brought to an end. Also affecting the law faculty was the fact that a grammar school education (*gymnasium*) was no longer a prerequisite for admission to law school. As already mentioned, the University Administration (Reform) Act came into force in 1970. It required the universities to introduce 'councils', which ensured the participation of all sections of the university (professors, staff and students). The Act was based on proposals from Nijmegen law students, who had set out their ideas about 'councils' in two papers in 1968. They were critical of the government's plans and were concerned that the participation model for large companies would be introduced into universities and universities of applied sciences (known as *hogescholen* at that time). These institutions would then be subject to the same requirements that companies had to meet, such as efficiency, cost reduction and returns.[127] In particular, the students wanted a say in the appointment of professors. They feared – not without justification – that their interests were not always properly considered in the appointment process. Although most law professors and students allowed these developments relating to governance to pass them by, there were also students for whom creating a revolution and demanding a voice was a full-time job.[128]

In Nijmegen, criticism about the lack of transparency reached boiling point with the events surrounding the appointment of Leijten in 1969. Leijten was a former student and assistant, but he did not have a PhD. The student paper *Morgen Meester* published a call to students to cut out a page from the paper, sign it and send it back to the editors. The page read: "The undersigned, a member of the law faculty in Nijmegen, requests that J. Leyten NOT be officially appointed as a professor, and, if this has already occurred [!], not to let this appointment

---

126. Brabers, *De Faculteit der Rechtsgeleerdheid van de Katholieke Universiteit Nijmegen 1923-1982*, p. 411 ff. (for the history of appointments).

127. See H.C. Boekraad, M.J. van Nieuwstadt, T. Regtien and H. Sips, *Universiteit en Onderneming: een analyse van het rapport Maris* (1968), p. 3. *Discussienota Bestuursstructuur* also appeared in 1968 and quickly became known as the 'Green Book' because of the colour of its cover; see 'Democratisering van Nijmeegse universiteit op komst. Geen eenstemmigheid over raden', *De Tijd* 21 November 1968, p. 5. Brabers, *De Faculteit der Rechtsgeleerdheid van de Katholieke Universiteit Nijmegen 1923-1982*, pp. 330-331.

128. The student newspaper *Morgen Meester* was the mouthpiece for critical law students.

proceed."[129] Students had organised a meeting that was attended by more than one hundred people, including Leijten himself. Those present asked him to hold back from his appointment until the students and staff had been heard. In this instance, their protest achieved little: a short time later, Leijten was appointed full professor in the introduction to jurisprudence and general law.[130] It was not only the lack of say in Leijten's appointment that came under criticism. The appointment of three other staff members had already been criticised for the same reason, with a fierce attack aimed at the individuals concerned.[131]

9   CONCLUSION

The first few years after the war were lean ones for the Nijmegen law faculty. The war had left its mark on the faculty and its staff, but as *De Volkskrant* wrote in 1948: "Young people have put their shoulders to the wheel and, with absolute commitment and youthful élan, they have made an immediate start on a new university." Was it not the hallmark of a citadel that it would be destroyed many times, but would nevertheless rise time and again in modified form?[132] The professors – aided in part by their Catholic faith – were on the right side of history, which meant that they were often given a role in the Special Courts and in the legal redress after the war. They formed a fairly close-knit group of intellectuals, inspired by neo-Thomist natural law and characterised by a close connection with legal practice and the KVP/RKSP.[133] Petit was the only outsider. He was less of a Catholic than the others, had little interest in natural law and had rather contrary views on abortion, divorce and adoption. The professors (including Petit) maintained close contacts with the student body (especially with Carolus Magnus), which some of them had belonged to themselves as students. Frans Duynstee, for example, was a member of HOEK and Willem van der Grinten of GONG in his student days. The first professors drawn from their own ranks were appointed after 1945, alongside Frans Duynstee, there were Van Eck, Joop van der Ven, Beel, Van Agt[134] and Willem van der Grinten. Following Jos van der Grinten and Van der Heijden from before the war, the faculty boasted two high flyers:

129. See 'Werkgroep Leyten', *Morgen Meester Extra Editie Mr. Jan Leyten* (17 June 1969), p. 5. Students could in no way 'verify' Leijten's 'expertise'.
130. Brabers, *De Faculteit der Rechtsgeleerdheid van de Katholieke Universiteit Nijmegen 1923-1982*, p. 352 ff.; see also Bulten, Hermans-Brand, Jansen, 'Kind van mijn tijd. Interview met mw. mr. Pia E.M.S. Lokin-Sassen', pp. 101-102.
131. J. Buskes, 'De welp volgt de oude wolf', *Morgen Meester* 1968/2, p. 20 ff.
132. 'Een kwart eeuw straalt het licht van de katholieke universiteit. Sluitstuk van de emancipatie', *De Volkskrant* 16 October 1948, p. 5.
133. See e.g. 'Interview met mej. Mr. W.C.E. Schoonderwoerd', *Morgen Meester* 1969/8, p. 46: "If I vote, it will be for the KVP."
134. Van Agt was professor of criminal law and criminal procedural law from 1968 to 1971. He was a student of Van Eck and hadn't yet obtained his PhD. See Brabers, *De Faculteit der Rechtsgeleerdheid van de Katholieke Universiteit Nijmegen 1923-1982*, p. 364 ff.

Frans Duynstee and Willem van der Grinten. The faculty built up a solid reputation in the Dutch legal sector. The 1923 mission of the university (and faculty) – to educate Catholic intellectuals who could take up a prominent position in society – had therefore succeeded. Graduates ended up not only in academia, but also made their way into high positions in the judiciary, business, the legal profession, the state and municipal administration, and politics. Stand-out appointments of 'Nijmegen' professors include Van den Brink, Beel, Cals, Veringa and Van Agt as ministers, and alumni Victor Marijnen (1917-1975) as Minister of Agriculture and Fisheries and Prime Minister and Emmanuel ('Maan') Sassen (1911-1995) as Minister of Overseas Territories (1947-1948), and later as a member of the European Atomic Energy Community (1958-1967) and of the European Commission (1967-1970).

In the late 1960s and early 1970s, Dutch society was in ferment. The Nijmegen law faculty was also affected. The 'law', like many institutions vested with authority (the Church and parents), was called into question. This criticism was accompanied by a far greater unwillingness to abide by the rules (civil disobedience). Confidence in the judiciary was also on the wane. Leijten, who had experienced the new era first-hand when appointed, accepted his professorship in 1970 with a speech entitled: *De rechter op de schopstoel* [Judges on the chopping block]. The era of the 'modern' Nijmegen Faculty of Law had dawned.

The 'modern' Faculty of Law (1970-1998)

1 Introduction

The introduction of the University Administration (Reform) Act (WUB) in 1970 changed the meaning of the concept of faculty from that of past centuries. It was no longer the professors alone who had the power to decide on the organisation of such matters as the teaching programme, examinations, staff appointments, academic counselling and study advice. Now, other academic and non-academic staff, as well as students, could also have a say. The changes weren't introduced without a fight. Student protests continued in Nijmegen until 1972/1973 but there was never a true revolution within the law faculty. Instead, the faculty enjoyed a high degree of continuity, in part because Willem van der Grinten held the position of dean from 1972 to 1983. Nevertheless, Brabers was not wrong to speak in his doctoral thesis of a cultural revolution.[1] The traditional law faculty of the 1950s and 1960s steadily evolved to become a modern centre of academic research and teaching. A new group of professors took up their posts around 1970.[2]

In the late 1960s and early 1970s, the university in Nijmegen became much more large-scale in many respects. There were 1000 students studying law in the 1967-1968 academic year; by 1970-1971 that number was 1500, as scholarships became available for students who couldn't afford to pay their own way. It was not until the mid-1980s that student numbers in Nijmegen declined, in part as a result of demographic changes. In 1971, Dessaur had been the first female professor (in criminology). The second such appointment, Willijne Hammerstein-Schoonderwoerd (b. 1943), was not made until 1987 (in personal and family law). Academic staff numbers grew exponentially – from 11 in 1965 to 69 in 1982.[3]

---

1. Brabers, *De Faculteit der Rechtsgeleerdheid van de Katholieke Universiteit Nijmegen 1923-1982*, p. 381.
2. Such as Petrus Mathijsen, (extraordinary) professor of European law in 1968; Van Agt, professor of criminal law in 1969; Geert van den Steenhoven, professor of folk law in 1972; Désiré Scheltens, professor of philosophy of law in 1973; and Leonardus de Leede, professor of social law and economic law in 1973.
3. J. Brabers, "Recht om mee te werken'. Een geschiedenis van de faculteit der rechtsgeleerdheid als academisch brandpunt en emancipatorisch vehikel (1923-1982)', in: Gitmans et al. (eds), *Te Recht in Nijmegen*, p. 47.

H.H. Franke was deputy director from 1965, assisted by Lidy Goddijn as secretary after 1969. Tutorials were held alongside the 'traditional' lectures. As a result, the 'faculty', which had been housed on the Oranjesingel since 1959, was bursting at the seams. Although the vast majority of professors worked from home, the faculty space had become too shabby and cramped. In 1982, the faculty moved to a much larger premises at Thomas van Aquinostraat 6-8 on the Heyendaal campus, although not everyone was happy about it. Maeijer felt that the best time was the first few years of his professorship (which began in 1963): "On the Oranjesingel in that beautiful building opposite café De Karseboom. Things were much livelier than at the Institute on the Thomas van Aquinostraat and we could also go to De Karseboom. (...). That was a good time back then."[4]

As well as greater democracy and a larger scale, secularisation and 'depillarisation' (*ontzuiling*) also affected the faculty at the end of the 1960s. As already mentioned, prayers had been dropped around 1970. Not all faculty professors or staff were Catholic or active within the KVP. The battle over the catholicity of prospective professors reached boiling point with the 1971 appointment of the non-Catholic Olav Moorman van Kappen (b. 1937) to the history of law. He was unanimously nominated by the appointments committee. The fact that Moorman van Kappen was not affiliated with a particular denomination sparked heated debate in a faculty meeting that lasted well into the night. Van der Grinten, who had a decided preference for a Catholic, was particularly opposed to Moorman van Kappen's candidacy. According to the appointments committee, however, no suitable Catholic was available. Maeijer proposed that the issue of principle – the appointment of non-Catholics – should first be addressed and then the 'specific case' of Moorman van Kappen. The vast majority of Nijmegen professors still preferred to have Catholic fellow professors. If there were no Catholics available, or if their academic credentials were much inferior to those of a non-Catholic, then the latter candidate was preferred. This became known as the 'two-track policy'. As the appointments committee had already established that there were no suitable Catholic candidates for the history of law, Moorman van Kappen came to join the faculty ranks.[5]

This preference for Catholics in professorial chairs continued for a long time. It was not until the 1990s that the 'two-track policy' faded into the background. This letting go of the Catholic faith as a prerequisite for professorial appointments also meant that the teaching was no longer inspired by Thomas Aquinas. A concern for the person within law remained, however. Thus there were chairs in personal and family law, immigration law (later migration law) and prison law. Hammerstein-Schoonderwoerd linked the establishment of her chair in personal and family law to the university's Catholic foundations: "In view of the university's identity, the

4. Bulten, Hermans-Brand, Jansen, ''Het leven is goed.' Interview met prof. mr. J.M.M. Maeijer', in: Hermans-Brand and Jansen (eds), *Te Recht in Nijmegen*, p. 94.
5. Brabers, *De Faculteit der Rechtsgeleerdheid van de Katholieke Universiteit Nijmegen 1923-1982*, p. 418 ff.

major social changes in that area, it seemed appropriate to create a chair for this purpose."[6]

The faculty took on a regional function. The number of Catholic students from northern regions had always been fairly small, but it now gradually dried up. Many Nijmegen law students were 'first-generation students' whose parents didn't have a university education, a very different situation from in Leiden, Utrecht and Amsterdam. The Nijmegen faculty was 'frugal' by nature, but in the 1980s it had to contend with budget cuts as a result of the economic crisis. The then dean, Antoon (Teun) Struycken (b. 1936), described the 1987-1991 period as the 'four lean years.' "There was a single message: cuts had to be made and people even had to be dismissed."[7]

The biggest change in education at that time related to the introduction of the University Education (Two-Tier System) Act of 1981, which entered into force in 1982 and was valid until 2002. Its introduction stemmed from the cuts in higher education that Struycken alluded to. The two-tier structure meant that the five-year law programme became a four-year one. The two-year *kandidaats* phase and the three-year *doctoraal* phase became a one-year propaedeutic phase and a three-year *doctoraal* programme, respectively. This shorter duration led to an impoverishment of the university programme and put pressure on the age-old ideal of a fully rounded academic education. The new Act was accompanied by a new system of control and monitoring of university education based on critical reflections and programme audits. The 1980s and 1990s thus marked the beginning of an unprecedented rise in bureaucracy and a complex system of organised distrust that continues to this day.[8]

2   PERSONALITIES FROM THE 1970S

In this section I will discuss the persona and work of Maeijer, who was appointed in 1963, Govaert van den Bergh (1926-2005), appointed in 1965, Leijten (in 1969) and Struycken (in 1971). All four professors were Catholic, but two of them (Van den Bergh and Leijten) struggled with their faith and broke away from the Catholic Church. They remained religious to the core, however. These professors no longer talked about natural law as the basis of positive law, although Maeijer, Leijten and Struycken had been trained in the Thomistic tradition and Leijten had even attended the seminary for a short time. They felt naturally at home with the KVP, although Van den Bergh and Leijten couldn't resist the appeal of the PvdA.

---

6.   W.C.E. Hammerstein-Schoonderwoerd, '25 jaar werken aan de faculteit (1969-1994)', in: Gitmans et al. (eds), *Te Recht in Nijmegen*, p. 118.

7.   W.J.M. Gitmans et al., 'In gesprek met J.M.M. Maeijer en A.V.M. Struycken: Nijmeegse juristen zijn in tal van sectoren toonaangevend', in: Gitmans et al. (eds), *Te Recht in Nijmegen*, p. 138.

8.   P.P.T. Bovend'Eert, 'De rechtenstudie in Nijmegen. Kanttekeningen bij enige ontwikkelingen', in: Gitmans et al. (eds), *Te Recht in Nijmegen*, pp. 150-151.

They felt a kinship with the movement that sought to 'break through' the pre-war pillarisation. The Episcopal Mandate of 1954, *De katholiek in het openbare leven van deze tijd* [Catholics in the public life of our time], which called on Catholics not to engage with social democracy, came as a shock to them. Nevertheless, Van den Bergh became a member of the PvdA and served as a city councillor for the party in Haarlem from 1959 to 1965. Van den Bergh wrote for and Leijten edited *Te Elfder Ure*, which began as a fairly progressive Catholic scientific and cultural journal. They were both editors of the 'progressive' *Nijmeegs Universiteitsblad*. Maeijer became a luminary in private law in the Nijmegen law faculty.

The following list of professorships from 1970 shows just how much the faculty (i.e. the number of professors) had grown compared to the previous period.

Employment law: F.J.H.M. van der Ven

Tax law: L.J.M. Nouwen

Tax law and economics: M.V.M. van Leeuwe

Administrative law: S.F.L. baron van Wijnbergen

Civil law and private international law: W.C.L. van der Grinten

Civil procedural law: L.E.H. Rutten

Canon law: P.J.M. Huizing

Economics, public finance and the economic cycle: G.W. Groeneveld

Commercial law: J.M.M. Maeijer

Introduction to law and general legal theory: J.C.M. Leijten

Notarial law: E.A.A. Luijten

Philosophy of law: A.T.B. Peperzak

History of law: F.F.X. Cerutti

Roman law: G.C.J.J. van den Bergh

Constitutional law: F.J.F.M. Duynstee

Criminal law: A.A.M. van Agt

Criminal procedural law: W.H.A. Jonkers

Rights of the indigenous people: G. van den Steenhoven

International law: A.M. Stuyt

2.1 Jozef (Sjef) Maeijer[9]

Maeijer had begun studying law in 1949 in Nijmegen, where Willem Duynstee made the deepest impression on him. Maeijer found him "an extraordinarily lucid

9.   See C.D.J. Bulten, C.J.H. Jansen and G. van Solinge (eds), 'Ten Geleide', in: *Verspreide geschriften van J.M.M. Maeijer*, Van der Heijden Institute Series Part 100, Deventer: Kluwer 2009, pp. XI-XV; G. van Solinge, 'Een vasthoudende en innemende strijder voor het redelijke en het billijke: Prof. Mr. J.M.M. Maeijer Breda 14 januari 1932 – 's Hertogenbosch 6 september 2018', *Ars Aequi* 2018, pp. 948-950; C.H. Sieburgh, 'In herinnering Jef Maeijer. Van rechtvaardigheid bezeten', *Tijdschrift voor Privaatrecht* 2018, pp. 875-879.

and wise man". Maeijer said that Duynstee revealed to his students a doctrine of natural law that derived from Thomas Aquinas. It contained norms that met humankind's naturally imperative aspirations, norms that people, as reasonable beings, must pursue. Regarding the natural virtue of justice, Duynstee – invoking the Roman jurist Ulpian – told his students that they should give everyone their due,[10] "whereby their due was everything that one's own individual personality demanded".[11] Maeijer read and heard related ideas from Savatier and Jean Carbonnier (1908-2003), the French professors of civil law in Poitiers, where he studied for a year in 1952 through the mediation of Petit, who – like Maeijer – came from Breda. He would spend another year in Poitiers after graduating in 1954. However, the Poitevin bookseller who sold him Savatier's textbook *Cours de droit civil* also "thrust into his hands books by Pascal, Voltaire and Camus", telling him: "ça vous changera du droit."[12] The work of Albert Camus (1913-1960) continued to fascinate Maeijer throughout his life, as he himself relates:

> What does Camus mean to me besides the scholastic thinking, governed in particular by reasonableness and rationality, with which I had previously become acquainted [in his student days in Nijmegen]. (...) His message is: in specific circumstances and conscious of our own imperfection, we must continue to work to achieve a little more justice in this unjust world. (...) In my view, Camus adds a dimension to the postulate of reasonableness located in people themselves.[13]

Maeijer transferred into law Camus' struggle for greater reasonableness. He regarded fairness as the basis of (private) law.[14] He shared with his colleague Willem van der Grinten the notion of reasonableness as a basic standard of private law proceedings. They separated it from natural law thinking. Maeijer believed that Christians or Roman Catholics could not claim exclusivity when it came to the 'prepositive principles of natural law'. These were human values. Catholic lawyers "working with other Dutch jurists from a different philosophical background" had to try to "put a definitive end to pure legal positivism, and (...) concern themselves

---

10.   See D. 1,1,10, pr : 'Justice is the unshakable and abiding will to give everyone their due' and D. 1,1,10,1 : 'The basic principles of the law are: to live decently, not to harm others and to give everyone their due.'

11.   Bulten, Hermans-Brand, Jansen, ''Het leven is goed'. Interview met prof. mr. J.M.M. Maeijer', in: Hermans-Brand and Jansen (eds), *Recht in Nijmegen*, p. 86; J.M.M. Maeijer, 'Albert Camus en de rechtvaardigheid', in: *Verspreide geschriften van J.M.M. Maeijer*, p. 563.

12.   Maeijer, 'Albert Camus en de rechtvaardigheid', p. 563.

13.   Maeijer, 'Albert Camus en de rechtvaardigheid', p. 568.

14.   L. Timmerman, 'Prof. Mr. J.M.M. Maeijer; jurist en mens van longue durée', in: *Verspreide geschriften van J.M.M. Maeijer*, p. 4. See J.M.M. Maeijer, 'De corrigerende werking van de goede trouw, in het bijzonder binnen rechtspersonen' (1984), J.M.M. Maeijer, 'Wil en vertrouwen bij de totstandkoming van verbintenissen' (1991) and J.M.M. Maeijer, 'Vertrouwen en rechtszekerheid in het overeenkomstenrecht' (1998), in: *Verspreide geschriften van J.M.M. Maeijer*, p. 247 ff., p. 129 ff. and p. 133 ff. respectively.

with the intrinsic content of human justice, without giving their own philosophy of life or that of their Church a dominant position in this endeavour and without explicitly acting as proclaimers of the Catholic faith."[15]

> Maeijer (1932-2018) was a Brabander in heart and soul, who felt at home throughout the old Duchy of Brabant.[16] The Flemish were also dear to him. He studied, of course, in Nijmegen. The Roman Catholic University was a symbol of Catholic emancipation. After his studies and his military service, Maeijer became a judicial officer in training in Amsterdam and Breda, and then a lawyer in Arnhem in 1962. In that same year, he obtained his PhD on a civil law topic, *Matiging van schadevergoeding* [Mitigation of damages], under the supervision of Willem van der Grinten. The subject was inspired by an 'issue' that Meijers had drawn up for the Dutch parliament in the context of his draft of the new civil code. Petit had encouraged Maeijer to study this subject. The issue wasn't regulated by Dutch law, although it was by the Swiss Civil Code (ZGB). Following the example of the Swiss legislator, Maeijer argued that the court should have the legal power to mitigate damages on the basis of the remedial effects of reasonableness and fairness. He had the satisfaction of seeing a provision along his suggested lines incorporated into Art. 6:109 of the Civil Law Code.
>
> Maeijer was appointed professor of commercial law (and private international law) at his *alma mater* in 1963. Like Van der Heijden, Kamphuisen and Willem van der Grinten, he was a private law generalist. He published on civil law, insurance law, intellectual property law, medical law and personal and company law. He was not afraid to take a stand. In an interview, Timmerman described Maeijer as a combative spirit, like Camus. "Maeijer has acknowledged Camus' militancy and admired it." Timmerman added: "Maeijer likes people of character who display courage."[17]
>
> Maeijer held many management positions inside and outside the faculty. He was vice dean of the faculty from 1973 to 1981 and dean from 1983 to 1987. In 1968 he joined the Company Law Committee, which he chaired from 1992 to 2005. In that capacity, he oversaw a number of fundamental changes in corporate law. From 1980 to 1992, Maeijer was president of the Commercial Law Association. In 1981 he was appointed a member of the Royal Netherlands Academy of Arts and Sciences (KNAW). From 1983 to 1997 he was president of the Dutch branch of the Association for the Comparative Study of Dutch and Belgian Law. In 1969, he and Willem van der Grinten co-founded the *Van der Heijden Institute series,* which is still published today. Maeijer was also at the inception of the biennial Van der Heijden conference (since 1971). And finally, he was a member of the supervisory board of several companies.

Maeijer was best known in the legal world for his work on three volumes in the Asser series, in which he covered the whole of company law and the law

---

15. J.M.M. Maeijer, 'Interventie over de identiteit van katholieke rechtsgeleerden' (1979), in: *Verspreide geschriften van J.M.M. Maeijer*, pp. 542-543.
16. Sieburgh, 'In herinnering Jef Maeijer. Van rechtvaardigheid bezeten', p. 878.
17. Timmerman, 'Prof. Mr. J.M.M. Maeijer; jurist en mens van longue durée', p. 3.

governing legal persons.[18] Volume 2-II was devoted to legal persons (eighth edition, 1997), volume 2-III dealt with public limited and private limited liability companies (first edition, 1994; second edition, 2000) and volume 5-V covered personal partnerships, partnerships, general partnerships and limited partnerships (fourth edition, 1981; fifth edition, 1989; sixth edition, 1995). Maeijer drafted a bill (28746) to regulate partnerships (intended for inclusion in Title 7.13 of the Dutch Civil Code), but it was never passed into law. He was also a prolific annotator of court decisions in the journal *Nederlandse Jurisprudentie*.

Perhaps the most important term coined by Maeijer was that of corporate interest, "the interest that the company has in its own healthy existence, expansion and survival with a view to its defined objective." He outlined the meaning of this concept in his inaugural address *Het belangenconflict in de naamloze vennootschap* [The conflict of interest in public limited companies] (1964) against the background of good faith, which in his view governed not only contractual relationships, but also internal relationships within a company. He referred to Art. 2:8 of the Civil Code, (Art. 2.1.7b of the Meijers bill), which was yet to be introduced. Maeijer departed from the contractual view of public limited companies (NVs) and aligned himself with an institutional one. Relationships within a public limited company had their own, non-contractual nature. The company's interest included not only the monetary interest of the joint shareholders, but also of employees, creditors and the organs of the company.[19] Timmerman pointed out that promoting institutions with a certain degree of sustainability was a key element in Maeijer's thinking about company law: Maeijer was a scholar and a man of the *longue durée*.[20] He considered it self-evident that the increasing concern in the society of his time demanded responsible action by companies. A company's freedom could be curtailed by legislation, but also by corrective infiltration through the existing norms of unwritten law, such as reasonableness, fairness and standards of due care. Moral standards provided in part the basis for law, but they never equated with it.[21] Thus, at the end of his academic career (1999), Maeijer drew on ideas that he had held at the beginning, in his 1962 thesis.

---

18.   The book that resulted from his lectures and which was later set reading for his students was entitled *Vennootschapsrecht in beweging* (first edition, 1971).

19.   J.M.M. Maeijer, 'Het belangenconflict in de naamloze vennootschap' (1964), *Verspreide geschriften van J.M.M. Maeijer*, pp. 141-142, p. 144 (containing a description of company interest), p. 158.

20.   Timmerman, 'Prof. Mr. J.M.M. Maeijer; jurist en mens van longue durée', pp. 8-9; Van Solinge, 'Een vasthoudende en innemende strijder voor het redelijke en het billijke: Prof. Mr. J.M.M. Maeijer', p. 950.

21.   J.M.M. Maeijer, 'Reflecties over verantwoordelijkheid en aansprakelijkheid zoals die tot uitdrukking komen in het recht', in: V. Poels (ed.), *Verantwoord ondernemen*, Best: Damon 1999, p. 37 ff., pp. 56-58. Maeijer referred in this contribution to Van der Heijden's 'natural standards'.

2.2   *Govaert van den Bergh*[22]

When Govaert van den Bergh succeeded Hermesdorf in 1965, the Nijmegen faculty wasn't acquiring the usual professor of Roman law. Van den Bergh was fascinated by language, law and history as all three represented the paradox of freedom and coercion. They were governed by more or less mandatory 'rules' and were both a restriction of and a condition for freedom. People made history, but history also made people. Van den Bergh believed that the paradox of freedom and coercion lay at the heart of what it meant to be human.[23] In his work, he would focus not on the dogmatics of Roman law nor stories from old Dutch law, but on the history of jurisprudence and of ideas. Like Leijten, Van den Bergh wrote poetry.[24] He also supplied poetry chronicles to *De Maasbode* from 1954 to 1957. He never entirely abandoned the Catholic faith, even though he developed an aversion to the Church as an institution. He called it letting go of God for God's sake. For him, Ulpian's celebrated basic principles were precepts for living: living honourably, not harming anyone else and rendering to each their own. He was especially inspired by this last precept.[25]

> Van den Bergh (1926-2005) was born in Haarlem. He completed a lengthy military service in Indonesia. He studied law at the University of Amsterdam, obtaining his PhD in 1964 under Pitlo's supervision with a thesis entitled *Themis en de Muzen. De functie van de gebonden vormen in het recht* [Themis and the Muses]. In Nijmegen he took a particular interest in Gerard Noodt (1647-1725), professor at the 'old' quarterly academy from 1671 to 1679, and the kind of Roman law practice that Noodt stood for. This practice was largely historical. Known as the Elegant School, it aimed to restore Roman law as applied in Roman times. Van den Bergh was there at the inception of the Gerard Noodt Instituut, which he co-founded with Moorman van Kappen in 1972. In 1975 Van den Bergh left for Utrecht, where he published profusely. His two best-known books are *Eigendom. Grepen uit de geschiedenis van een omstreden begrip* [Property. Examples from the history of a controversial concept] (first edition, 1979; second edition, 1988) and *Geleerd recht. Een geschiedenis van de Europese rechtswetenschap in vogelvlucht* [Learned law. A history of European legal science at a glance] (first edition, 1980; fourth edition, 2000). His two

---

22. C.J.H. Jansen and B.H. Stolte, 'G.C.J.J. van den Bergh (1926-2005)', *Pro Memorie* 8.1 (2006), p. 135 ff.
23. G.C.J.J. van den Bergh, 'Voorwoord', in: *Bibliografie van Prof. Mr. Govaert C.J.J. van den Bergh*, Nijmegen: editio ad familiares 2005, pp. vi-vii.
24. Several sonnets appeared in *Roeping*. He published under the pseudonym Govaert van Haarlem, *Sic et nondum*, Op de Brandon Pers 1975. The Tilburg and Nijmegen professor of employment law, F. van der Ven, known as a poet under the pseudonym Frank Valkenier, was printer and publisher of the Brandon Press.
25. D. 1,1,10,1. See G. and M. van den Bergh-Neelissen, *Wat leven ons leerde*, second edition, Nijmegen 2003, p. 15 and p. 24. Augustine was never far away: 'Schoonheid is orde, orde is God.' See G.C.J.J. van den Bergh, 'Jedem das Seine', in: J.B.J.M. ten Berge et al. (eds), *Recht als norm en als aspiratie: Opstellen over recht en samenleving ter gelegenheid van het 350-jarig bestaan van de Utrechtse juridische faculteit*, Nijmegen: Ars Aequi 1986, p. 258 ff.

principal works appeared after he retired in 1988: *The Life and Work of Gerard Noodt (1647-1725).*
Dutch Legal Scholarship between Humanism and Enlightenment (1988) and *Die holländische elegante*
Schule. Ein Beitrag zur Geschichte von Humanismus und Rechtswissenschaft in den Niederlanden
1500-1800 [The Dutch Elegant School: a contribution to the history of humanism and legal
science in the Netherlands 1500-1800] (2002).

Van den Bergh had a reputation in the Nijmegen law faculty as a 'progressive'. In
1968, he took part in an anti-Vietnam war demonstration, where he also had
himself fined in solidarity with students who had had the book thrown at them for
shouting 'Johnson murderer'. He felt that the police action infringed freedom of
expression. Van den Bergh felt a kinship with the student movement in many
ways. He was sympathetic to the ideals of the 'critical university'. The university
should be an institution that trained students to become critical, socially engaged
intellectuals. In his view, reflection on the role of the law and the university in
society should be part of a university education. On the other hand, he deplored
the lack of intellectual independence of some of the student leaders, viewing them
as slavish followers of foreign role models.[26] As editor of the *Nijmeegs*
Universiteitsblad, the magazine of the radical Nijmegen student movement, he
became the whipping boy for his colleagues, who made no bones about what they
thought of him.[27] Van den Bergh had few friends within the faculty. Nor was he
any good at sensing the mood. Without consulting his colleagues, he was the first
to abandon the traditional prayer at the opening of his lectures, a practice that later
fell into disuse.
A dogmatic approach to law was characteristic of the method of many Nijmegen
professors. Hermesdorf, with his cultural-historical approach, was an exception.
Van den Bergh was a 'true' child of his time. He was particularly interested in the
social structures and the social embedding of law, including in the case of Roman
law. His focus was not on dogmatic analysis, for example of liability for *custodia* (a
high degree of care), but on the social reasons why one debtor was liable for
custodia and another was not.[28] During his time in Nijmegen, and fuelled by his
experiences in the 'Dutch East Indies', he developed a great interest in 'folk law',
the workings of non-statutory law, such as folk and adat law, people's courts, legal
pluralism and legal anthropology. He had a god deal of contact with Geert van den
Steenhoven (1919-1998), who was appointed professor of folk law and legal

26.   G.C.J.J. van den Bergh, 'Roodkapje gaat studeren', *Nijmeegs Universiteitsblad* 17 (1967-1968), no. 13
      (8 December 1967). See also G.C.J.J. van den Bergh, 'Studentenbeweging en crisis der
      universiteit', *Universiteit en hogeschool* 16 (1970), p. 347 ff.
27.   Brabers, *De Faculteit der Rechtsgeleerdheid van de Katholieke Universiteit Nijmegen 1923-1982*, p. 352 ff.
      To the annoyance of many of his Nijmegen colleagues, Van den Bergh also wrote in *De Katholiek*
      in de P.v.d.A. and *De Nieuwe Linie*, a progressive weekly that the Jesuits had founded in 1946 as *De*
      Linie.
28.   G.C.J.J. van den Bergh, 'Custodiam praestare. Custodia-Liability or Liability for failing Custodia',
      Tijdschrift voor Rechtsgeschiedenis 43 (1975), p. 59 ff.

development in non-Western societies a year after his own appointment to the Nijmegen faculty. In 1980, Van den Bergh and others published *Staphorst en zijn gerichten. Verslag van een juridisch-antropologisch onderzoek* [Staphorst and its public trials. Report of a legal-anthropological study], a large-scale, interdisciplinary study in which lawyers, sociologists and cultural anthropologists joined forces.[29] In 1968, Van den Bergh argued for a greater focus on the methodological and theoretical aspects of jurisprudence, in particular legal theory and the sociology of law. His plea was well received: Cornelis (Kees) Schuyt (b. 1943) was appointed lector at the Nijmegen law faculty in 1972 and professor of sociology of law in 1974.[30] In 1969, in addition to introduction to jurisprudence, Leijten was given general legal theory as part of his teaching and research remit.[31]

2.3　　　*Johannes (Jan) Leijten*[32]

If there is one word that characterises Leijten's legal habitus, it is 'generalist'. Like some of his Nijmegen predecessors, he was active in many areas of the law: civil law (including personal and family law), constitutional law, criminal and criminal procedural law, civil procedural law, general legal theory, human rights and theory of law. As advocate general, he had a preference for civil law, in particular the writing of civil summations: "a summation under civil law is infinitely more fascinating to make than a summation under criminal law. Because of its age, civil law is extremely highly developed; it demands more of your ingenuity than criminal law. Decisions are also easily suggested in rational terms. Much more so than criminal law, civil law has the quality of a chess game with consequences."[33] Leijten shared the view of his Nijmegen predecessors and colleagues that scholarship could not manage without practice, nor practice without scholarship. Leijten practised law in Nijmegen for ten years (from 1952 to 1962). Johannes (Jan) Vranken (b. 1948), one of Leijten's supervisors, wrote that Leijten would cultivate

---

29.　Law was not a monolithic whole. It was difficult to separate and distinguish law, religion, morality, folk law and popular entertainment from one another.

30.　See G. Hoogeboom, 'De noodzaak van een kritiese rechtssociologie', *Morgen Meester* 1970/1, p. 11 ff.; Brief Groep Rechtssociologie, *Morgen Meester* 1970/3, p. 21 ff.

31.　Brabers, *De Faculteit der Rechtsgeleerdheid van de Katholieke Universiteit Nijmegen 1923-1982*, p. 400.

32.　G.J.M. Corstens et al. (eds), *Met hoofd en hart. Opstellen aangeboden aan prof. mr. J.C.M. Leijten ter gelegenheid van zijn afscheid als hoogleraar aan de Katholieke Universiteit Nijmegen*, Zwolle: W.E.J. Tjeenk Willink 1991; A. Hammerstein & J.B.M. Vranken (eds), *Het kan ook anders. Een keuze uit het juridische werk van Jan Leijten*, Deventer: W.E.J. Tjeenk Willink 1996; Caroline Lindo in conversation with J.C.M. Leijten, *De NJB Interviews*, Deventer: Kluwer 2011, p. 158 ff.; A. Hammerstein & J.B.M. Vranken, 'Jan Leijten (14 januari 1926 – 4 mei 2014)', *NJB* 2014/980; W.J.M. Davids, 'Jan Cornelis Maria Leijten. Etten-Leur 14 januari 1926 – Nijmegen 4 mei 2014', *Jaarboek Maatschappij der Nederlandse Letterkunde*, Leiden: Maatschappij der Nederlandse Letterkunde 2014, p. 124 ff. and www.janleijten.nl. Part of his archive is held in the KDC.

33.　Caroline Lindo in conversation with J.C.M. Leijten, p. 165.

a lawyer's way of thinking throughout his life.[34] Leijten was also interested in politics, although the bishops' mandate of 1954 alienated him from the KVP. He continued nevertheless to feel an affinity with the party, even though – as mentioned above – he voted for the PvdA: "as you grow older, you notice that although an everlasting characteristic or stamp may not have been imprinted on your soul, a good deal still lingers of what seemed lost forever."[35] Leijten said that his Catholic faith had very slowly died away. "I am not a believer, but I believe." (...) "What I do want to believe is that there is someone who rules, that it's not all just chance." He considered Christianity in its original form to be a very respectable faith.[36]

> Leijten (1926-2014) was born in Etten-Leur in West Brabant. Like Maeijer, he regarded studying at the Roman Catholic University as a clear act of catholic emancipation. After graduating in 1952, he became an assistant for Petit (in personal and family law) and for Van Eck.[37] At the same time, he practised law in Nijmegen. He also published poems. As Van den Bergh wrote in *Met hoofd en hart* [With head and heart], the *liber amicorum* for Leijten, their first "literary love, which never entirely faded, was not law but poetry. Poet-lawyers, in other words, except that the demands of professional life meant that the lawyer won out over the poet."[38] In 1962, Leijten switched to the judiciary and became a judge in the District Court of Den Bosch. In 1969 he was appointed professor in the introduction to jurisprudence and general legal theory. This teaching remit changed to civil procedural law, with effect from 1976. Peter Tak (b. 1944) succeeded him in the introduction to jurisprudence (Tak's research interest was comparative criminal law).[39] Leijten combined the (extraordinary) professorship with being a judge in the Arnhem Court of Appeal. In 1981 he was appointed advocate general at the Supreme Court.
>
> Leijten was also a man of the *longue durée*. From 1972 to 1996 he was editor of the *Nederlands Juristenblad*. He was a member of the Ethics Committee of the UMC St Radboud, a member of the Advisory Board of the NJCM (the Dutch section of the International Commission of Jurists), president of the Supervisory Board of the Dutch Association of Real Estate Agents and a member of many other committees. Leijten was appointed to the Royal Netherlands Academy

---

34.   J.B.M. Vranken, 'Levensbericht van Johannes Cornelis Maria Leijten', in: *Levensberichten en herdenkingen*. Koninklijke Nederlandse Akademie van Wetenschappen, 2016, p. 62.

35.   J.C.M. Leijten, 'Een 'oude liefde'?', *Christen Democratische Verkenningen* 7-8/83, pp. 402-403.

36.   Caroline Lindo in conversation with J.C.M. Leijten, p. 162.

37.   His first two articles were also in this field: 'De huwelijkstoestemming van grootouders voor hun minderjarige kleinkinderen (art. 92 en 94 BW)' and 'De erkenning van natuurlijke kinderen in strijd met de waarheid en het nieuwe kinderrecht van 10 juli 1947' in *WPNR* 1951/4205 and *WPNR* 1952/4268 and 4269.

38.   *Met hoofd en hart*, p. 15.

39.   On Tak: Y. Buruma et al., 'Woord vooraf', in: Y. Buruma et al. (eds), *Op het rechte pad. Liber amicorum Peter J.P. Tak*, Nijmegen: Wolf Legal Publishers 2008, pp. v-vii. Tak was appointed Secretary General of the International Penal and Penitentiary Foundation in 2006. He was a specialist in German criminal law. He wrote about comparative law, or in English, about euthanasia, crown witnesses, DNA evidence, the settlement of criminal cases and lay justice in the Netherlands. He published *The Dutch criminal justice system* (first edition, 1999, 2003 and 2008). He was dean from 1995 to 1998.

of Arts and Sciences in 1988. After his legal career, he wrote seven works of a more literary nature but which often touched on legal topics (such as *De verschrikkelijke eenzaamheid van de inbreker* [The terrible loneliness of the burglar] in 1992, *Brullen als een nachtegaal* [Roaring like a nightingale] in 1993 and *Kleine hebzucht loont niet* [Petty greed doesn't pay] in 2003).

Like other forms of authority in society, the law and its magistrates didn't escape criticism from the late 1960s and early 1970s on. 'Openness' (today we would say 'transparency') in governmental institutions, opportunities for public scrutiny and the pursuit of greater democracy were the catch cries of the time. Trust in the judiciary was on the wane: judges – in the words of Leijten – were on the chopping block. In 1972 the Working Group on the Review of the Judicial System published its report *Gedachten over de toekomst van de rechtspleging* [Thoughts on the future of justice], which probably prompted the Dutch Lawyers Association (NJV) in 1975 to elicit preliminary opinions "on the performance of judges in society".[40] In his preliminary report, Schuyt spoke without compunction of the juxtaposition of the judge and the law.[41] As he had already done in his inaugural lecture, Leijten frankly opposed the judge's power to make decisions in violation of the law on the grounds of fairness. His speech was reminiscent of Utrecht professor Suijling's fierce fight against the 'free interpretation of the law'.

> I absolutely do not appreciate that my conduct in society is governed by the totality of views on reasonableness of 500 judges. My confidence in justice resides largely in the fact that I expect that although judges *are able* – to some degree – to make *their* reasonableness as an autonomous phenomenon 'the law', they will very emphatically not do so.[42]

Leijten didn't like to see the formal authority of the legislator replaced by the formal authority of the judge. He considered this contrary to Art. 11 of the Law on General Precepts and Regulations (Wet AB).

> As soon as judges are required to make political decisions *in the sense* that they take a position – and thus make a binding decision – in the fundamental conflicts of society by virtue of their own formal authority – and thus rejecting the authority of the law – that is the end of their authority or our freedom.[43]

---

40. The following argument is based on C.J.H. Jansen, *De wetenschappelijke beoefening van het burgerlijke recht tussen 1940 en 1992*, Deventer: Wolters Kluwer 2016, pp. 144-145.
41. C.J.M. Schuyt, 'De rol van de rechtspraak en rechterlijke macht in een democratische samenleving', *HNJV* 1975-I, p. 198.
42. J.C.M. Leijten, 'De rol van de rechtspraak en rechterlijke macht in een democratische samenleving', *HNJV* 1975-I, p. 129.
43. *HNJV* 1975-I, pp. 131-132. Also J.C.M. Leijten, *De rechter op de schopstoel*, Deventer: Kluwer 1970, p. 19.

Bernd Rüthers (b. 1930) – inspired by his study of the stance of the German judiciary in the Second World War – wrote that judges were not permitted to test the law against a supra-legal positivist standard:

> The conflict between the judicial sense of justice and the applicable law presents judges, if they wish to act in accordance with the Constitution, with the choice of either applying the law that they disapprove of or quitting the service.[44]

Leijten was not a legalist, however. In his opinion, judges both made and interpreted the law. The legal system was an open system. In *We need stories*, his farewell speech in 1991, Leijten returned to the theme of the judge's relationship to the law and pointed out the importance of stories in administering justice: "It is the story element that ensures that the judge – in these exceptional cases – does not judge according to the law, but according to justice."[45]

Leijten's philosophy of teaching is revealed in his preface to the seventeenth edition (1972) of Lambertus (Bert) van Apeldoorn's (1886-1979) *Inleiding tot de studie van het Nederlandse recht* [Introduction to the study of Dutch law; hereafter referred to as *Introduction*]. Leijten said that he admired the work as a whole (although he didn't always agree with Van Apeldoorn's basic premises). His admiration stemmed mainly from the fact that the book dealt with the introduction to law from the rationale of legal theory. According to Leijten, Van Apeldoorn had borrowed this idea from the historical school of Friedrich Carl von Savigny (1779-1861). In Savigny's view, law was a historical phenomenon, an organism that developed in and with the people for whom it applied, as a tree grows from its roots.[46] Van Apeldoorn's *Introduction*, he wrote:

> compels readers to agree if they don't wish to quickly go astray. And whoever agrees. may also disagree. Van Apeldoorn's *Introduction* takes first-year law students completely au sérieux, it demands their effort and commitment (...).

Thus Leijten regarded the book as a remedy against the infantilisation of academic studies and made students allergic to the glorification of formulae and to legalism.[47]

---

44.   B. Rüthers, *Die unbegrenzte Auslegung. Zum Wandel der Privatrechtsordnung im Nationalsozialismus*, 3. Aufl., Heidelberg: C.F. Müller 1988, p. 433. See J.C.M. Leijten, 'Rechtspraak en topiek', in: W. van Gerven and J.C.M. Leijten, *Theorie en praktijk van de rechtsvinding*, second edition, Zwolle: W.E.J. Tjeenk Willink 1981, p. 101, who endorsed "much of" Rüthers' argument.

45.   J.C.M. Leijten, *We need stories*, Zwolle: W.E.J. Tjeenk Willink 1991, p. 10.

46.   See F. Brandsma, 'De Historische School in het privaatrecht. Misschien wisten zij alles', in: R. Schutgens et al. (eds), *Canon van het Recht*, Nijmegen: Ars Aequi Libri 2010, p. 33 ff.

47.   J.C.M. Leyten, 'Voorbericht voor de zeventiende druk', in: L.J. van Apeldoorn, *Inleiding tot de studie van het Nederlandse recht*, edited by J.C.M. Leyten, Zwolle: W.E.J. Tjeenk Willink 1972, pp. VI-VIII. See C.J.H. Jansen, 'L.J. van Apeldoorn (1886-1979), Inleiding tot de studie van het Nederlandsche recht (1933)', *Ars Aequi* 2021/1, p. 93 ff.

When asked by *NJB* editor Caroline Lindo (b. 1946) how lawyers wrote best, Leijten replied:

> When writing about a general subject in a good style and from a wealth of experience. Looking at legal matters from a meta-legal point of view. You need to have an excellent mastery of your subject if you wish to shine a new light on it.[48]

This legal-theoretical perspective was exactly what Leijten found attractive in Van Apeldoorn's *Introduction*. Although in many ways a typical Brabander, if asked whether he had written fine articles, Leijten would no doubt have responded with a typical Groningen expression: *het kon minder* (it could be worse).

2.4   *Antoon (Teun) Struycken*[49]

Brabers described Struycken as "a devoutly religious, young, idealistic professor".[50] The internationally oriented Struycken, who obtained his doctorate under Van der Grinten, stood for the practice of law based on Catholic values. A lawyer should never forget what the law was for and should not insist on details. "People should not suffer under unnecessary formalism. You must try to display some flexibility. I know that that is a difficult choice."[51] Struycken was the *auctor intellectualis* of a preliminary draft of an abortion law, which he had presented to the KVP and to parliament on behalf of a number of Catholic professors from Nijmegen. Underpinning the bill was the respect for the life of the unborn child, based on Church teaching. Struycken wanted to place the decision as to whether or not an abortion was permitted with the civil courts, which should make a decision in each specific case. But there had to be 'clear' grounds. With this bill, Struycken was going against the spirit of the times, which called for abortion to be legalised. Struycken's bill did not become law. Within his own faculty, Maeijer and Leijten

---

48.   Caroline Lindo in conversation with J.C.M. Leijten, p. 164.
49.   Cf. S.C.J.J. Kortmann et al. (eds), *Op recht. Bundel opstellen aangeboden aan prof. mr. A.V.M. Struycken ter gelegenheid van zijn zilveren ambtsjubileum aan de Katholieke Universiteit Nijmegen*, Zwolle: W.E.J. Tjeenk Willink 1996; J. van den Berg and H. Spath, 'Interview met prof. mr. A.V.M. Struycken en mr. J.G.A. Struycken', *Ars Aequi* 50 (2001) 10, p. 741 ff. Struycken's archive is held in the KDC.
50.   Brabers, *De Faculteit der Rechtsgeleerdheid van de Katholieke Universiteit Nijmegen 1923-1982*, p. 456. Struycken would also look back with great pleasure on Brabers' commission to write the history of the faculty. See Gitmans et al., 'In gesprek met J.M.M. Maeijer en A.V.M. Struycken. Nijmeegse juristen zijn in tal van sectoren toonaangevend', *Te Recht in Nijmegen*, p. 139.
51.   Van den Berg and Spath, 'Interview met prof. mr. A.V.M. Struycken en mr. J.G.A. Struycken', p. 743.

saw nothing in his initiative. As Van den Bergh was expected to oppose the bill (this was correct), his views were not even canvassed.[52]

> Struycken (b. 1936) was born in Ginneken-en-Bavel, now Breda. He knew Maeijer from the parish church, where they had both served as altar boys. Struycken studied law in Nijmegen from 1954 to 1959. From 1955 until his graduation, he was editor of *Ars Aequi*, where he succeeded Maeijer's brother. He then studied in Bologna and for a year in Paris, where he was impressed by the Catholic professor Henri Battifol (1905-1989), a well-known civil law expert and a distinguished practitioner of international private law. From 1963, Struycken was employed by his *alma mater*. He obtained his PhD in 1970 with a thesis entitled *De gracieuze jurisdictie in het internationaal privaatrecht* [Gracious jurisdiction in international private law]. He was appointed professor in 1971 and was dean of the faculty from 1987 to 1991.
>
> Struycken has held numerous ancillary positions in the field of private international law. He was a member of the Standing Committee for Private International Law, which he also chaired from 2003 to 2011. He was president of the Conférence de La Haye de Droit International Privé and was affiliated with the Hague Academy of International Law. Struycken published two international reference works: *Les conséquences de l'intégration européenne sur le développement du droit international privé*, Recueil des Cours, Vol. 232 (1992) and *Co-ordination and Co-operation in Respectful Disagreement. General Course on Private International Law*, Collected Courses, Vol. 311 (2004), published in 2009.

In his academic work, Struycken was known as the master of sober, dogmatic analysis, averse to speculation and esoteric theory. And like many of his Nijmegen colleagues, he was a generalist in private law. He was flexible and pragmatic in his approach to international private law, focusing on European law. The closing sentences of his contribution to the *liber amicorum* for Leijten are typical of him: "Justice is a serious matter. (...). Judgements by foreign judges must also be taken seriously. If proceedings conducted abroad have led to a decision that merits recognition, it is not the parties' place to ignore it."[53]

3   PERSONALITIES FROM THE 1980S

A new generation of professors took office in the early 1980s: Tijn Kortmann (1944-2016) for constitutional law and general constitutional theory in 1981, Groenendijk (b. 1943) for sociology of law in 1982, Corstens (b. 1946) for criminal and criminal procedural law in 1982, Hennekens (b. 1938) for constitutional and administrative law in 1983, Bas Kortmann (b. 1950) for civil law in 1984 and Van

---

52.   Brabers, *De Faculteit der Rechtsgeleerdheid van de Katholieke Universiteit Nijmegen 1923-1982*, p. 455 ff. Struycken enjoyed the support of Willem van der Grinten, Frans Duynstee, Jonkers and Luijten within his own faculty.
53.   A.V.M. Struycken, 'Vreemde vonnissen zijn geen houten fietsen. Over het ambtshalve doen gelden van vreemde vonnissen', in: *Met hoofd en hart*, p. 352.

Mourik (b. 1943) for notarial and private law in 1987. Corstens, an alumnus of the university (1964-1969), was a professor in Nijmegen for only a fairly short time as he was appointed a Supreme Court judge in 1995.[54] In 2008 he succeeded another Nijmegen alumnus, Willibrord Davids (b. 1938), as president of the Supreme Court. His chief work is *Het Nederlands Strafprocesrecht* [Dutch criminal procedural law] (first edition, 1993). Hennekens was also an alumnus of the university in Nijmegen (1960-1965).[55] Under Willem van der Grinten's supervision, he obtained his PhD in 1977 with a thesis entitled *De openbare weg en het privaatrecht* [Public roads and private law]. He had written it while holding the office of mayor of Cuyk, not with a view to an academic career but because, as mayor, he found it difficult to sleep in the absence of mental stimulation. "It was quiet at night and I could work well. I felt content in the morning if I had entrusted something to paper the night before. Practice and theory came together in my work and that gave me a good feeling."[56] Hennekens left for the Council of State in 2001.

3.1 Constantijn (Tijn) Kortmann[57]

Tijn Kortmann liked to provoke. He was averse to 'pedantry', bureaucracy and any curtailment of his freedom as a researcher and teacher. He was polemical by nature and dismissed overblown rhetoric as bunkum. His student years in Nijmegen, the 1960s, had made him allergic to vague and woolly language and to any flirtation with multidisciplinary, sociological and political science research. Many of his articles had extremely short titles.[58] His beliefs about the desirable method in the practice of constitutional law can be found in the preface to the second edition of his reference work *Constitutioneel recht* [Constitutional law]: "The legal positivist

---

54. On his career and ancillary positions: P.J. van Koppen and J. ten Kate, *De Hoge Raad in persoon. Benoeming in de Hoge Raad der Nederlanden 1838-2002*, Deventer: Kluwer 2003, no. 415. Corstens commissioned the author of this centenary volume to write a book about the Supreme Court during the Second World War. The publication of that book (*De Hoge Raad en de Tweede Wereldoorlog. Recht en rechtsbeoefening in de jaren 1930-1950*) in 2011 gave Corstens many suggestions for articles on the judiciary and the rule of law.
55. On his student years, see: H.Ph.J.A.M. Hennekens, 'Studeren in de eerste helft van de jaren zestig en doceren in de laatste twee decennia van de vorige eeuw in Nijmegen', in: Hermans-Brand and Jansen (eds), *Recht in Nijmegen*, p. 111 ff.
56. Hennekens, 'Studeren in de eerste helft van de jaren zestig (...)', p. 115.
57. P. Bovend'Eert, 'Een bijzondere positivist uit Nijmegen. In Memoriam Tijn Kortmann (1944-2016)', *Tijdschrift voor Constitutioneel Recht* 2016, p. 72 ff.; R. Schutgens and J.J.J. Sillen, 'In memoriam Tijn Kortmann', *Ars Aequi* 2016, p. 308 ff.; E.M.H. Hirsch Ballin, 'Levensbericht van Constantinus Albertus Josephus Maria Kortmann', *Levensberichten en herdenkingen*. Koninklijke Nederlandse Akademie van Wetenschappen, 2016, p. 47 ff. See for a bibliography: P.P.T. Bovend'Eert, J.W.A. Fleuren and H.R.B.M. Kummeling (eds), *Grensverleggend staatsrecht. Opstellen aangeboden aan prof. mr. C.A.J.M. Kortmann*, Deventer: Kluwer 2001.
58. 'Leve het toetsingsrecht' (*NJB* 1992, p. 728), 'Zwangere volksvertegenwoordigers'(*NJB* 1996, p. 290 ff.); 'Het gezin: liefde en haat' (*RM Themis* 1997, p. 121 ff.), 'Wegwerprecht' (*NJB* 1998, p. 205 ff.), 'Juridisering' (*RM Themis* 1999), p. 223 ff., 'Vaderlandse mystiek' (*NJB* 2000, p. 13 ff.), etc.

character has been preserved, despite the risk of 'legal compartmentalisation'. Philosophers, political scientists and public administration experts will have to seek their salvation elsewhere, unless they also have an interest in positive law. Politicians already know it all. For that matter, some confrères seem to loathe positivists and positivism. To me, however, they seem preferable to negativists and negativism, not to mention fantasists who present all manner of their own fabrications and (political) desires as valid law."[59] Kortmann's aversion to woolly and vague language was not a question of art for art's sake. It was precisely in public law that pure language, logical reasoning and clear conceptualisation mattered: it brought certainty. And certainty helped to provide citizens with legal protection against the government.[60] His 2009 farewell speech had a predictive value in this respect. It contained the following quips:

> More importantly, government institutions should be staffed by people who are skilled, who have an eye for practice, who are upright and honest, who don't allow themselves to be 'read to' or blathered to by consultants, communicators and journalists, but who think, speak and write for themselves. (...) Nor should we refer to the relationship between the state and citizens as a horizontal one. That's not true, and nor should it be. A government is not a 'partner' but is always a potential opponent, an armed gang or worse. A government must therefore present itself modestly and set a good example in matters both large and small. (...). If the government requires citizens to act in a correct and timely manner, it must certainly do so itself. These are the requirements of fair play and of setting a good example.[61]

In particular, the Dutch childcare benefits scandal of 2020 underlined the truth of Kortmann's words: the Tax and Customs Administration had classified tens of thousands of citizens as fraudsters and denied them almost any form of legal protection.

> Kortmann (1944-2016) was the eldest son of a Catholic family in which both parents had studied law in Nijmegen. Following his own law studies there – during which time he spent six months studying in Paris in 1964 – he spent a year in Poitiers working on his thesis. He obtained his PhD in 1971, under Van Wijnbergen's supervision. In 1976 Kortmann was appointed lector in constitutional law at the University of Amsterdam, where he became professor in 1980. He also held the position of dean. In 1981 he was appointed as Duynstee's successor to Nijmegen. Kortmann had a reputation among students for his annual propaedeutic lecture, which he delivered in rhyme at Sinterklaas time. He twice held the position of dean, from 1991 to 1993

---

59. C.A.J.M. Kortmann, 'Voorwoord', in: C.A.J.M. Kortmann, *Constitutioneel recht*, sixth edition, Deventer: Kluwer 2008, p. VI.
60. See C.A.J.M. Kortmann, 'Positivisme, soevereiniteit en recht', *NJB* 1997, p. 482 ff.; Cf. Schutgens and Sillen, 'In memoriam Tijn Kortmann', p. 310.
61. C.A.J.M. Kortmann, *Staatsrecht en raison d'Etat*, Deventer: Kluwer 2009, p. 28.

and from 2001 to 2003. From 2004 to 2009 he was a KNAW professor; he had been a member of KNAW (Royal Netherlands Academy of Arts and Sciences) since 2000.

Kortmann said that Harry Beekman (1932-2010) was his true mentor in constitutional law. From 1967 to 1987 Beekman was on the academic staff for constitutional law. Kortmann described him as a brilliant teacher. He had also written a compendium of constitutional law for students, which had continued to circulate among students for many years. This compendium formed the basis for Kortmann's book *Constitutioneel recht* [Constitutional law].[62] Thom de Graaf, the current vice president of the Council of State, said about him: "For a host of reasons, he (Beekman) never became a professor, unjustly so. I have never met anyone who could explain constitutional law as well, as consistently and in such conceptual terms as he could."[63]

During his academic career, Kortmann was involved in numerous ancillary activities. He was government commissioner for the review of legislative projects, a member of the Dutch Education Council and of the Council for Home Administration. He was a member of the Standing Committee on the 'relationship between voters and policy-making' (1982) and of the Standing Committee for Constitutional Review (2009). He was chair of the Referendum Committee in 2005. Kortmann was a member of the KVP and the CDA for many years. While he became estranged from the CDA, he remained a Catholic.

Kortmann was a generalist in the field of public law. He published widely on almost all areas of constitutional law, administrative law, case law and general constitutional theory. He also had an interest in European law. His major work was *Constitutioneel recht* [Constitutional law] (first edition, 1990), for which he was awarded the Thorbecke medal in 1996. *De Grondwetsherzieningen van 1983 en 1987* [The constitutional reforms of 1983 and 1987], a fundamental commentary on (amendments to) the Constitution, was published in 1987. With Amsterdam professor Lucas Prakke (b. 1938), he co-edited *Het staatsrecht van de landen van de EU* [The constitutional law of EU countries] (first edition, 1981, under a slightly different title), which was also translated into English. Kortmann was editor of *RM Themis* for many years. He had a great fondness for France and for snails (whose propagation he approached in true scholarly fashion).

For several decades (1990-2010), Kortmann was the standard bearer for the practice of Dutch constitutional law. He loved to challenge the usurpation of powers by state institutions. He became wound up about the law-making role assumed by the Supreme Court, and in its wake the Administrative Law Division of the Council of State. "That law-making task cannot be found in the Constitution

---

62. 'De keuze van Tijn Kortmann', *De Academische Boekgids* May 2010, p. 18.

63. 'Interview oud-vicepremier en oud-burgemeester van Nijmegen: mr. Th.C. (Thom) de Graaf', *Bulletineke Justitia* 27 March 2017 (available online); cf. also the words of Pia Lokin-Sassen in Bulten, Hermans-Brand, Jansen, 'Kind van mijn tijd. Interview met mw. mr. Pia E.M.S. Lokin-Sassen', in: Hermans-Brand and Jansen (eds), *Recht in Nijmegen*, p. 106 on Beekman: "an outstanding teacher who taught me a love for constitutional law." See B.F. de Jong, C.A.J.M. Kortmann, H.R.B.M. Kummeling (eds), *Nijmeegs staatsrecht. Opstellen aangeboden aan H.J.M. Beekman*, Nijmegen: GNI 1987. Another distinguished lecturer in constitutional law, , from 1965 to 1982, was Jan Boeren (1919-1991).

or the law; on the contrary, the Law on General Precepts and Regulations suggests at the very least that judges may not make laws."[64] In doing so, he piqued many a Supreme Court judge, which he clearly enjoyed.

3.2   Cornelius (Kees) Groenendijk[65]

Central to Groenendijk's academic work was the fight against unequal access to legal protection, with the unsolicited and unwelcome exercise of power by the government as a recurring theme. A book on this subject, which he co-wrote in 1976 with Schuyt and Bernardus Sloot (b. 1949), became one of the best-known empirical studies within Dutch jurisprudence in the final quarter of last century: *De weg naar het recht, een rechtssociologisch onderzoek naar de samenhangen tussen maatschappelijke ongelijkheid en juridische hulpverlening* [The pathway to law, a legal-sociological study of the links between social inequality and legal aid]. Groenendijk focused at an early stage on strengthening the weak legal position of foreign nationals. In this, he had recourse – often successfully – to European rules and principles. Although the official Dutch government policy tended to be one of tolerance, 'on paper' at least, it proved intractable in practice: discrimination and structural social inequalities were never far away, especially where litigation was concerned. Groenendijk shared Tijn Kortmann's notion that the government should observe fair play, especially with regard to refugees and displaced persons who frequently fell victim to excessive government hard-handedness. In 2003, Groenendijk and Kortmann published a joint article in the *NJB* on the increase in fees for residence permits. They accused the minister (and parliament) of bullying, "whereby the Netherlands risks doing itself harm."[66] In 1975 Groenendijk had co-written a report for the Association for Refugees, *Naar een nieuw vluchtelingenrecht* [Towards a new refugee law]. In that same year, together with A. (Bert) Swart (1941-2011), he began publishing *Rechtspraak Vreemdelingenrecht*[Jurisprudence on immigration law], a loose-leaf collection of judicial decisions, which would become an annual collection from 1979 to 1992. Groenendijk never shied away from influencing public debate and politics through his academic work.

Groenendijk (b.1943) studied law in Utrecht from 1961 to 1967. He then worked as a lawyer in Amsterdam, focusing mainly on legal aid. Schuyt brought him to Nijmegen in 1973. In 1981 Groenendijk obtained his PhD under the supervision of Leijten and Schuyt; it was entitled

---

64.   Kortmann, *Staatsrecht en raison d'Etat*, p. 11. At length: C.A.J.M. Kortmann, 'De rechtsvormende taak van de Hoge Raad', in: W.M.T. Keukens (ed.), *Raad en Daad. Over de rechtsvormende taak van de Hoge Raad*, Nijmegen: Ars Aequi Libri 2008, p. 31 ff.
65.   For a brief biography, see P. Minderhoud & T. Havinga, 'Inleiding', in: A. Böcker et al. (eds), *Migratierecht en rechtssociologie, gebundeld in Kees' studies*, Nijmegen: Wolf Legal Publishers 2008, p. 1 ff.
66.   C.A. Groenendijk & C.A.J.M. Kortmann, 'Nieuwe verhoging leges voor verblijfsvergunningen: wederom onredelijk, onverstandig en onrechtmatig', *NJB* 2003, p. 314 ff.

Bundeling van belangen bij de burgerlijke rechter [Pooling of interests in civil courts]. In 1982 he succeeded Schuyt in the chair of sociology of law. Groenendijk was dean of the Faculty of Law from 1993 to 1995.

Like almost all his Nijmegen colleagues, Groenendijk engaged in many ancillary activities. He was a member of the Dutch Research Council's Research Committee on Ethnic Minorities, the Zeevalking Committee on illegal immigrant legislation and the Mulder Committee on revision of the asylum procedure, the Social and Economic Council (SER) committee on the revision of the Foreign Nationals Employment Act (WAV) and the Standing Committee of Experts on International Immigration, Refugee and Criminal Law (the Meijers Committee), which he chaired for some time.

Groenendijk was involved in the Centre for Migration Law (CMR) since its very beginning in 1995. His field of research and that of his staff and PhD students had broadened to include migrants and minorities. The CMR had and continues to have an international and European focus, with a practice-oriented, multidisciplinary and comparative law emphasis (see section 6).[67]

3.3 Sebastiaan (Bas) Kortmann[68]

In 1984 Bas Kortmann was appointed professor of civil law, the successor to Willem van der Grinten. He had big shoes to fill – and he more than succeeded. Kortmann became a leading professor of civil law in the Netherlands, a much sought-after director, commissioner, arbitrator, and a member and chair of foundations with a protective role. He was also a deputy judge in the Court of Appeal and district courts. Like Van der Heijden, Kamphuisen, Van der Grinten and Maeijer, he is a civil law generalist. He has worked in almost all areas of private law: property and contract law, financing and securities, personal and family law, non-contractual liability, financial law, corporate law and insolvency law. He was the uncrowned king in this latter area of law for many years.[69] Kortmann was chair of the Insolvency Law Committee, which drafted a new

---

67. See for example C.A. Groenendijk, E. Guild & R. Barzilay, *The Legal Status of Third Country Nationals who are Long Term Residents in a Member State of the European Union* (2001); C.A. Groenendijk, E. Guild & P. Minderhoud, *In search of Europe's borders* (2003); C.A. Groenendijk & E. Guild (eds), *Observatory on free movement of workers within the European Union* (2004) and C.A. Groenendijk, R. Cholewinsky, E. Guild & P. Minderhoud, *European report on the freedom of workers in Europe* (2005).

68. 'Woord vooraf', in: S.E. Bartels et al. (eds), *Vertrouwen in het burgerlijk recht. Liber Amicorum Prof. Mr. S.C.J.J. Kortmann*, Deventer: Wolters Kluwer 2017, pp. V-X (with bibliography and list of former PhD students. In addition to this collection, the following publications appeared at his farewell: C.D.J. Bulten et al. (eds), *Vertrouwen in het ondernemingsrecht en het financiële recht. Liber Amicorum Prof. Mr. S.C.J.J. Kortmann* (2017) and Dennis Faber et al. (eds), *Trust and good faith across borders. Liber Amicorum prof. dr. S.C.J.J. Kortmann* (2017).

69. Cf. the collections he co-edited with others: *De curator, een octopus* (Serie Onderneming en Recht, Part 6, 1996) and *De bewindvoerder, een octopus* (Serie Onderneming & Recht, Part 44, 2008).

insolvency law. Published in 2007, the bill never became law due to the fickleness of politics. Kortmann continued the Nijmegen tradition of collaboration between theory and practice. As he himself said, he had made the switch from the legal profession to academia in order to have more time for study. "I enjoy the extra opportunities I have here to really come to grips with the dogmatic problems of civil law. If there was no contact with legal practice, however, I wouldn't wish to stay here. It's practice that inspires me."[70]

Bas Kortmann (b. 1950) is the youngest son of a family (Tijn Kortmann is his older brother). After studying law in Groningen, Kortmann became a research assistant for Van der Grinten in 1973, who he regarded – alongside Peter Birks. (1941-2004) – as his major source of inspiration. They taught him the value of systematising jurisprudence. He obtained his PhD *cum laude* in 1977 under Van der Grinten's supervision, with a thesis entitled *'Derden-werking' van aansprakelijkheidsbedingen*. [The 'third-party effect' of liability clauses]. After his PhD, he practised as a lawyer at Dirkzwager in Nijmegen for seven years. Following his return to the faculty in 1984, he became a leading national and international figure.

After 1985 Kortmann assumed responsibility for the postgraduate teaching of law at Nijmegen. He became chair of what today is called the Centre for Professional Legal Education (CPO). It grew quickly under his stewardship, becoming the biggest university provider of education for legal professionals. Kortmann was chair of the Grotius Academy Foundation, established in 1985, which offers legal specialisation courses. In 1994, together with N. (Dennis) Faber, he founded the Radboud Business Law Institute (OO&R) (see section 6). In 1996, Kortmann was involved from the beginning in the authoritative journal *Jurisprudentie Onderneming & Recht* (a case law journal on business law). He founded the *Serie Onderneming & Recht* [Business and Law series][71] (the 'red' series) and the *Law of Business and Finance series* (the 'blue' series). His Asser series volume *Vertegenwoordinging* [Representation] is a classic law text. He was president of the Dutch Lawyers Association (NJV) in 2018.

Kortmann was dean of the Faculty of Law from 1998 to 2001 and was appointed rector magnificus of Radboud University Nijmegen in 2007. As rector, he was a strong advocate of the internationalisation of teaching and research, educational quality, developing programmes for talented students and promoting the university's research excellence. He invariably made offerings to Saint Clare of Assisi (1194-1253) to ensure that all university celebrations could be celebrated under clear skies. As a 'good, Den Bosch Catholic', Kortmann loved celebrations at the appropriate time. From 2018 he dedicated himself to the people of Groningen who had suffered damage to their property, chattels and wellbeing as a result of gas extraction. He became chair of the Temporary Committee on Mining Damage Groningen (TCMG) and since 2020 has been board chair of the Institute for Mining Damage Groningen (IMG) (with which the TCMG merged). As a young man, he had wanted to be chair of everything.

---

70.   'Recht moet eenvoudig zijn'. R. Willemsen & R. van Breevoort, 'Interview met prof. mr. S.C.J.J. Kortmann, hoogleraar burgerlijk recht', *Actioma* 11 (1989)/3, p. 5.
71.   The first part, published in 1994, was entitled *Financiering en Aansprakelijkheid*. The series was preceded in 1991 by a zero number: *Onderneming en Nieuw Burgerlijk Recht*.

Kortmann worked hard to make research at the OO&R more international. In the late 1990s, he founded international working groups, which enabled him to establish contacts with many well-known English and German professors. These working groups led to the publication of *Principles of European Trust Law* (1999) and *Principles of European Insolvency Law* (2003). This international collaboration sparked Kortmann's interest in legal concepts applied in practice from Anglo-American law, such as leasing, factoring and trust.[72] There is an inextricable link between the driving force of Kortmann's intellect and Nijmegen's focus on commercial private law.

3.4   *Martin Jan van Mourik*[73]

Van Mourik was fully immersed in the law – or notarial law, to be precise. There was no such thing as a law-free space in his orbit. He either talked about the law or wrote about it. However, he barely had time for writing because he was continuously talking about the law to anyone wanting to hear it: students, notaries, directors, housewives, 'ordinary' people, young and old. "So I'm always preoccupied with law, from early in the morning till late at night. Law is in fact my world, my life – although I also often sit in cafés and think about other things and I really like to play sports."[74] He was a man of seeming contradictions: academia and the notary profession, professor and notary, lawyer's office and university, church and pub, humour and gravity, theory and practice, sports and beer, *WPNR* and *Telegraaf*, *Lederhosen* and a three-piece suit.[75] Van Mourik's moral compass never failed him. He regarded the law as having a subservient function. For that very reason, it needed to be fair. Positive law didn't always succeed in meeting the demands of justice. In addition to legal standards, there were ethical standards, such as those arising from fairness, care and integrity. These were inherent to the nature of humankind (natural law). They were also part of the law. All lawyers had to be acquainted with them and to develop a sense of ethics. Van Mourik criticised notaries who had a questionable sense of values and a wavering independence and impartiality.[76]

---

72.   See D.J. Hayton, S.C.J.J. Kortmann, A.J.M. Nuytinck, A.V.M. Struycken, N.E.D. Faber (eds), *Vertrouwd met de Trust. Trust and Trust-like Arrangements* (1996).
73.   For more on his life and work: S.C.J.J. Kortmann et al. (eds), *Yin –Yang. Bundel opstellen, op 12 mei 2000 aangeboden aan prof. mr. M.J.A. van Mourik ter gelegenheid van zijn 25-jarig ambtsjubileum als hoogleraar*, Deventer: Kluwer 2000 and S. Roes and F. Schols (eds), *Recht met sfeer. Bloemlezing uit eigen werk. Bundel ter gelegenheid van het afscheid van prof. mr. M.J.A. van Mourik als hoogleraar notarieel- en privaatrecht aan de Radboud Universiteit Nijmegen*, Kluwer: Deventer 2008.
74.   C. Coppens and B. Duinkerken, 'Het recht is voor het volk'. Interview with Martin-Jan van Mourik, recorded in: *Recht met sfeer*, p. 495.
75.   Kortmann et al., 'Woord vooraf', in: *Ying – Yang*, p. V.
76.   See his farewell address: *Recht, Rechtvaardigheid en Ethiek, in het bijzonder in de notariële praktijk*, Deventer: Kluwer 2008. Van Mourik harked back to Willem Duynstee's conception of natural law.

Van Mourik (b. 1943) was born in Ravenstein in Brabant. He never wished to be disturbed at carnival time. His mother tongue was Brabants. He studied notarial law from 1961 to 1967. From 1968 to 1975 he worked part-time as an academic and part-time as a lawyer in a notary practice. In 1970 he gained his PhD under Luijten's supervision. From 1975 to 1987 Van Mourik was professor of notarial law in Leiden, where he introduced beer-drinking to the faculty. In 1987 he was appointed to Nijmegen for half of his 'working time' and he worked as a civil-law notary for the other half (1989-2006). He proved to be a brilliant teacher, who could explain complex matters simply. There is no aspect of notary law on which he hasn't written: inheritance law, notary tax law, matrimonial property law, corporate law, real estate law, disciplinary law, etc. In that respect he is a true notary generalist. His main publications, which have appeared in many editions, are *Huwelijk en vermogensrecht* [Marriage and property law] (first edition, 1972), *Handboek voor het Nederlands vermogensrecht bij echtscheiding* [Handbook for Dutch property law in cases of divorce] (first edition, 1989), *Rondom depersonenvennootschap* [On private partnerships] (first edition, 1981), *Erfrecht* [Inheritance law] (first edition, 1985), *Handboek Nieuw Erfrecht* [New inheritance law handbook] (first edition, 1998) and *Nieuw Erfrecht* [New inheritance law] (first edition, 1999).

As well as speaking and writing, Van Mourik was fond of 'leading' and 'directing'. From 1986 to 2009 he was a member and chair (until 2014) of the *WPNR* editorial board. For many years he was president of the Association for Family and Juvenile Law and the Association for Agricultural Law, and their associated journals. For more than twelve years, he was also president of the Groot Ravenstein Carnaval Foundation. He wrote a column in the *Telegraaf*, starting in 1978. Like many of his colleagues, Van Mourik was by inclination a member of the Christian Democratic Appeal (CDA), although he too, unsurprisingly, became rather disenchanted with the party.

Van Mourik had a major influence on the content of the new inheritance law (Book 4 of the Dutch Civil Code), which came into force in 2003. The fact that women increasingly worked outside the home hadn't yet led to their economic independence. Husband and wife had often built up the family wealth together. For Van Mourik, therefore, when the husband or wife died, the principle was 'absolutely' clear: "In a normal marriage, the survivor just wants everything and no hassle." He wrote a series of fiery articles on the subject, couched in strong rhetoric: "The compelling adventures of the surviving spouse" (*NJB* 1982, 1991 and 1997, and *WPNR* 2003). A strong right to inherit on the part of the surviving spouse has become the principle that underpins existing inheritance law.[77] The 'boss' of the Nijmegen notaries and an avid 'squeezebox' player, Van Mourik was one of the most colourful and iconic professors in the history of the Nijmegen law faculty.

---

77.   Like Willem van der Grinten, Van Mourik strongly advocated the abolition of the statutory share, which he considered contrary to human freedom and a parent's power of disposition. See M.J.A. van Mourik, 'De legitieme portie: weg ermee!', *WPNR* 1991/6018, p. 621 ff.

4   CENTRE FOR PROFESSIONAL LEGAL EDUCATION (CPO)

The history of continuing education in Nijmegen began with a committee for
postgraduate legal education (PAO), set up at Struycken's behest in 1972/1973.
Moorman van Kappen was appointed chairman of the committee, which included
both faculty lecturers and practising lawyers. The Restructuring of Higher
Education Act of 12 November 1975 (*Staatsblad* 656), which took effect on
1 September 1978, ushered in a new era for continuing education. The universities
were now charged with this task. In the summer of 1979, the faculty appointed a
PAO coordinator in the person of J. (Fien) Edixhoven-Majoor. She was also
secretary of the PAO committee. Her appointment is seen as the start of continuing
education in Nijmegen and of the current CPO. The PAO committee became the
Continuing Education Office in 1980. Edixhoven-Majoor – and soon with the help
of Louk Hermans-Brand (b. 1955) – organised refresher courses for alumni and
legal professionals, initially in the Nijmegen region. The combination of lecturers
from legal practice and from the university was seen as the key to the Office's
success. The atmosphere and the quality of education in Nijmegen attracted
growing numbers of lawyers from all over the Netherlands. To mark the 10th
anniversary in 1989, the Office was renamed the Centre for Continuing
Education.[78]

The 1982 introduction of the two-phase structure in academic education gave a
new impetus to continuing education. The study of law became a four-year degree
programme, thus acquiring the character of 'basic training'. The Act gave
responsibility for organising teaching in the second phase to the professional
organisations, preferably in conjunction with a university. The Nijmegen faculty
and the CPO were convinced that neither the universities nor the professional
organisations could provide further training by themselves. The CPO therefore
sought collaboration from law practitioners. The ideal person in Nijmegen for this
role was Bas Kortmann, who was appointed professor of civil law in 1984 and who
came from the legal profession. He became president of the Continuing Education
Office in 1985, succeeding Nève, who had replaced Van den Bergh as professor of
Roman law in 1975, when the latter left for Utrecht. Kortmann wasted no time. He
began with a committee on Training in the Legal Profession, in which professors,
lawyers, civil-law notaries and company lawyers worked together. In 1987, three
courses for legal professionals were launched, one in collaboration with the Dutch
Bar Association (NOvA), one with the (then) Royal Dutch Association of Civil-law

---

78.   Brabers, *De Faculteit der Rechtsgeleerdheid van de Katholieke Universiteit Nijmegen 1923-1982*,
      pp. 477-478 and J.C.W.J. Edixhoven-Majoor, '23 jaar Postdoctoraal juridisch onderwijs', *Te Recht in
      Nijmegen*, p. 199 ff. See also: M.L.A. van den Bosch, '29 jaar Postacademisch juridisch onderwijs.
      Over de combinatie van theorie en praktijk, kwaliteit en de Nijmeegse ambiance', in: Bulten,
      Hermans-Brand, Jansen (eds), *Meesterlijk Nijmegen*, p. 155 ff. Van den Bosch succeeded
      Edixhoven-Majoor in 2003.

Notaries (KNB) and one with the Dutch Society of Company Lawyers. In order to maintain a degree of distance from the law faculties and the professional organisations, they were organised in foundations, for which the CPO provided the management. All programmes not only taught skills but offered a deeper and broader knowledge of substantive law and procedural law.

In 1990, the Grotius Academy Foundation began offering specialisation courses, which the Nijmegen faculty and the CPO helped to set up. Other law faculties and a major publisher were also involved in the initiative. Once again, it was a collaboration between academics and practitioners. For a period of four years, the Grotius Academy provided a one-year full-time post-Master's programme in commercial private law involving a rigorous selection process. The lecturers were 'top lawyers' and professors from the law faculties affiliated with the Academy. There was no stampede on enrolments. After four years, specialist training in commercial law replaced the full-time programme. Academics and practising lawyers continue to provide the teaching, while the CPO provides the management for the Grotius Academy.

An amendment to the Traineeship Regulation in 1988, which took effect on 1 March 1989, heralded a tumultuous period in continuing education.[79] From then on, professional training was made compulsory for new (first-year) lawyers. Later, in their second and third years, they were required to complete the Continuing Education Programme for Trainees (VSO), which involved in-depth and profiling courses. The continuing education made compulsory by the NOvA and the KNB in 1996 ensured a continuous influx of practising lawyers who were keen to learn.

Since 1992, the CPO has occupied an independent position in the faculty. Although not a legal entity, the Centre has its own decision-making powers wherever possible, in terms of both organisation and finances. This was deemed necessary because of the speed required to act in the market in which the CPO operates. For that reason, the Centre continues to have its own three-member board (comprising professors from the faculty).[80] At the end of 1993, the Board established a CPO rotating chair, which Birks was the first to hold. Intensive PAO courses began in Curaçao in 1994.[81] Thanks to its high-quality education, excellent teaching staff and the fact that it organises major conferences (such as the biennial Van der Heijden conference), the CPO has made a major contribution to the good reputation that the Nijmegen Faculty of Law has built up among legal practitioners. Continuing education, and the CPO, have become an integral part of the day-to-day lives of practising lawyers.

---

79.   S.C.J.J. Kortmann, 'De juridische opleiding, pre- en postdoctoraal', *NJB* 1990, p. 587 ff.
80.   As already mentioned, Bas Kortmann was the first chairman.
81.   From 1995, the CPO offered an international LL.M programme in European Business Law, in collaboration with the Pallas Consortium, which for more than a decade was a partnership of seven European universities, including Nijmegen.

5   Special law programmes in Nijmegen

5.1   *Law in Europe*

In the early 1990s, the Nijmegen Faculty of Law offered two 'regular' programmes: Dutch law and notarial law. Both programmes were of a generalist nature and led to the acquisition of *civiel effect*, which gave graduates access to the bar or judiciary on completion of the relevant courses. The 1970s saw the rise of European law, and competition law in particular.[82] In 1968, the faculty appointed Leiden lawyer Pierre Mathijsen (1924-2015), director of the European Economic Community Commission on Competition, as extraordinary professor of European law. His publication *A Guide to European Community Law* (first edition, 1985) brought him some renown. Competition law, aimed at the efficient working of the economic market, was at that time part of a broader area of law: socioeconomic law.[83] Socioeconomic law was primarily of a public law nature. Mathijsen was succeeded in 1987 by the Leuven lawyer Jules Stuyck (b. 1948), whose primary focus was competition law. Because of the growing importance of European law, the law faculty decided around 1990 to establish a new programme, Law in Europe, an off-shoot of the Dutch law programme. It proved a huge drawcard for students. This was because – in order to distinguish it from similar programmes offered by other Dutch law faculties – it led to a Master's degree and students spent six months studying abroad as a compulsory part of the curriculum.[84] This specialisation exists to this day, but its name has changed to International and European Law. Compulsory study abroad is no longer a curriculum component. The introduction of the Law in Europe programme coincided with moves to further internationalise

---

82. The European Communities comprised the European Coal and Steel Community (established in 1951), the European Atomic Energy Community (established in 1957) and the European Economic Community (also established in 1957). They had an identical organisational structure from 1967 on.

83. See P. VerLoren van Themaat, 'Het decennium van de grenzen der westerse groei. De ontwikkeling van het sociaal-economisch recht in de zeventiger jaren', in: *Recente rechtsontwikkelingen (1970-1980)*, Zwolle: W.E.J. Tjeenk Willink 1983, p. 111 ff. The legal historian Cerutti was very interested in socioeconomic law. Unfortunately, he was killed in a car accident in 1970. The faculty purchased part of his library, which was housed in a separate room in the law library (the Cerutti room). D. (Feer) Verkade (b. 1944) was appointed lector in commercial law in Nijmegen in 1974. He became professor of economic law in 1980. His successor Antoon Quaedvlieg (b. 1958) acquired the teaching and research remit for commercial law in 1990, in particular commercial and economic law, industrial property and copyright law.

84. C.G. van der Plas, 'De Nijmeegse rechtenfaculteit vanuit het perspectief van één van haar studenten die er bovendien ook promovenda werd: een impressie' and N. Jagtenborg and A.G.A. Cuijpers, 'In gesprek met een student Internationaal en Europees recht', *Te Recht in Nijmegen*, p. 209 ff. and p. 215 ff.

education during Struycken's deanship, through the Socrates (later the Erasmus) programme and other initiatives.[85]

5.2   Other new programmes

From the late 1990s, the Nijmegen Faculty of Law, in conjunction with Nijmegen School of Management, created two educational programmes that served students who were interested in working in the corporate world. These combined a full law programme with courses from business administration or economics. Some courses were jointly developed and there was also a joint graduation project. The fact that students (with some exemptions) had to undertake a full programme in law again meant that *civiel effect* was guaranteed. The total programme took five and a half years. The two programmes, which became known as Law and Management and Law and Economics, still exist today and enjoy some degree of popularity.[86]

5.3   Nijmegen Law School

The dual Master's programme in Business & Law was launched in 1998, under the name Nijmegen Law School. N. (Dennis) Faber (b. 1969) and Louk Hermans-Brand (1955) were responsible for the training.[87] The programme aligned with the OO&R. The basic plan for the programme is still the same today. It includes an internship and a stint working at a law firm and notary office (often in the Amsterdam Zuidas business district) or with a company involved in the programme as a partner. The cross-pollination between teaching and the practice of law is the basic concept underpinning the programme, with lecturers hailing from both the university and legal practice. Because practising lawyers and company lawyers are often more likely than university lawyers to encounter new legal concepts and complex legal problems, their involvement adds further depth to the legal training. These days, alumni who practise law often teach on one of the courses (such as Finance & Securities, Corporate Law, International Private Law, Financial Law, Contract Law and Insolvency Law) and provide skills training, such as writing annotations or preparing a case study. The teaching takes place in small groups. Admission to the dual Master's programme is preceded by a

---

85.   The efforts to internationalise education still further resulted in a combination of the Dutch and Belgian law programmes (in collaboration with KU Leuven) and in 2002 in a joint programme in Dutch and German law (in collaboration with the Westfälische Wilhelmsuniversität in Münster).
86.   Bovend'Eert, 'De rechtenstudie in Nijmegen. Kanttekeningen bij enige ontwikkelingen', in: Gitmans et al. (eds), *Te Recht in Nijmegen*, pp. 153-154. It was possible for a time to do a five-year programme that combined notarial law from Nijmegen with tax law in Tilburg.
87.   In 2005, Prof. Corjo Jansen and M. (Irene) Larooy took on responsibility for the programme. Prof. Ben Schuijling joined the team in 2016. Annika Boh replaced Larooy in 2019. For a short time, there was also a dual Master's programme in administrative law, but it proved unviable.

rigorous selection process. An excellent knowledge and thorough understanding of commercial private law are key to the programme.[88] Because many lawyers know graduates from the dual Master's programme, it has become an excellent advertisement for the Nijmegen faculty, with law firms and notary offices queuing up for an opportunity to join the partnership between the faculty and its programme partners.

6   RADBOUD BUSINESS LAW INSTITUTE (OO&R) AND CENTRE FOR
           MIGRATION LAW (CMR)

From the mid-1960s, professors such as Van Eck and Maeijer favoured the creation of focal points for research. Before that time, research was predominantly a private matter for individual professors who explored subjects of interest to them. The Nijmegen faculty acceded to the wishes of Maeijer and others and allowed research institutes to be established, headed by one or more faculty professors. The early 1970s saw the emergence of several study centres, as they were called, in Nijmegen. They worked in the areas of criminal law and criminology (1965; renamed the Criminological Institute in 1971 following Dessaur's intervention), legal entities and company law (1966), parliamentary history (the Centre for Parliamentary History founded by Frans Duynstee in 1970), and the history of law (1972). The two most prominent institutes were the Van der Heijden Institute (study centre for legal entities and company law) and the Gerard Noodt Institute (study centre for the history of law). The founders also wanted to call this latter study centre the Van der Heijden Institute because of Van der Heijden's keen interest in the history of law but professors involved in the two centres felt that this was confusing. Gerard Noodt was an attractive alternative. In the 1990s, two new research centres were added that have admirably stood the test of time: the OO&R (1994) and the CMR (1995). Their creation was partly a response to ministerial and university calls for academic research to be pooled in research schools.

6.1   Radboud Business Law Institute (OO&R)

The OO&R is a partnership between the Nijmegen Faculty of Law and a number of prominent law firms, notary offices, companies and financial institutions. It was recognised as a research school by the Royal Netherlands Academy of Arts and Sciences in 1998. The success of cooperation with leading law firms and notary offices in the field of professional education sparked the notion that the same could be done with systematic research into commercial law. After all, many excellent lawyers with a PhD worked in offices, banks and companies. The OO&R's mission was therefore to carry out national and international research in the field of

---

88.   The dual Master's programme in business & law won the University Education Award in 2000.

business and law that was relevant to legal practice. The cross-pollination between theory and practice was the idea behind the establishment of the OO&R. This collaboration soon led to the identification of new legal developments in areas such as leasing, trusts and assignments. The research carried out by the OO&R relates mainly to positive law but also utilises insights from other disciplines (such as economics, philosophy and history). The OO&R's main focus areas are general property law and European private law, corporate law, financing, securities and insolvency law, civil procedural law and financial law. Traditionally, research in the fields of international private law, comparative law, employment law, insurance law, tax law and the history of law has also fallen under the aegis of the OO&R. To this has been added the research carried out by the Van der Heijden Institute. Prominent practitioners from the Netherlands and abroad have contributed to the OO&R's publications.[89] The OO&R research centre is unique in the Netherlands and in Europe, with its three book series: the *Van der Heijden Institute Series*, the *Serie Onderneming & Recht* [Series on Business and Law] and the *Law of Business and Finance Series*. OO&R researchers have also been closely involved from the outset with volumes in the authoritative Asser series. The 'leading' figure from the earliest days of the OO&R was Bas Kortmann, with Dennis Faber as his right-hand man. The first professor/director of the OO&R, in 1996, was H. (Rick) Verhagen (b. 1962).

6.2   Centre for Migration Law (CMR)

CMR's research has traditionally focused on two closely linked themes: minorities and migration. The theme of minorities looks at analysing the legal situation of people (groups) who occupy a disadvantaged position in Dutch and European society, frequently members of ethnic minorities and refugees. The theme of migration is mainly concerned with migration within and to the European Union. The CMR's approach has never been a simply legal positivist one. Traditionally, there was a close relationship with sociology of law, which soon broadened to become a multidisciplinary collaboration. CMR research is also characterised by an international focus and an emphasis on the relationship between international developments and national legal practice. The 'leading' figures of the earliest days of the CMR were Cees Groenendijk and Roel Fernhout (b. 1947), who was professor of European law in Nijmegen from 1991, in particular European migration law.

---

89.   S.C.J.J. Kortmann, 'Woord vooraf', in: C.J.H. Jansen, B.A. Schuijling and I.V. Aronstein (eds), *Onderneming & Digitalisering*, Serie Onderneming & Recht, Part 116, Deventer: Wolters Kluwer 2019, p. V.

7   CONCLUSION

The Nijmegen faculty of the early 1990s bore little resemblance to that of the 1970s. It had grown into a medium-sized centre (by Dutch standards) of academic teaching and research, with a sizeable number of academic and non-academic staff and professors. Increasing bureaucracy, the influx of students, the campus with its large lecture theatres, tutorial-based teaching, the growth in staff numbers (due in part to the ever-increasing demands of 'quality assurance' and 'quality management plans'), the maze of offices both large and small in the meandering corridors of the buildings on Thomas van Aquinostraat – all this gave the faculty of the 1990s a different appearance from the 1970s faculty on the Oranjesingel. The professors' freedom to organise teaching and examine their students as they saw fit had vanished. Students, too, had less freedom of choice.[90] The steady rise in student numbers from the 1970s on made the administration of oral tests and exams a demanding and time-consuming task. Oral exams disappeared from the main subjects, except in the notarial programme and the course on constitutional law, in what is known as the D1 phase (*basisdoctoraal*).[91]

Despite all these changes, some common characteristics could still be identified, among the professors at least. Professors paid close attention to, and worked with, law practitioners. The cohesion within the faculty and the concern for 'decency' in law remained. The Nijmegen professors no longer linked this decency to the Catholic faith as a matter of course (although the majority were still Catholic). The once self-evident affiliation with the KVP (later the CDA) also disappeared. As Catholics, most professors no longer felt at home in the party. In the key areas of law, the approach remained a legal-positivist and dogmatic one. The approach was generalist in nature, although legal specialism gradually crept into the faculty's teaching and research remits (personal and family law, European migration law, European tax law). Some professors, such as Van den Bergh, Schuyt and Groenendijk, were involved in social science research. Natural law (with a few exceptions) had disappeared from the faculty's research and teaching.[92]

The leading post-war figures were Frans Duynstee and Willem van der Grinten. Alongside and after them, the Nijmegen faculty still had professors who not only adapted their teaching and research to the spirit of the times, but who exerted their own influence. They were the 'movers and shakers' in the academic debate. This

---

90.   See Brabers, *Een kleine geschiedenis van de Radboud Universiteit.*
91.   See Lokin, *De Groninger Faculteit der Rechtsgeleerdheid (1596-1970),* p. 592 ff.; p. 603 ff. For most subjects, however, oral exams continued to form part of the D-II phase (Master's phase).
92.   The legal philosopher Scheltens still devoted some attention to it in his research. He also wrote a good deal about the ethical foundations of law and human rights. See L. Heyde, J. Leijten, Th. Mertens, B.P. Vermeulen (eds), *Begrensde Vrijheid. Opstellen over mensenrechten aangeboden aan prof. dr. D.F. Scheltens bij zijn afscheid als hoogleraar aan de Katholieke Universiteit Nijmegen,* Zwolle: W.E.J. Tjeenk Willink 1989. Scheltens himself contributed an essay on secularisation and religion to this collection.

was true, for example, of Maeijer and Leijten, and also of the Kortmann brothers and Van Mourik. Nor was there a shortage of colourful professors in the last quarter of the 20th century. Here I will mention only Frans Duynstee and Van Mourik, who reached a large audience through *DeTelegraaf* and who are the subject of many stories. Looking back on their time as professors in an interview, Maeijer and Struycken commented with great satisfaction that Nijmegen lawyers were valued in the job market and were leaders in many sectors. They had developed the skills of the profession, but with a sense of social responsibility.[93]

On 1 July 1998 there was another change in the area of governance: the University Administration (Reform) Act (WUB) of 1970 was replaced by the Modernisation of University Administrative Organisation Act (MUB) of 27 February 1997 (*Staatsblad* 117), which came into force on 1 July 1998. The democratisation of power within universities was replaced by a centralisation of power in the Executive Board. The dean had to become a single 'head'. However, the Nijmegen Faculty of Law stubbornly continued with a three-member faculty board, with the dean as *primus inter pares*. From the mid-1990s, a new generation of Nijmegen professors started arriving.[94] Their task, together with Tijn and Bas Kortmann, was to usher the law faculty into the new millennium. They included the later deans Jansen (b. 1961), Buruma (b. 1955) and Bovend'Eert (b. 1957). After the deanships of Bas Kortmann (1998-2001) and Tijn Kortmann (2001-2003, his second), the three of them constituted the administrative face of the law faculty from 2003 to 2014.

---

93.   Gitmans et al., 'In gesprek met J.M.M. Maeijer en A.V.M. Struycken: Nijmeegse juristen zijn in tal van sectoren toonaangevend', *Te Recht in Nijmegen*, p. 140.
94.   They are Ybo Buruma (appointed in 1995), André Nuytinck (1995), H.(Rick) Verhagen (1996), Frank van den Ingh (1997), Gerard van Solinge (1997), Corjo Jansen (1998), Paul Bovend'Eert (1999), Thomas Mertens (1999), Carla Klaassen (1999) and Martin van Olffen (1999).

6 CONCLUDING REMARKS (1998-2023)

1 INTRODUCTION

The Nijmegen Faculty of Law partied into the new millennium with a swing festival on 11 November 1999 to celebrate the move into the new faculty 'library', the Studeon. The Limburg band Rowwen Hèze was the main act.[1] The Studeon occupied the site of a draughty bicycle cellar under Thomas van Aquinostraat 6. The new space – which contained books, computers, an OO&R study centre, teaching and meeting rooms, and the Cerutti room with its old, rare books – represented a major improvement in the faculty's facilities. The construction of the Studeon was symbolic of the concern now demonstrated by each faculty board for the quality of education and of the study and working environment. From 1998 on, the Office for Internal and External Relations (BIEB), a unique office within the university, helped the faculty boards professionalise their contact with students, teaching staff and the outside university world, in matters such as internships.[2] This desire for optimum workplaces for staff and excellent facilities for students led in 2014 to the completion of the Grotius building, a new, modern and sustainable building for the Nijmegen law faculty. The move into this building was also celebrated with a party.

There were many administrative and organisational changes in terms of teaching and research in the first quarter of the 21st century. Although the focus was on quality improvement, professionalisation and internationalisation, the changes often related to commercialisation, the 'bureaucratisation' of the university 'business' and developments surrounding digitisation, privacy and the growth of new supervisory institutions and the like. Terms like 'framework', 'best practice', 'valorisation' and 'efficiency' were always hovering in the wings.[3]

---

1. J. Brands (compiler), *Een splinter van de ziel. Rowwen Hèze en het grote dorpsverlangen*, Nijmegen: SUN 1995.
2. Louk Hermans-Brand headed the BIEB from 1998 until her retirement. The BIEB's tasks are broader than just communication. Today, it is also responsible for contract education, alumni affairs, talent programmes and fundraising.
3. Cf. Y. Buruma, *Wat is een goede rechter? Een mentaliteitsgeschiedenis (1900-2020)*, Nijmegen: CPO, Radboud University 2016, p. 42 ff.

2   Administrative and organisational changes

2.1   *General*

The two-phase structure of university education that had been introduced in 1982 disappeared again in 2002. In 2003, the Bachelor's and Master's system saw the light of day. This model elaborated on agreements made by the ministers of education from 29 European countries in Bologna on 19 June 1999 to create uniform, and thus comparable, university degrees. The result was a three-year basic programme (Bachelor's) and a one- or two-year specialisation programme (Master's) within universities. It was no coincidence that Bologna was chosen as the venue for the ministers to sign the declaration. The city, which had built up its immense wealth through trade, boasted one of the oldest academic institutions in Europe. The University of Bologna was founded in 1088 and is regarded as the birthplace of European jurisprudence.[4] As with many other European projects, the efforts to bring about uniformity in European education have failed miserably. Not every country has honoured the agreements made in Bologna. The introduction of the Bachelor's and Master's model in the Netherlands was accompanied by a new system for assessing the quality of law education. A national accreditation body decides, based on a review involving a faculty self-reflection, whether a programme can continue or should end.

2.2   *Education*

The Faculty of Law in Nijmegen offers three main programmes: Dutch Law (Law), Notarial Law, International and European Law. The faculty launched a Master's programme in tax law in 2009. The programmes share two general characteristics: they are legal positivist and generalist in nature, a feature that has in fact remained unchanged since 1923. The teaching focuses mainly on the 'core subjects', which coincide with the main areas of law. They are taught on a semester basis. The Bachelor's programmes devote considerable attention to legal skills, such as in the *Rota Carolina*, the moot court for private law set up by Van der Heijden by sealed private deed in 1924. Its purpose was to practise law and to train students for the legal profession.[5] Moot courts for criminal, administrative and international law have been added in recent decades.

---

4.   H. Lange, *Römisches Recht im Mittelalter*, I (glossators), München: C.H. Beck 1997, p. 35 ff., p. 151 ff.; G.C.J.J. van den Bergh/C.J.H. Jansen, *Geleerd recht. Een geschiedenis van de Europese rechtswetenschap in vogelvlucht*, 7th edition, Deventer: Wolters Kluwer 2018, p. 25 ff.
5.   See A.C.A. van Kuijck, 'De Rota Carolina', in: Gitmans et al. (eds), *Te Recht in Nijmegen*, p. 99 ff. As a Nijmegen lawyer, Van Kuijck was the registrar of *Rota Carolina* from 1951 to 1985, succeeding Van Cals, whose law practice he worked for. He was there when Jurgens, Petit and Willem van der Grinten held the post of president. *Rota Carolina* was named after the *Rota Romana*, the ecclesiastical court of the Vatican City.

Other specific features of the Nijmegen law programmes are the firmly established place of philosophy of law and history of law (Roman law) in the curriculum, a practical orientation, small-scale teaching, the use of ICT and interactive teaching (while maintaining the transfer of knowledge). Education occurs along long lines, with an increasing degree of difficulty from the first to the third year.[6] The outbreak of the coronavirus pandemic in March 2020 prompted a switch from face-to-face teaching to hybrid teaching, and at times fully online teaching, much to the dismay of students and teaching staff.

The Research Master's in Business & Law was launched in 2005 under the auspices of the OO&R. This two-year programme aims to impart knowledge and understanding about commercial (private) law. Students are expected to acquire a critical, principled approach to research and research skills that will enable them, after graduation, to carry out independent academic research at a university or in a similar role within legal practice. Its focus on commercial (private) law and its legal positivist orientation make this Research Master's unique in the Netherlands.[7]

Today's Centre for Professional Legal Education (CPO) is a rather different organisation from that of 40 years ago – not just in terms of size but also in its approach to teaching. Digitisation was already in full swing in 2020 when the coronavirus pandemic made all forms of face-to-face teaching impossible. Continuing education in Nijmegen is characterised by blended learning, which combines face-to-face and online forms of teaching. Almost all professional training programmes have their own online learning environment. Teaching staff are also encouraged to use video clips, podcasts and digital 'tools'. No-one knew when the pandemic struck in 2020 that this would become the future for all university teaching. The biggest change for the CPO came in 2012, when it was made the implementing body for *Beroepsopleiding Advocaten*, the professional training for the Netherlands Bar Association. A three-year programme offered training to some 1000 lawyers a year. The CPO is now an integral part of the post-graduate legal landscape of the Netherlands. Its motto is: 'Think further, be sharper.'[8]

---

6.   See P.P.T. Bovend'Eert, 'De rechtenstudie in Nijmegen. Kanttekeningen bij enige ontwikkelingen', in: Gitmans et al. (eds), *Te Recht in Nijmegen*, p. 147 ff. and P.P.T. Bovend'Eert, 'Schets van de rechtenstudie in Nijmegen', in: Bulten, Hermans-Brand and Jansen (eds), *Meesterlijk Nijmegen*,p. 117 ff.

7.   Qanu, *Onderzoeksmaster Onderneming en Recht, Faculteit der Rechtsgeleerdheid Radboud Universiteit*, 2021, p. 11. Prof. Corjo Jansen and Louk Hermans-Brand have been involved in the programme from the beginning. Jansen and Irene Larooy (and Annika Boh from 2019) are responsible for the Master's programme. Since 2014, the Nijmegen faculty has also offered students interested in public law research an opportunity to do a Research Master's programme. To this end, the faculty works with the University of Groningen and VU Amsterdam. The person responsible for the Research Master's in Nijmegen is Dr Joost Sillen.

8.   See M.L.A. van den Bosch and C. Korbeld, 'Het CPO in de laatste 5 jaar', in: Hermans-Brand and Jansen (eds), *Recht in Nijmegen*, p. 133 ff.

2.3   *Legal research*

Since 2007, the Nijmegen Faculty of Law has had three research centres: the Radboud Business Law Institute (OO&R), the Research Centre for State & Law (SteR) and the Centre for Notarial Law (CNR).[9] The OO&R celebrated its 25th anniversary in 2019, while its 'daughter institute', the Van der Heijden Institute, celebrated its 50th anniversary in 2016. The OO&R offers four programmes: Business & Patrimonial Law (focusing on the foundations and key concepts of private law), Finance, Security Rights & Insolvency Law (offered by the Institute for Insolvency Law), Company Law (offered by the Van der Heijden Institute) and Financial Law (offered by the Institute for Financial Law). Exploring the implications that European law and treaty law have for national law is one of the central research themes at the OO&R.[10] In recent years, the OO&R has paid particular attention to the impact of digitisation, diversity and sustainability on the doctrines, principles and concepts of civil law, insolvency law, corporate law and financial law. The OO&R has partnered with Radboud University's Interdisciplinary Hub for Security, Privacy and Data Governance in the area of digitisation.

Research on national and international public law, criminal law and criminology, migration law and philosophy of law was clustered within the SteR in 2007. SteR's overarching research programme, 'Foundations of Public Law', is made up of four sub-programmes: supporting principles and fundamental rights, the interplay between national and international law, conflict-solving institutions, and migration and citizenship. Research at the Centre for Migration Law (CMR) is conducted within the last sub-programme. The CMR has twice been recognised as a Jean Monnet Centre of Excellence.

There is a close connection between teaching and research in the vision of the Nijmegen faculty. As with teaching, legal research in the faculty is legal positivist and generalist in nature. Generalist research is coming under pressure, however. Today, there are almost no lawyers who are proficient in more than one area of law. The current generation of Nijmegen professors is increasingly made up of specialists. To Tijn Kortmann's horror, the research centres are subject to comprehensive quality assessments. His comments in 2009 echo the sentiments of many of his colleagues: "With the dictatorship of the evaluations, the rankings, the reviews, the wretched programming, in fact the whole shebang, all humour and

---

9.   G. van Solinge, 'Rechtswetenschappelijk onderzoek in Nijmegen', in: Bulten, Hermans-Brand, Jansen (eds), *Meesterlijk Nijmegen*, p. 141 ff. The CNR's research covers (national) notarial law, and in particular family property law. In addition to the three research centres, there is an 'other research' category.
10.   On this: A.S. Hartkamp, 'Sede vacante. Een terugblik op twaalf jaar onderwijs en onderzoek in het Europese Privaatrecht aan de Radboud Universiteit', in: C.J.H. Jansen (et al.) (eds), *Nijmeegs Europees Privaatrecht*, Deventer: Wolters Kluwer 2018, p. 1 ff.

imagination will go to the dogs. There's little room for the Einzelgänger in this system. It has all become very serious and bureaucratic."[11]

The debate about whether law is a true 'science' has flared up in the first few decades of the 21st century.[12] It hasn't left the Nijmegen lawyers untouched. From the late 19th century, legal research in the Netherlands was based on two pillars: a dogmatic and an empirical one. The OO&R, the SteR and the CNR have placed the former at the centre of their approach to research. Since its inception, however, the Centre for Migration Law – one of the SteR programmes – has relied heavily on empirical research. In recent decades, all the research centres have begun devoting more attention to comparative law, European law, economics and the use of social science methodologies (borrowed from psychology, sociology, and the like). The interplay between theory and practice continues to occupy a central place within the approach of the Nijmegen research centres. It is a bone of contention for some other scholars and scientists (as well as for some politicians, who nevertheless go on about the benefits that universities offer to society). However, the 'fertilisation' by legal practice doesn't detract from the 'scientific' nature of legal research. On the contrary, it sheds light on new research problems and solutions.

2.4   *Roman Catholic?*

In 2004, the university bade farewell to the name bestowed at its foundation in 1923. The Roman Catholic University became Radboud University. The name change symbolised the disintegrating ties with Roman Catholicism. The ties with the Church seem to have been definitively severed in 2020 when the Dutch bishops' conference withdrew the predicate 'Catholic'. The pope has decided in 2022 that the Radboud University is still a catholic university. The Dutch bishops had no power to deprive the Radboud University of the 'predicate' catholic. Although that decision of the bishops saddened some members of the law faculty, it was a matter of indifference to many professors and students, who for years had barely felt a connection with the Catholic past of the university and faculty. The question remains as to what it means to be a special university, and a special Catholic university in particular. Given the history of the faculty, this is a sad observation.

---

11.   Caroline Lindo in conversation with Prof. Tijn Kortmann, 'Een korte Grondwet graag!', *De NJB interviews*, p. 286.

12.   It began with an article by Leiden professor Carel Stolker, ''Ja, geléérd zijn jullie wel!' Over de status van de rechtswetenschap', *NJB* 2003, p. 766 ff. This was followed by many articles in the *NJB* and other law journals. See, for example, J.H.A. Lokin, 'Regtskunde, rechtsgeleerdheid, rechtswetenschap', *RM Themis* 2008/2, p. 49 ff.; J.M. Smits, *Omstreden rechtswetenschap. Over aard, methode en organisatie van de juridische discipline*, The Hague: Boom Juridische uitgevers 2009.

3   CONCLUSION AND RECAP

As I have said a good deal in the concluding sections of the individual chapters of this book, the recap can be brief. In 1923, the mission of the Roman Catholic University, and hence of the Faculty of Law, was to put an end to the shortage of Catholic intellectuals able to occupy prominent positions in the legal profession, the judiciary, academia, the government, business and politics. The university has more than succeeded: the emancipation of Catholic lawyers (trained in Nijmegen) is a success story (alumni include four prime ministers, three presidents of the Supreme Court and a vice-president of the Council of State).[13] The university has also shone in academic terms: many alumni have become professors in and outside Nijmegen, book series have been launched, and Nijmegen academics have written prestigious textbooks and filled countless columns in authoritative journals. The number of people obtaining a PhD degree has risen sharply. Students in the Master's programmes (especially alumni of the dual Master's and the Research Master's in Business & Law) enjoy an excellent reputation in the professional field.

The first generations of Nijmegen professors felt that they had something to prove to the outside world. Until well into the 1970s, they were proud, socially active and socially committed Catholics (at some distance from the episcopal authority). They worked from a shared scholarly perspective: a focus on positive law, with attention to the foundations of this law within natural law, believing in the cross-fertilisation between theory on the one hand and practice and society on the other, and with a high degree of involvement in the education and training of students. They often opposed legalism (with the exception of Jurgens). They were politically active within the RKSP/KVP. The professors stood for the Catholic pillar, which the university had made possible. They occupied countless ancillary positions both within that pillar and outside it: on standing committees, in the Social and Economic Council of the Netherlands (SER), the judiciary, etc. Despite depillarisation, these characteristics are still in evidence in today's teaching and research at the university and among the university's employees, except that they are now much more pluralistic when it comes to faith, political interests (inasmuch as this is apparent in today's world) and scholarly foundations. Since the faculty was founded, it has boasted undisputed major players, who were influential in academia and with legislators, the judiciary and politics. I will simply mention Van der Heijden and Jos van der Grinten, Willem van der Grinten, Frans Duynstee, Maeijer and the Kortmann brothers.

The zeitgeist could not help but exert its influence on professorial teaching and research. In the 1930s, the rise of fascism and National Socialism prompted protests by the Nijmegen professors. The planned incomes policy and the concern for

---

13.   The names are well-known: Beel, Victor Marijnen, Cals and Van Agt (prime ministers), Charles Moons, Davids and Corstens (presidents of the Supreme Court) and Thom de Graaf (vice-president of the Council of State).

security of livelihood led to the establishment of a chair in employment law after the Second World War. The call for democratisation created a different kind of faculty, with participation bodies, while the law faculty was also a beacon of calm during the period of student unrest. The rise of the European Community brought a teaching and research assignment in socio-economic law and a programme in International and European Law. The call for research schools led to the clustering of research within research centres. As is typical of our time, abbreviations now dominate the language of the faculty (OO&R, CMR, CPO, SteR, CNR, etc.). Nijmegen professors took a strong stance during the Second World War. Rector magnificus Hermesdorf, in particular, deserves greater acknowledgement in the history of Dutch universities during the Second World War than he is usually accorded.

The changing social circumstances (influenced by such things as digitisation and the desire to eliminate social inequalities), political developments, the shorter duration of studies, technological and demographic changes, Europeanisation, internationalisation and globalisation, the rise of continuing education and the requirement for lifelong learning in the various legal professions – all have significantly changed the teaching and research of the Nijmegen faculty in recent decades. The differences between programmes offered by Dutch law faculties have increased rapidly, as have the number of focal points for legal research. Some faculties wanted to drop *civiel effect* from their programmes. They felt that society needed a different kind of lawyer, not someone who was dogmatically trained, but someone who felt at home in a wide range of academic fields (such as psychology and public administration). There was even doubt as to whether lawyers were 'true scientists'. For the professors, this issue was a 'no brainer' until well into the 1970s. The Nijmegen Faculty of Law has chosen to maintain its course, nurtured by the tradition in which it has evolved and with the emphases from the past that it holds dear. This means that knowledge of positive law and an understanding of the systematics of law play an important role in teaching. Research continues to focus on the main areas of law and has not become a repository of specialisms.[14] For many, this continuity of teaching and research makes the Nijmegen Law Faculty a wonderful place to study and work. The faculty doesn't stand still, but moves boldly forward in uncertain times.

---

14.   Lokin, *De Groninger Faculteit der Rechtsgeleerdheid (1596-1970)*, p. 605, p. 607.

Overview of the teaching responsibilities of the Nijmegen law professors

Labor Law

J.J.M. van der Ven	**1947-1951**
F.J.H.M. van der Ven	1952-1972
L.J.M. de Leede	1972-1994
Asscher-Vonk, I.P.	1994-2010
L.G. Verburg	2010-2021
F.G. Laagland	2018-present

Fiscal Law

G.M.G.H. Russel	**1928-1961**
L.J.M. Nouwen	1961-1973
M.V.M. van Leeuwe	1965-1985
D.C. Smit	1973-1990
H.M.N. Schonis	1985-2005
G.T.K. Meussen	2003-present

Administrative Law

J.H.P.M. van der Grinten	**1923-1932**
P.W. Kamphuisen	**1933-1945**
F.J.F.M. Duynstee	**1948-1950**
L.J.M. Beel	1949-1951
S.F.L. van Wijnbergen	1954-1984
H.Ph.J.A.M. Hennekens	1983-2001
R.J.N. Schlössels	2002-present
A.G.A. Nijmeijer	2008-present

Civil Law[1]

E.J.J. van der Heijden	**1923-1941**
C.J.J.M. Petit	**1945-1957**
W.C.L. van der Grinten	**1957-1984**
S.C.J.J. Kortmann	**1984-2007**[2]
C.H. Sieburgh	2003-2010
S.E. Bartels	2008-present
J.B. Spath	2012-2019

Law of Civil Procedure[3]

J.H.P. Bellefroid	**1923-1939**
J.W.J.P. Jurgens	**1940-1960**
L.E.H. Rutten	1960-1974
J.C.M. Leijten	**1976-1991**
W.H.D. Asser	1992-1999
C.J.M. Klaassen	1999-present

European Law

P.S.R.F. Mathijsen	1968-1985
A.T.S. Leenen	1985-1986
J.H.V. Stuyck	1987-2013
R. Fernhout	1911-1999
A.M.A.P. van den Bossche	2000-2006
J.W. van de Gronden	2007-2014
J.H. Gerards	2014-2016[4]
J.W. van de Gronden	2017-present

European Private Law

A.S. Hartkamp	2006-2010
C.H. Sieburgh	2010-2017[5]
A.U. Janssen	2018-present

---

1. Other professors have also had Civil Law in their teaching duties. A.J.M. Nuytinck, appointed in 1995, was professor of Family Law, P.M. Veder, appointed in 2012, professor in Insolvency Law.
2. Kortmann was the *rector magnificus* of the Radboud University from 2007 until 2014.
3. Always in combination with another teaching assignment.
4. Gerards was appointed in 2011 as professor of 'Fundamental Rights.
5. Sieburgh is also a judge in the Dutch Supreme Court from 2017 onwards.

Commercial Law/Company Law[6]

E.J.J. van der Heijden	**1923-1941**
J.W.G.P. Jurgens	**1940-1963**
J.M.M. Maeijer	**1963-1997**
G. van Solinge	1997-present
F.J.P. van den Ingh	1997-2012
M.P. Nieuwe Weme	2005-present
C.D.J. Bulten	2012-present

Commercial Law/Economic Law

F.F.X. Cerutti	1969-1970
P.S.F.R. Mathijsen	1971-1985
L.J.M. de Leede	1972-1983
D.W.F. Verkade	1980-1990
A.A. Quaedvlieg	1990-present

Jurisprudence

J.H.P. Bellefroid	**1923-1939**
W.J.A.J. Duynstee	**1939-1956**
J.J.H. Nieskens	1956-1958 (lecturer)
F.F.X. Cerutti	1958-1969
J.C.M. Leijten	**1969-1975**
P.J.P. Tak	1976-2009
R.J.B. Schutgens	2010-present

Private International Law

J.H.P. Bellefroid	**1923-1939**
J.W.G.P. Jurgens	**1940-1963**
J.M.M. Maeijer	**1963-1964**
W.C.L. van der Grinten	**1964-1971**
A.V.M. Struycken	**1971-2001**
H.L.E. Verhagen	2001-present[7]

---

6. D. Busch (2011) and S.N. Grünewald (2020) are the professors of Financial Law.
7. Verhagen was between 1996 and 2001 professor of Business and Law.

NOTARIAL LAW

L.J.M. Nouwen	1959-1961
E.A.A. Luijten	1961-1987
M.J.A. van Mourik	**1987-2013**
F.W.J.M. Schols	2008-present[8]

BUSINESS AND LAW

H.L.E. Verhagen	1996-2001
N.E.D. Faber	2007-2015
B.A. Schuijling	2019-present

PHILOSOPHY OF LAW

J.H.E.J. Hoogveld	**1923-1942**
W.J.A.J. Duynstee	**1948-1956**
D. van Eck	**1958-1968**
A.T.B. Peperzak	1970-1972
D.F. Scheltens	1973-1989
P.J.M. van Tongeren	1990-1993
B.P. Vermeulen	1993-1998
T.J.M. Mertens	1999-2021
R.J.B. Tinnevelt	2021-present

HISTORY OF LAW AND ROMAN LAW

E.J.J. van der Heijden	**1923-1938 (History of Law)**
B.H.D. Hermesdorf	**1928-1965 (Roman Law and History of Law)**
G.C.J.J. van den Bergh	**1965-1975 (Roman Law)**
F.F.X. Cerutti	1965-1970 (History of Law)
O. Moorman van Kappen	1971-2000 (History of Law)
P.L. Nève	1975-1998 (Roman Law)
C.J.H. Jansen	1998-present (Roman Law and History of Law)

SOCIOLOGY OF LAW

C.J.M. Schuyt	1974-1980

---

8. Schols was between 2007 and 2008 professor of *Estate planning*.

C.A. Groenendijk	**1982-2008**
A.B. Terlouw	2008-present

CONSTITUTIONAL LAW

J.H.P.M. van der Grinten	**1923-1932**
P.W. Kamphuisen	**1932-1945**
F.J.F.M. Duynstee	**1945-1981**
C.A.J.M. Kortmann	**1981-2010**
P.P.T. Bovend'Eert	1999-present

CRIMINAL LAW AND LAW OF CRIMINAL PROCEDURE

W.P.J. Pompe	**1923-1928**
W.J.A.J. Duynstee	**1928-1948**
D. van Eck	**1947-1968**
W.H.A. Jonkers	1970-1986
G.E. Mulder	1972-1981
G.J.M. Corstens	1982-1995
A.J.M. Machielse	1986-2013
Y. Buruma	1996-2011
P.H.P.H.M.C. van Kempen	2009-present
P.M. Frielink	2012-2017
M. Fedorova	2018-present

VOLKENRECHT

J.H.P. Bellefroid	**1923-1939**
R.W.H. Regout	**1939-1942**
F.J.F.M. Duynstee	**1946-1948; 1950-1970**
L.J.C. Beaufort	1946-1960
A.M. Stuyt	1960-1981
B.K.J. Vitànyi	1980-1983
K.C. Wellens	1982-2012
J. Bast	2012-2013
H.C.F.J.A. de Waele	2014-present

Deans of the Nijmegen Law Faculty since 1970 and Alumni Deans (since 2007)

F.J.F.M. Duynstee	1970-1972
W.C.L. van der Grinten	1972-1983
J.M.M. Maeijer	1983-1987
A.V.M. Struycken	1987-1991
C.A.J.M. Kortmann	1991-1993
C.A. Groenendijk	1993-1995
P.J.P. Tak	1995-1998
S.C.J.J. Kortmann	1998-2001
C.A.J.M. Kortmann	2001-2003
C.J.H. Jansen	2003-2005
Y. Buruma	2005-2008
C.J.H. Jansen	2008-2010
P.P.T. Bovend'Eert	2010-2014
S.E. Bartels	2014-2018
P.H.P.H.M.C. van Kempen	2018-2022

Alumni Deans Since 2007

M.J.A. van Mourik	2007-2014
A.J.M. Nuytinck	2014-2020
P.P.T. Bovend'Eert	2020-present

Adresslist of Professors in 1946[1]

Faculty of Law

W.J.A.J. Duynstee	Van Oldenbarneveltstraat 4 (Tel. 26964)
B.H.D. Hermesdorf	Groesbeeksche Weg 195 (Tel. 21139)
J.W.G.P. Jurgens	St. Annastraat 170 (Tel. 26096)
J.R.M. van den Brink	Tafelberg 10, Laren N.H. (Tel. K. 2953 – 3156)
F.J.F.M. Duynstee	Graadt van Roggenstraat 6 (Tel. 20023)
Ch.J.J.M. Petit	Groesbeeksche Weg 70 (Tel. 20636)
G.M.G.H. Russel	Willemsparkweg 205, Amsterdam Z (Tel. K. 2900 – 26609)
L.J.C. Beaufort	RK Gymnasium I.C., Venray (Tel. 366)

Faculty of Theology

F.A.M. van Welie	Van Slichtenhorststraat 93 (Tel. 22855)

Faculty of Arts and Philosophy (Psychology)

J.J.G. Prick	Canisiussingel 25 (Tel. 22067)

Emeriti

J.H.P. Bellefroid	Nijhoffstraat 9
Ch.A.M. Raaijmakers	Stijn Buysstraat 11

---

1. *Nijmeegsche Studenten-Almanak* 1947, p. 66, p. 76, p. 79 e.v.

LECTOR

D. van Eck   Van Oldenbarneveltstraat 38 (Tel. 22954)

LECTURER

A.J.J.C. Begheyn   Zomerstraat 1, Heerlen

Bibliography

A.A.M. van Agt, 'D. van Eck (1911-1968)', in: Hermans-Brand en Jansen (red.), *Recht in Nijmegen*, p. 69 e.v.

M. Ahsmann, 'Teaching the ius hodiernum: Legal education of advocates in the Northern Netherlands (1575-1800)', *Tijdschrift voor Rechtsgeschiedenis* 65 (1997), p. 423 e.v.

L.J. van Apeldoorn, 'De fundamenten van een grootsch bouwwerk. Het Duitsche Volkswetboek. Grondregels en Boek I', *Het Rechtsfront* 1943, p. 18, p. 26-27, p. 37-39, p. 45-46, p. 54-55.

S.E. Bartels e.a. (red.), *Vertrouwen in het burgerlijke recht. Liber Amicorum Prof. Mr. S.C.J.J. Kortmann*, Deventer: Wolters Kluwer 2017.

J.H.P. Bellefroid, *De Bronnen van het Stellig Recht en haar Onderlinge Verhoudingen*, Nijmegen: G.C. Richelle 1927.

J.H.P. Bellefroid, *Inleiding tot de rechtswetenschap in Nederland*, vijfde druk, Nijmegen-Utrecht: Dekker & Van de Vegt 1948.

B. von Benda-Beckmann, Rapport verkennend onderzoek 'De rooms-katholieke kerk en de grenzen van verzet in Nederland tijdens de Tweede Wereldoorlog' (digitaal raadpleegbaar).

I.J.M. van den Berg, 'In memoriam Mgr. Prof. dr. J.Th. Beysens', *Tijdschrift voor Philosophie* 8 (1946)-2/3, p. 379 e.v.

J. van den Berg en H. Spath, 'Interview met prof. mr. A.V.M. Struycken en mr. J.G.A. Struycken', *Ars Aequi* 50 (2001) 10, p. 741 e.v.

G.C.J.J. van den Bergh, 'Roodkapje gaat studeren', *Nijmeegs Universiteitsblad* 17 (1967-1968), nr. 13.

G.C.J.J. van den Bergh, 'Studentenbeweging en crisis der universiteit', *Universiteit en hogeschool* 16 (1970), p. 347 e.v.

G.C.J.J. van den Bergh, 'Custodiam praestare. Custodia-Liability or Liability for failing Custodia', *Tijdschrift voor Rechtsgeschiedenis* 43 (1975), p. 59 e.v.

G.C.J.J. van den Bergh, 'Jedem das Seine', in: J.B.J.M. ten Berge e.a. (red.), *Recht als norm en als aspiratie: Opstellen over recht en samenleving ter gelegenheid van het 350-jarig bestaan van de Utrechtse juridische faculteit*, Nijmegen: Ars Aequi 1986, p. 258 e.v.

G.C.J.J. van den Bergh, 'Simon Groenewegen van der Made (1613-1652), Petrus de Greve (1621-1677) and law teaching in Nijmegen', *Zeitschrift für Neuere Rechtsgeschichte* 2002/3-4, p. 273 e.v.

G.C.J.J. van den Bergh, *The Life and Work of Gerard Noodt (1647-1725). Dutch Legal Scholarship between Humanism and Enlightenment*, Oxford: Oxford University Press 1988.

G.C.J.J. van den Bergh/C.J.H. Jansen, *Geleerd recht. Een geschiedenis van de Europese rechtswetenschap in vogelvlucht*, zevende druk, Deventer: Wolters Kluwer 2018.

J.Th. Beysens, *Hoofdstukken uit de Bijzondere Ethiek*, II, *Wijsgeerige Staatsleer*, Hilversum: P. Brand 1917.

J. Bluyssen, *Oorlogsdagboek, Nijmegen september t/m december 1944*, bewerkt door P. Kriele, 's-Hertogenbosch: Uitgeverij Bastion Oranje 2013.

J. Bosmans e.a., *Tot hier en niet verder! De RK Universiteit in oorlogstijd*, Katholieke Universiteit Nijmegen 70 jaar: Nijmegen 1993.

M.L.A. van den Bosch, '29 jaar Postacademisch juridisch onderwijs. Over de combinatie van theorie en praktijk, kwaliteit en de Nijmeegse ambiance', in: Bulten, Hermans-Brand en Jansen (red.), *Meesterlijk Nijmegen*, p. 155 e.v.

M.L.A. van den Bosch en C. Korbeld, 'Het CPO in de laatste 5 jaar', in: Hermans-Brand en Jansen (red.), *Recht in Nijmegen*, p. 133 e.v.

H. Bots & T. Kerkhoff, *De Nijmeegse Pallas. De geschiedenis van de kwartierlijke academie en medische faculteit, 1655-1679*, UMC St Radboud 2001.

P.P.T. Bovend'Eert, 'De rechtenstudie in Nijmegen. Kanttekeningen bij enige ontwikkelingen', in: Gitmans e.a. (red.), *Te Recht in Nijmegen*, p. 147 e.v.

P.P.T. Bovend'Eert, 'Schets van de rechtenstudie in Nijmegen', in: Bulten, Hermans-Brand en Jansen (red.), *Meesterlijk Nijmegen*, p. 117 e.v.

P. Bovend'Eert, 'Een bijzondere positivist uit Nijmegen. In Memoriam Tijn Kortmann (1944-2016)', *Tijdschrift voor Constitutioneel Recht* 2016, p. 72 e.v.

P.P.T. Bovend'Eert, J.W.A. Fleuren en H.R.B.M. Kummeling (red.), *Grensverleggend staatsrecht. Opstellen aangeboden aan prof. mr. C.A.J.M. Kortmann*, Deventer: Kluwer 2001.

J. Brabers, *De Faculteit der Rechtsgeleerdheid van de Katholieke Universiteit Nijmegen 1923-1982*, Nijmegen: GNI 1994.

J. Brabers, "Recht om mee te werken'. Een geschiedenis van de faculteit der rechtsgeleerdheid als academisch brandpunt en emancipatorisch vehikel (1923-1982)', in: Gitmans e.a. (red.), *Te Recht in Nijmegen*, p. 25 e.v.

J. Brabers, *Een zoet juk. Rectores magnifici van de Radboud Universiteit over hun rectoraat 1923-2014*, Nijmegen: Valkhofpers 2014.

J. Brabers, 'Studeren in bezet Nijmegen', *Vox* 05/2018, p. 6 e.v.

J. Brabers, *Een kleine geschiedenis van de Radboud Universiteit*. Nijmegen: Radboud University, 2021.

J. Brabers en L. Savenije, 'Radboud bevrijd. Afstuderen in een frontstad', in: *Impressie. Nieuwsbrief van het KDC* 2019, p. 4 e.v.

J. Brands (samenstelling), *Een splinter van de ziel. Rouwen Hèze en het grote dorpsverlangen*, Nijmegen: SUN 1995.

F. Brandsma, 'De Historische School in het privaatrecht. Misschien wisten zij alles', in: R. Schutgens e.a. (red.), *Canon van het Recht*, Nijmegen: Ars Aequi Libri 2010, p. 33 e.v.

T. Brandsma, *De Katholieke Universiteit in 1932-1933*, Nijmegen-Utrecht: N.V. Dekker & Van de Vegt en J.W. van Leeuwen 1933.

J.J. Brinkhof, 'Enkele opmerkingen over de geldigheid van de aan de Kwartierlijke Academie behaalde doctorsgraad in de rechten', *Numaga* 1972, p. 14-17.

F. Broeyer, *Het Utrechtse universitaire verzet * 'Heb je Kafka gelezen? 1940 * 1945*, tweede druk, Matrijs: Utrecht 2015.

J. de Bruijn, S. Faber en A. Soeteman (red.), *Ridders van het Recht. De juridische faculteit van de Vrije Universiteit, 1880-2010*, Amsterdam: Prometheus*Bert Bakker 2010.

C.D.J. Bulten, L.J.T.M. Hermans-Brand en C.J.H. Jansen (red.), *Meesterlijk Nijmegen*, Den Haag: Boom Juridische uitgevers 2008.

C.D.J. Bulten, L.J.T.M. Hermans-Brand, C.J.H. Jansen, "Het leven is goed'. Interview met prof. J.M.M. Maeijer', in: Bulten, Hermans-Brand en Jansen (red.), *Meesterlijk Nijmegen*, p. 87 e.v.

C.D.J. Bulten, L.J.T.M. Hermans-Brand, C.J.H. Jansen, 'Kind van mijn tijd. Interview met mw. mr. Pia E.M.S. Lokin-Sassen', in: Bulten, Hermans-Brand, Jansen (red.), *Meesterlijk Nijmegen*, p. 99 e.v.

C.D.J. Bulten, C.J.H. Jansen en G. van Solinge (red.), *Verspreide geschriften van J.M.M. Maeijer*, Serie vanwege het Van der Heijden Instituut Deel 100, Deventer: Kluwer 2009.

Y. Buruma (red.), *100 jaar strafrecht. Klassieke teksten van de twintigste eeuw*, Amsterdam: Amsterdam University Press 1999.

Y. Buruma e.a. (red.), *Op het rechte pad. Liber amicorum Peter J.P. Tak*, Nijmegen: Wolf Legal Publishers 2008.

Y. Buruma, *Wat is een goede rechter? Een mentaliteitsgeschiedenis (1900-2020)*, Nijmegen: CPO, Radboud Universiteit 2016.

G.J.M. Corstens e.a. (red.), *Met hoofd en hart. Opstellen aangeboden aan prof. mr. J.C.M. Leijten ter gelegenheid van zijn afscheid als hoogleraar aan de Katholieke Universiteit Nijmegen*, Zwolle: W.E.J. Tjeenk Willink 1991.

W.J.M. Davids, 'Jan Cornelis Maria Leijten. Etten-Leur 14 januari 1926 – Nijmegen 4 mei 2014', *Jaarboek Maatschappij der Nederlandse Letterkunde*, Leiden: Maatschappij der Nederlandse Letterkunde 2014, p. 124 e.v.

J.M. van Dunné, P. Boeles, A.J. Heerma van Voss, *Acht civilisten in burger*, Zwolle: W.E.J. Tjeenk Willink 1977.

J.M. van Dunné, *Ex tunc, ex nunc. Twee generaties juristen aan het woord over de ontwikkeling van het recht*, Zwolle; W.E.J. Tjeenk Willink 1990.

F.J.J.M. Duynstee, 'Is het gewenst wijziging te brengen in de bestaande bepalingen in grondwet en wet betreffende de vrijheid van meningsuiting door middel van drukpers, toneel, film, en radio, zo ja, in welke zin?', *HNJV* 1949-I (tweede stuk), p. 1 e.v.

W.J.A.J. Duynstee, 'Natuurrecht', *Handelingen van de Vereeniging voor de Wijsbegeerte des Rechts* 1929, p. 161 e.v.

W.J.A.J. Duynstee, *Over recht en rechtvaardigheid*, 's-Hertogenbosch: Malmberg 1956.

D. van Eck, 'Enkele beschouwingen omtrent het nulla-poena-beginsel', in: *Opstellen over recht, wet en samenleving op 1 October 1948 door vrienden en leerlingen aangeboden aan Prof. Mr. W.P.J. Pompe*, Nijmegen-Utrecht: Dekker & Van de Vegt 1948, p. 55 e.v.

D. van Eck, *De strafrechter tegenover het gewetensbezwaar*, Nijmegen-Utrecht: Dekker & Van de Vegt 1956.

D. van Eck, 'Het universele karakter van het strafrecht', *Opstellen over recht en rechtsgeschiedenis aangeboden aan Prof. Mr. B.H.D. Hermesdorf*, Deventer: Kluwer 1965, p. 135 e.v.

J.C.W.J. Edixhoven-Majoor, '23 jaar Postdoctoraal juridisch onderwijs', in: Gitmans e.a. (red.), *Te Recht in Nijmegen*, p. 199 e.v.

J. Elgershuizen, 'Pater Prof. Mr. Willem Duynstee', in: *Een kroniek van vijfenzeventig jaar Nebo*, Nijmegen: Paters Redemptoristen 2003, p. 50-53.

P.H.J. Essers, *Het Nederlandse belastingrecht onder nationaalsocialistisch regime*, Deventer: Kluwer 2013.

T. Gerritse, *Rauter. Himmlers vuist in Nederland*, Amsterdam: Boom 2018.

W.J.M. Gitmans, A.A.H.M. Gommers, L.J.T.M. Hermans-Brand, C.J.H. Jansen, S.C.J.J, Kortmann en Y.A.J.M. van Kuijck, *Te Recht in Nijmegen*, Deventer: Kluwer 2003.

W.J.M. Gitmans e.a., 'In gesprek met J.M.M. Maeijer en A.V.M. Struycken: Nijmeegse juristen zijn in tal van sectoren toonaangevend', in: Gitmans e.a. (red.), *Te Recht in Nijmegen*, p. 135 e.v.

Goed en trouw. Opstellen aangeboden aan Prof. mr. W.C.L. van der Grinten ter gelegenheid van zijn afscheid als hoogleraar aan de Katholieke Universiteit Nijmegen, Zwolle: W.E.J. Tjeenk Willink 1984.

W.C.L. van der Grinten, 'Moraal en billijkheid als bron van verbintenis', *Donum Lustrale*, Nijmegen-Utrecht: Dekker & Van de Vegt 1949, p. 435 e.v.

W.C.L. van der Grinten, 'Handelen te goeder trouw', in: *Opstellen over recht en rechtsgeschiedenis aangeboden aan Prof. mr. B.H.D. Hermesdorf*, Deventer: Kluwer 1965, p. 155 e.v.

W.C.L. van der Grinten, 'Boek 6 van het nieuwe BW', *NJB* 1976, p. 1189 e.v.

C.A. Groenendijk & C.A.J.M. Kortmann, 'Nieuwe verhoging leges voor verblijfsvergunningen: wederom onredelijk, onverstandig en onrechtmatig', *NJB* 2003, p. 314 e.v.

A. Hammerstein & J.B.M. Vranken (red.), *Het kan ook anders. Een keuze uit het juridische werk van Jan Leijten*, Deventer: W.E.J. Tjeenk Willink 1996.

A. Hammerstein & J.B.M. Vranken, 'Jan Leijten (14 januari 1926 – 4 mei 2014)', *NJB* 2014/980.

W.C.E. Hammerstein-Schoonderwoerd, '25 jaar werken aan de faculteit (1969-1994)', in: Gitmans e.a. (red.), *Te Recht in Nijmegen*, p. 117 e.v.

A.S. Hartkamp, 'Sede vacante. Een terugblik op twaalf jaar onderwijs en onderzoek in het Europese Privaatrecht aan de Radboud Universiteit', in: C.J.H. Jansen (e.a.) (red.), *Nijmeegs Europees Privaatrecht*, Deventer: Wolters Kluwer 2018, p. 1 e.v.

A. Haverkamp, 'Ode aan gemartelde studentenvriend Robert Regout', *Vox* 09/2015, p. 30 e.v.

E.J.J. van der Heijden, *Handboek voor de naamlooze vennootschap naar Nederlandsch recht*, tweede druk, Zwolle: W.E.J. Tjeenk Willink 1931.

E.J.J. van der Heijden, 'Voldoet de universitaire opleiding van den jurist aan de daaraan uit wetenschappelijk oogpunt te stellen eischen? Zoo neen, welke wijzigingen behooren daarin dan te worden aangebracht?', *HNJV* 1931-I (tweede stuk), p. 1 e.v.

E.J.J. van der Heijden, *Gezag en Vrijheid*. Uitgave van het secretariaat der R.K. Staatspartij. Den Haag 1933.

E.J.J. van der Heijden, *Aanteekeningen bij de geschiedenis van het oude vaderlandsche recht*, eerste druk, Nijmegen/Utrecht: Dekker & Van de Vegt 1933.

H.Ph.J.A.M. Hennekens, *Overheidsaansprakelijkheid op de weegschaal*, Deventer: W.E.J. Tjeenk Willink 2001.

H.Ph.J.A.M. Hennekens, 'Studeren in de eerste helft van de jaren zestig en doceren in de laatste twee decennia van de vorige eeuw in Nijmegen', in: Hermans-Brand en Jansen (red.), *Recht in Nijmegen*, p. 111 e.v.

L.J.T.M. Hermans-Brand en C.J.H. Jansen (red.), *Recht in Nijmegen. Lustrumbundel ter gelegenheid van het 90-jarig bestaan van de Faculteit der Rechtsgeleerdheid van de Radboud Universiteit Nijmegen*, Den Haag: Boom Juridische uitgevers 2013.

B.H.D. Hermesdorf, 'Een voortreffelijk ambassadeur', *Rechtskundig Weekblad* 13 (1949/1950), kol. 923 e.v.

L. Heyde, J. Leijten, Th. Mertens, B.P. Vermeulen (red.), *Begrensde Vrijheid. Opstellen over mensenrechten aangeboden aan prof. dr. D.F. Scheltens bij zijn afscheid als hoogleraar aan de Katholieke Universiteit Nijmegen*, Zwolle: W.E.J. Tjeenk Willink 1989.

E.M.H. Hirsch Ballin, 'Levensbericht van Constantinus Albertus Josephus Maria Kortmann', *Levensberichten en herdenkingen*. Koninklijke Nederlandse Akademie van Wetenschappen, 2016, p. 47 e.v.

H.J. Hommes, *Een nieuwe herleving van het natuurrecht*, Zwolle: W.E.J. Tjeenk Willink 1961.

A. Jacobs, *Kroniek van de Karmel in Nederland 1840-1970*, Hilversum: Verloren 2017.

N. Jagtenborg en A.G.A. Cuijpers, 'In gesprek met een student Internationaal en Europees recht', in: Hermans-Brand en Jansen (red.), *Te Recht in Nijmegen*, p. 215 e.v.

C.J.H. Jansen, 'P.W. Kamphuisen (1897-1961)', in: C.J.H. Jansen, J.M. Smits, L.C. Winkel (red.), *16 juristen en hun filosofische inspiratie*, Nijmegen; Ars Aequi Libri 2004, p. 129 e.v.

C.J.H. Jansen, 'De Kwartierlijke Academie van Nijmegen (1655/1656-1679)', in: Hermans-Brand en Jansen (red.), *Recht in Nijmegen*, p. 3 e.v.

C.J.H. Jansen, *De Hoge Raad en de Tweede Wereldoorlog. Recht en rechtsbeoefening in de jaren 1930-1950*, met medewerking van D. Venema, Amsterdam: Boom 2011.

C.J.H. Jansen, 'W.J.A.J. Duynstee (1886-1968)', in: Hermans-Brand en Jansen (red.), *Recht in Nijmegen*, p. 71 e.v.

C.J.H. Jansen, *De wetenschappelijke beoefening van het burgerlijke recht tussen 1940 en 1992*, Deventer: Wolters Kluwer 2016.

C.J.H. Jansen, 'Nederlandse protesten tegen het Duitse antisemitisme in de jaren dertig van de vorige eeuw en de rol van de Rooms-Katholieke kerk daarin', *RMThemis* 2016/6, p. 289-291.

C.J.H. Jansen, 'Prof. mr. E.J.J. van der Heijden (1885-1941) in het licht van zijn tijd', in: *50 jaar Van der Heijden Instituut 1966-2016*, Serie vanwege het Van der Heijden Instituut, deel 148, Deventer: Wolters Kluwer 2017, p. 17 e.v.

C.J.H. Jansen, 'L.J. van Apeldoorn (1886-1979), Inleiding tot de studie van het Nederlandsche recht (1933)', *Ars Aequi* 2021/1, p. 93 e.v.

C.J.H. Jansen, S.C.J.J. Kortmann, G. van Solinge (red.), *Verspreide geschriften van W.C.L. van der Grinten*, Deventer: Kluwer 2004.

C.J.H. Jansen, S.C.J.J. Kortmann, G. van Solinge, 'Willem Leonard Christiaan van der Grinten (1913-1994)', in: Jansen, Kortmann, Van Solinge (red.), *Verspreide geschriften van W.C.L. van der Grinten*, p. XVII e.v.

C.J.H. Jansen en E. Poortinga, 'Het onderwijs in de rechtsfilosofie van Paul Scholten', *Recht en kritiek* 19 (1993) 2, p. 191 e.v.

C.J.H. Jansen en W. Rijnenberg, 'Slechts de "principieele" houding lijkt mij in dezen "doelmatig". Boekbeschouwing naar aanleiding van Kees Schuyt, *R.P. Cleveringa. Recht, onrecht en de vlam der gerechtigheid'*, *Ars Aequi* 2019/11, p. 919 e.v.

C.J.H. Jansen en G. van Solinge, *Verspreide Geschriften van E.J.J. van der Heijden*, Serie Monografieën vanwege het Van der Heijden Instituut, deel 67, Deventer: Kluwer 2001.

C.J.H. Jansen en B.H. Stolte, 'G.C.J.J. van den Bergh (1926-2005)', *Pro Memorie* 8.1 (2006), p. 135 e.v.

P.W. Kamphuisen, C.Ch.A. van Haren en F.G.J.M. Peters (red.), *Verspreide Opstellen van Prof. Mr. Dr. J.H.P.M. van der Grinten*, Nijmegen-Utrecht: Dekker & Van de Vegt en J.W. van Leeuwen 1934.

P.W. Kamphuisen, *Beschouwingen over rechtswetenschap*, Nijmegen-Utrecht: Dekker & Van de Vegt 1938.

P.W. Kamphuisen, 'Mr. E.J.J. van der Heijden (Gouda, 12 Augustus 1885-Nijmegen, 24 Mei 1941)', in: *Jaarboek van de Maatschappij der Nederlandsche Letterkunde* 1941, p. 38-42.

C. Kelk, 'Willem Petrus Josephus Pompe (1893-1968)', in: T.J. Veen en P.C. Kop (red.), *Zestig juristen. Bijdragen tot een beeld van de geschiedenis der Nederlandse rechtswetenschap*, Zwolle: W.E.J. Tjeenk Willink 1987, p. 345 e.v.

C. Kelk, 'W.P.J. Pompe (1893-1968)', in: C.J.H. Jansen, J.M. Smits, L.C. Winkel (red.), *16 juristen en hun filosofische inspiratie*, Nijmegen: Ars Aequi Libri 2004, p. 89 e.v.

G.Th. Kempe, 'Levensbericht Willem Petrus Joseph Pompe (10 maart 1893-26 juli 1968)', *Jaarboek van de Koninklijke Nederlandse Akademie van Wetenschappen* 1968-1969, p. 3 e.v.

P.J. Knegtmans, 'Onderwijspacificatie in de Nieuwe Orde Jan van Dam (1896-1979)', in: P.J. Knegtmans, P. Schulten, J. Vogel, *Collaborateurs van niveau. Opkomst en val van de hoogleraren Schrieke, Snijder en Van Dam*, Amsterdam: Vossiuspers AUP 1996, p. 223 e.v.

T. Koopmans, 'De rol van de wetgever' (1970), in: T. Koopmans, *Juridisch stippelwerk*, Deventer: Kluwer 1991, p. 151 e.v.

P.J. van Koppen en J. ten Kate, *De Hoge Raad in persoon. Benoeming in de Hoge Raad der Nederlanden 1838-2002*, Deventer: Kluwer 2003.

C.A.J.M. Kortmann, 'Positivisme, soevereiniteit en recht', *NJB* 1997, p. 482 e.v.

C.A.J.M. Kortmann, *Constitutioneel recht*, zesde druk, Deventer: Kluwer 2008.

C.A.J.M. Kortmann, 'De rechtsvormende taak van de Hoge Raad', in: W.M.T. Keukens (red.), *Raad en Daad. Over de rechtsvormende taak van de Hoge Raad*, Nijmegen: Ars Aequi Libri 2008, p. 31 e.v.

C.A.J.M. Kortmann, *Staatsrecht en raison d'Etat*, Deventer: Kluwer 2009.

C.A.J.M. Kortmann, 'J.H.P.M. van der Grinten (1885-1932)', in: Hermans-Brand en Jansen (red.), *Recht in Nijmegen*, p. 57 e.v.

C.A.J.M. Kortmann, 'F.J.F.M. Duynstee (1914-1981)', in: Hermans-Brand en Jansen (red.), *Recht in Nijmegen*, p. 73 e.v.

S.C.J.J. Kortmann, 'De juridische opleiding, pre- en postdoctoraal', *NJB* 1990, p. 587 e.v.

S.C.J.J. Kortmann e.a. (red.), *Op recht. Bundel opstellen aangeboden aan prof. mr. A.V.M. Struycken ter gelegenheid van zijn zilveren ambtsjubileum aan de Katholieke Universiteit Nijmegen*, Zwolle: W.E.J. Tjeenk Willink 1996.

S.C.J.J. Kortmann e.a. (red.), *Yin –Yang. Bundel opstellen, op 12 mei 2000 aangeboden aan prof. mr. M.J.A. van Mourik ter gelegenheid van zijn 25-jarig ambtsjubileum als hoogleraar*, Deventer: Kluwer 2000.

S.C.J.J. Kortmann, 'W.C.L. van der Grinten (1913-1994)', in: Hermans-Brand en Jansen (red.), *Recht in Nijmegen*, p. 77 e.v.

S.C.J.J. Kortmann, 'Woord vooraf', in: C.J.H. Jansen, B.A. Schuijling en I.V. Aronstein (red.), *Onderneming & Digitalisering*, Serie Onderneming & Recht, Deel 116, Deventer: Wolters Kluwer 2019, p. V.

F.W.H.M. Kusters, 'Ach toen, ja', in: Gitmans e.a. (red.), *Te Recht in Nijmegen*, p. 125-126.

A.C.A. van Kuijck, 'De Rota Carolina', in: Gitmans e.a. (red.), *Te Recht in Nijmegen*, p. 99 e.v.

H. Lange, *Römisches Recht im Mittelalter*, I (Glossatoren), München: C.H. Beck 1997.

G.E. Langemeijer, '[Bespr. van:] W.C.L. van der Grinten, Recht en rechtsgemeenschap', *NJB* 1954, p. 263-265.

J.C.M. Leijten, *De rechter op de schopstoel*, Deventer: Kluwer 1970.

J.C.M. Leyten, 'Voorbericht voor de zeventiende druk', in: L.J. van Apeldoorn, *Inleiding tot de studie van het Nederlandse recht*, bewerkt door J.C.M. Leyten, Zwolle: W.E.J. Tjeenk Willink 1972.

J.C.M. Leijten, 'De rol van de rechtspraak en rechterlijke macht in een democratische samenleving', *HNJV* 1975-I, p. 129.

J.C.M. Leijten, 'Rechtspraak en topiek', in: W. van Gerven en J.C.M. Leijten, *Theorie en praktijk van de rechtsvinding*, 2ᵉ druk, Zwolle: W.E.J. Tjeenk Willink 1981, p. 63 e.v.

J.C.M. Leijten, *We need stories*, Zwolle: W.E.J. Tjeenk Willink 1991.

J.C.M. Leijten, 'Een 'oude liefde'?', *Christen Democratische Verkenningen* 7-8/83, p. 402-403.

Ph.B. Libourel, 'Ons honderdjarige Burgerlijk Recht en het Notariaat', *Correspondentie-blad van de Broederschap der Notarissen in Nederland* 1938/11, p. 281 e.v.

A.van Liempt, *Aan de Maliebaan. De kerk, het verzet, de NSB en de SS op een strekkende kilometer*, Amsterdam: Balans 2015.

Caroline Lindo in gesprek met [...], *De NJB Interviews*, Deventer: Kluwer 2011.

J.H.A. Lokin, 'Nijmeegs privaatrecht, bestaat?', in: *Nijmeegs recht bestaat (niet)!*, Nijmegen: GNI 1999, p. 1 e.v.

J.H.A. Lokin, 'Regtskunde, rechtsgeleerdheid, rechtswetenschap', *RM Themis* 2008/2, p. 49 e.v.

J.H.A. Lokin, *De Groninger Faculteit der Rechtsgeleerdheid (1596-1970)*, Den Haag: Boom juridisch 2019.

E.A.A. Luijten, 'De notariële studierichting aan de KU Nijmegen in retrospectief', in: Gitmans e.a. (red.), *Te Recht in Nijmegen*, p. 103 e.v.

J.M.M. Maeijer, 'Willem Christiaan Leonard van der Grinten 7 september 1913 – 1 juni 1994', *Levensberichten en herinneringen* (Koninklijk Nederlandse Akademie van Wetenschappen) 1994, p. 43 e.v.

J.M.M. Maeijer, 'Reflecties over verantwoordelijkheid en aansprakelijkheid zoals die tot uitdrukking komen in het recht', in: V. Poels (red.), *Verantwoord ondernemen*, Best: Damon 1999, p. 37 e.v.

J.M.M. Maeijer, 'C.J.J.M. Petit (1896-1978)', in: Hermans-Brand en Jansen (red.), *Recht in Nijmegen*, p. 65-67.

E. van Meerkerk, 'Nijmegen en de Harderwijkse academie, 1648-1679', in: J.A.H. Bots e.a. (red.), *Het Gelders Athene. Bijdragen tot de geschiedenis van de Gelderse universiteit in Harderwijk (1648-1811)*, Hilversum: Verloren 2000, p. 124 e.v.

J. Meihuizen, *Smalle marges. De Nederlandse advocatuur in de Tweede Wereldoorlog*, Amsterdam: Boom 2010.

J. Meihuizen, *Richard Fiebig en de uitbuiting van de Nederlandse industrie 1940-1945*, Amsterdam: Boom 2018.

T. Mertens, 'Rechtspositivisme, nazisme en Radbruchs these van het wettelijk onrecht', in: Y. Buruma e.a. (red.), *Recht door de eeuw. Opstellen ter gelegenheid van het 75-jarig jubileum van de Faculteit der Rechtsgeleerdheid van de Katholieke Universiteit Nijmegen*, Deventer: Kluwer 1998, p. 263 e.v.

T. Mertens, *Mens & Mensenrechten. Basisboek Rechtsfilosofie*, Amsterdam: Boom 2012, p. 63 e.v.

P. Minderhoud & T. Havinga, 'Inleiding', in: A. Böcker e.a. (red.), *Migratierecht en rechtssociologie, gebundeld in Kees' studies*, Nijmegen: Wolf Legal Publishers 2008, p. 1 e.v.

M.J.A. van Mourik, 'De legitieme portie: weg ermee!', *WPNR* 1991/6018, p. 621 e.v.

M.J.A. van Mourik, *Recht, Rechtvaardigheid en Ethiek, in het bijzonder in de notariële praktijk*, Deventer: Kluwer 2008.

P.L. Nève, 'Toetsing van het belastingrecht aan een/het rechtvaardigheidscriterium. Enkele kanttekeningen', in: Y. Buruma e.a. (red.), *Recht door de eeuw. Opstellen ter gelegenheid van het 75-jarig bestaan van de Faculteit der Rechtsgeleerdheid van de Katholieke Universiteit Nijmegen*, Deventer: Kluwer 1998, p. 291 e.v.

P.L. Nève, 'Een surnumerair in toga: Laurent Nouwen (1903-1997)', *Pro Memorie* 8.1 (2006), p. 115 e.v.

C.M.O. van Nispen tot Sevenaer, 'De strijd om de grenzen van het natuurrecht', *NJB* 1934, p. 673 e.v. en p. 685 e.v.

A.J.M. Nuytinck en A.H.N. Stollenwerck, 'In memoriam prof. mr. E.A.A. Luijten', *WPNR* 2016/7130.

Opstellen over recht en rechtsgeschiedenis aangeboden aan Prof. Mr. B.H.D. Hermesdorf, Deventer: Kluwer 1965.

W. Otterspeer, *Het horzelnest. De Leidse universiteit in oorlogstijd*, Amsterdam: Prometheus 2019.

Ch.J.J.M. Petit, *Het beeld van den mensch in de burgerlijke wetgeving*, Nijmegen-Utrecht: Dekker & Van de Vegt 1947.

Ch.J.J.M. Petit, 'De belanghebbenden bij een beslissing over abortus', *NJB* 1972, p. 484 e.v.

A. Pitlo, *De geschiedenis der notariële wetenschap*, Geschiedenis der Nederlandsche Rechtswetenschap, deel V, afl. 2, Amsterdam: Noord-Hollandsche Uitgevers Mij 1956.

C.G. van der Plas, 'De Nijmeegse rechtenfaculteit vanuit het perspectief van één van haar studenten die er bovendien ook promovenda werd: een impressie', in: Bulten, Hermans-Brand, Jansen (red.), *Recht in Nijmegen*, p. 209 e.v.

G. Radbruch, 'Gesetzliches Unrecht und übergesetzliches Recht', *Süddeutsche Juristenzeitung* 1946, S. 105-108.

R.H.W. Regout, *Is er grond voor het vertrouwen in de toekomst van het volkenrecht?*, Nijmegen-Utrecht: Dekker & Van de Vegt 1940.

R. Reussing, 'De vroege geschiedenis van de (lokale) bestuurswetenschappen. Jos van der Grinten als bondgenoot van Gerrit van Poelje', *Bestuurswetenschappen* 2018 (72) 1, p. 64 e.v.

S. Roes en F. Schols (red.), *Recht met sfeer. Bloemlezing uit eigen werk. Bundel ter gelegenheid van het afscheid van prof. mr. M.J.A. van Mourik als hoogleraar notarieel- en privaatrecht aan de Radboud Universiteit Nijmegen*, Kluwer: Deventer 2008.

J.S.L.A.W.B. Roes, *De zaakwaarnemer. Een notarieel-historische terugblik*, Ars Notariatus 157, Deventer: Kluwer 2014.

B. Rüthers, *Die unbegrenzte Auslegung. Zum Wandel der Privatrechtsordnung im Nationalsozialismus*, 3. Aufl., Heidelberg: C.F. Müller 1988.

H. van Run, 'Van Welie en de Daad', in: *Met recht meer meester*, CPO, Radboud Universiteit 2004, p. 68.

G.M.G.H. Russel, *Confiscatoire belastingtarieven en misbruik van strafwetgeving*, Utrecht: Dekker & Van der Vegt 1961.

A.N. Ruuls, 'Vier vragen omtrent de disputaties binnen het juridisch onderwijs aan de Nijmeegse Kwartierlijke Academie verdedigd onder P. de Greve (periode 1663-1676), benevens een poging tot beantwoording', *Batavia Academica* 1988, p. 31 e.v.

L. Savenije, *Nijmegen, collaboratie en verzet. Een stad in oorlogstijd*, Vantilt: Nijmegen 2018.

L. Savenije, 'In de voetsporen van Jozef van Hövell', *Vox* 05/2018, p. 16 e.v.

C.M. Scheuren-Brandes, *Der Weg von nationalsozialistischen Rechtslehren zur Radbruchsen Formel. Untersuchungen zur Geschichte der Idee vom "Unrichtigen Recht"*, F. Schöning: Paderborn [etc.] 2006.

F.W.J.M. Schols en B. Snijder-Kuijpers, 'De academische juridische opleiding; verleden, heden en vooral de toekomst', in: C.J.H. Jansen en J.S.L.A.W.B. Roes (red.), *175 jaar KNB*, Den Haag: Sdu 2018, p. 65 e.v.

P. Scholten en E.M. Meijers (red.), *Gedenkboek Burgerlijk Wetboek 1838-1938*, Zwolle: W.E.J. Tjeenk Willink 1938.

R. Schütz, *Kille mist. Het Nederlandse notariaat en de erfenis van de oorlog*, Amsterdam: Boom 2016.

G.H.A. Schut, 'W.C.L. van der Grinten – Een pragmatisch realist', in: *Juristenportretten*, Zutphen: Uitgeverij Paris 2014, p. 59 e.v.

R. Schutgens en J.J.J. Sillen, 'In memoriam Tijn Kortmann', *Ars Aequi* 2016, p. 308 e.v.

K. Schuyt, *R.P. Cleveringa. Recht, onrecht en de vlam der gerechtigheid*, Amsterdam: Boom 2019.

M. Schwegman, 'Cleveringa en Meijers. Een weerbarstige geschiedenis van getuigen en overleven', Cleveringarede 27 november 2017, via internet raadpleegbaar.

C.H. Sieburgh, 'In herinnering Jef Maeijer. Van rechtvaardigheid bezeten', *Tijdschrift voor Privaatrecht* 2018, p. 875-879.

D. Simons, 'Bezuiniging en rechterlijke macht', *Weekblad van het Recht* 1923/10994, p. 1-2.

D. Simons, 'De wet der vergelding', *W.* 1925/11322, p. 2.

D. Simons, 'Straf- en beveiligingsmaatregel', *W.* 1925/11358, p. 8.

R. te Slaa & E. Klijn, *De NSB. Ontstaan en opkomst van de Nationaal-Socialistische Beweging, 1931-1935*, Amsterdam: Boom 2009.

J.M. Smits, *Omstreden rechtswetenschap. Over aard, methode en organisatie van de juridische discipline*, Den Haag: Boom Juridische uitgevers 2009.

G. van Solinge, 'Rechtswetenschappelijk onderzoek in Nijmegen', in: Hermans-Brand en Jansen (red.), *Meesterlijk Nijmegen*, p. 141 e.v.

G. van Solinge, 'Vijftig jaren Nijmeegs vennootschapsrecht', in: *50 jaar Van der Heijden Instituut 1966-2016*, Deventer: Wolters Kluwer 2017, p. 1 e.v.

G. van Solinge, 'Een vasthoudende en innemende strijder voor het redelijke en het billijke: Prof. Mr. J.M.M. Maeijer Breda 14 januari 1932 – 's Hertogenbosch 6 september 2018', *Ars Aequi* 2018, p. 948-950.

A. Stadhouders, 'Willem Duynstee', *Jaarboek Numaga* 2004, p. 43-44.

C.J.J.M. Stolker, ''Ja, geléérd zijn jullie wel!' Over de status van de rechtswetenschap', *NJB* 2003, p. 766 e.v.

J.C.M. van Stratum, *Bevolking in beweging 1750-1920. Historische demografie van Geldrop in economisch perspectief*, Tilburg: Stichting Zuidelijk Historisch Contact 2004, p. 483-484, p. 488, p. 489-490, p. 497 e.v.

C.E.M. Struyker Boudier e.a., *De "oude Duyn" herdacht*, Nijmegen: Katholieke Universiteit Nijmegen 1987.

B.M. Telders, '[Bespr. van:] J.H.P. Bellefroid, Inleiding tot de rechtswetenschap', *Rechtsgeleerd Magazijn* 1937, p. 421.

Van blad tot boek. Verzameld Werk van Dr. A.C.B. Arts met inleidingen van Professor Mr. W. Pompe en Wouter Lutkie, Pr., Tilburg: Nieuwe Tilburgsche Courant 1937.

T.J. Veen, 'Inleiding', in: T.J. Veen en P.C. Kop (red.), *Zestig juristen. Bijdragen tot een beeld van de geschiedenis der Nederlandse rechtswetenschap*, Zwolle: W.E.J. Tjeenk Willink 1987, p. 1 e.v.

J.J.M. van der Ven, 'Overzicht van de nieuwste sociale wetgeving', I, *De Naamlooze Vennootschap*, 1941/1942, p. 282 e.v.

J.J.M. van der Ven, 'De eenheid van het arbeidsrecht' (1947), in: *Van sociale politiek naar sociaal recht. Een bundel arbeidsrechtelijke oraties*, Alphen aan den Rijn: Samsom 1966, p. 259 e.v.

J.J.M. van der Ven, 'De beoefening van het privaatrecht als discipline van juridisch denken', in: *Van Opstall-Bundel. Opstellen aangeboden aan Prof. Mr. S.N. van Opstall*, Deventer: Kluwer 1972, p. 189 e.v.

J.J.M. van der Ven, 'Willem Duynstee, de juridische-wijsgerige denker', in: Struyker Boudier e.a., *De "oude Duyn herdacht"*, p. 30 e.v.

W. Veraart, *Ontrechting en rechtsherstel in Nederland en Frankrijk in de jaren van bezetting en wederopbouw*, Deventer: Sanders Instituut/Kluwer 2005.

P. VerLoren van Themaat, 'Het decennium van de grenzen der westerse groei. De ontwikkeling van het sociaal-economisch recht in de zeventiger jaren', in: *Recente rechtsontwikkelingen (1970-1980)*, Zwolle: W.E.J. Tjeenk Willink 1983, p. 111 e.v.

M. Verburg, *Geschiedenis van het Ministerie van Justitie 1940-1945. Een departement in oorlogstijd*, Amsterdam: Boom 2016.

F. Verhagen, *Toen de katholieken Nederland veroverden. Charles Ruijs de Beerenbrouck 1873-1936*, diss. Radboud Universiteit, Amsterdam: Boom 2015.

Verspreide Opstellen [van] prof. mr. W.J.A.J. Duynstee CssR, verzameld en ingeleid door P.J.A. Calon, Roermond: J.J. Romen & Zonen 1963.

Verzameld Werk van Prof. Mr. P.W. Kamphuisen, Zwolle: W.E.J. Tjeenk Willink 1962.

R. Victor, 'Een verjaardag. Prof. J.H.P. Bellefroid', *Rechtskundig Weekblad* 13 (1949/1950), kol. 913 e.v.

Vita Radbodi. Het leven van Radboud, toegelicht, bezorgd en vertaald door P. Nissen en V. Hunink, Nijmegen: Vantilt 2004.

J.B.M. Vranken, 'Levensbericht van Johannes Cornelis Maria Leijten', in: *Levensberichten en herdenkingen*. Koninklijke Nederlandse Akademie van Wetenschappen, 2016, p. 62.

H. de Waele, 'Grond voor vertrouwen. Regout als jurist', in: M.J.F. Lindeijer en A. Welle (red.), *Robert Regout Maastricht 1896 – Dachau 1942*, Drachten: Vriendenkring van Robert Regout en Omnia Faustia 2004, p. 103 e.v.

H. de Waele, 'Commemorating Robert Regout (1896-1942). A chapter from the history of public international law revisited', *Journal of History of International Law* 2005, p. 81-92.

H. de Waele, 'A New League of Extraordinary Gentlemen? The Professionalization of International Law Scholarship in the Netherlands, 1919-1940', *European Journal of International Law* 2020, p. 1005-1024.

H. Weinkauff, 'Der Naturrechtsgedachte in der Rechtsprechung des Bundesgerichtshofes', *Neue Juristische Wochenschrift* 1960, 2. Halbband, 1691 ff.

H. Westra, 'Het plan voor het nieuwe Duitsche Volkswetboek', *Nieuw Nederland* 1941, p. 431-434.

W.J. Zwalve, 'De klassieke propedeuse van de jurist', *Groninger Opmerkingen en Mededelingen* 1986, p. 1 e.v.

W.J. Zwalve, 'Luijten's plaats in de rechtsgeschiedenis', in: *Luijten en Kleijn nader bekeken*, Deventer: Kluwer 2001, p. 3 e.v.

W.J. Zwalve, 'The cultivation of Incompetence", *Groninger Opmerkingen en Mededelingen* 2003, p. 1 e.v.

INDEX